D1470647

THE CREATORS

Role Models of Creativity

Emerson Klees

Cameo Press, Rochester, New York

Cameo Press
P. O. Box 18131
Rochester, New York 14618

Library of Congress Control Number 2015944616

ISBN 978-1-891046-24-7

Printed in the United States of America
9 8 7 6 5 4 3 2 1

DEDICATION

This book is dedicated to today's creators whose creations add to and improve our lives.

OTHER BOOKS BY EMERSON KLEES

Role Models of Human Values Series

One Plus One Equals Three—Pairing Man / Woman Strengths:
  Role Models of Teamwork
Entrepreneurs In History—Success vs. Failure: Entrepreneurial
  Role Models
Staying With It: Role Models of Perseverance
The Drive to Succeed: Role Models of Motivation
The Will to Stay With It: Role Models of Determination
Paul Garrett: Dean of American Winemakers
A Song of the Vine: A Reflection on Life
Emotional Intelligence: People Smart Role Models
Emotional Intelligence: People Smart Role Models II
Emotional Intelligence: People Smart Role Models III
Rebounding From Setbacks: Role Models of Resilience

The Moral Navigator: Stories From Around the World
Inspiring Legends and Tales With a Moral I
Inspiring Legends and Tales With a Moral II
Inspiring Legends and Tales With a Moral III

Books About New York State and the Finger Lakes Region

People of the Finger Lakes Region
Legends and Stories of the Finger Lakes Region
The Erie Canal in the Finger Lakes Region
Underground Railroad Tales With Routes Through the Finger Lakes
  Region
More Legends and Stories of the Finger Lakes Region
The Women's Rights Movement and the Finger Lakes Region
Persons, Places, and Things In the Finger Lakes Region [6 lakes]
The Crucible of Ferment, New York's "Psychic Highway"
The Iroquois Confederacy: History and Legends
Rochester Lives
Wineries of the Finger Lakes Region—100 Wineries
Persons, Places, and Things Of the Finger Lakes Region [11 lakes]
Finger Lakes Wineries: A Pictorial History

THE ROLE MODELS OF HUMAN VALUES SERIES

"Example teaches better than precept. It is the best modeler of the character of men and women. To set a lofty example is the richest bequest a man [or woman] can leave behind."

Samuel Smiles

The Role Models of Human Values Series provides examples of role models and of lives worthy of emulation. The human values depicted in this series include perseverance, motivation, determination, resilience, and creativity. Role models are presented in biographical sketches of historical figures that describe the environment within which they strived and delineate their personal characteristics.

These profiles illustrate how specific human values helped achievers reach their goals in life. We can learn from these examples in strengthening the human values that are so important to our success and happiness. The Introduction in each book highlights the factors that contributed to these achievers' success.

PREFACE

"Creation—that is the great redemption from suffering, and life's growing light. But that the creator may be, suffering is needed and much change."

Nietzche, *Thus Spoke Zarathustra*

This book provides role models of creativity via profiles of thirty individuals who were creators. The thirty biographical sketches represent six areas of endeavor:

Painters / Sculptors

Songwriters / Composers

Authors / Poets

Inventors / Researchers

Architects / Entrepreneurs

Engineers / Scientists

Although the subject of this book is creativity, these individuals displayed other strong personal characteristics, including perseverance, motivation, determination, and resilience, discussed in other books in the Human Values Series. We can learn from these individuals to be more creative in our own lives.

TABLE OF CONTENTS

Page No.

Page No.

INTRODUCTION

"The reason creativity is so fascinating is that when we are involved in it, we feel that we are living more fully than during the rest of life. The excitement of the artist at the easel or the scientist in the lab comes close to the idea of fulfillment we all hope to get from life, and so rarely do. Perhaps only sex, sports, music, and religious ecstasy— even when these experiences remain fleeting and leave no trace— provide as profound a sense of being a part of an entity greater than ourselves. But creativity leaves an outcome that adds to the richness and complexity of the future."

Mihaly Csikszentmihalyi, *Creativity: Flow and the Psychology of Discovery and Invention*

Creativity is the quality from which something novel and useful is created, such as a work of art, a dance routine, a literary work, or a musical composition We all view architects and designers as being creative. When many think of the word "creative," they think of the word "artistic." They are certain that architects and designers are creative, but may question whether CEOs and entrepreneurs are. They are creators. Also, no one questions whether inventors are creative.

The world of technology has many creative individuals. Companies in Silicon Valley not only hire creative people, they strongly encourage their employees to strive to improve their creativity.

Creativity is involved when we have the opportunity to generate new ideas, new approaches to a situation needing improvement, and new solutions to a problem. Creativity is not wholly an inherited trait. A wide range of academic interests in the subject of creativity exists, including business administration, cognitive science, economics, education, philosophy of science, psychology, songwriting, and technology.

In *Defying the Crowd,* Robert Sternberg and Todd Lubart ask the question, "Who Needs Creativity?" " Our answer is that everyone does—for creativity is the spring that propels technological, cultural, financial, intellectual, and certainly personal leaps. How much more creativity might we see in the world if only those who should support creativity really did—if they only wanted to hear it?"

Unfortunately, creativity is generally underappreciated in society and in our education system. International education leader Sir Ken Robinson noted in his 2006 TED (Technology, Education, Design) Talk, "Do Schools Kill Creativity," (the most popular TED talk until that time): Creativity is as important in education as literacy and we should treat it with the same status."

Many factors are involved in determining how creative we are, including intelligence, feedback, knowledge, styles of thought, personality, motivation and environmental influences.

Intelligence helps us to see a problem in a way that has not been perceived before. Intelligence allows us to use existing information and concepts in a new and unique way. Procedures that have been known before can be modified and used differently. Intelligence allows us to use the information with which we are familiar in a different approach, making something unique with it.

We must be able to determine which of our new ideas is a good idea, that is, to use existing resources efficiently, possibly using a new idea to solve existing problems. Another role of intelligence is to be able to effectively present a new idea to an audience. Packaging and presenting a new idea is crucial.

Feedback on the new idea is important as is the manner of reacting to the feedback. Feedback from others is important because other members of a team may have different thoughts that can improve the idea. Unfortunately, no one is strong in all areas. The need to team with others with strengths in our areas of weakness is vital.

Knowledge in one's field of endeavor is important to being creative because in order to extend beyond earlier contributions to a field, one must know what they are or merely repeat them. Thus, lack of knowledge contributes to individuals perceiving ideas or concepts that are new to them but have been perceived before.

Styles of thought are important because they determine how our intelligence is going to be used. Frequently, creative people like to make up their own rules rather than following existing ones. Style must be distinguished from ability. Even though people have creative ability, they may prefer doing things in the existing way, or perhaps they don't have the intellectual ability to utilize new ideas effectively.

Creativity involves personality traits as well as mental traits. Some individuals are not geared to making changes. They prefer the status quo. They do not want to stand up and defend their new ideas. They may not have the persistence and determination to take on those who are opposing or questioning their ideas.

Motivation is critical to the creative process. In order to progress beyond the potential for being creative to actually being creative, people must be motivated toward their goals. These goals might be external goals, such as fame, money, or power, or they may be internal goals, including personal challenges or self-expression.

Creative people tend to be much more productive than individuals who are average. In academia, they publish more papers and books. In technical fields, they design and invent much more. Creative people tend to be doing something that they love doing. They discovered early in life that if you are doing what you want to be doing and what you are good at doing, your chances of achieving success are significantly elevated.

The environment in which we are performing can promote creativity or squelch it. In part, creativity is the result of an interaction between the ones doing the creating and their environment. Some environments do not nurture out-of-the-ordinary ideas. The creative process needs an environment that stimulates new ideas and concepts, encourages their presentation, and rewards new and nonconformist thinking.

Occasionally, creativity results from an epiphany, or a "bolt from the blue." Two examples of this are discussed in this book: John Atanasoff and the invention of the computer and Robert Goddard and his rocket development efforts.

We can and should all strive to improve our creativity. It assists in leading a productive and happy life. In *The Creativity Book,* Eric Maisel observes:

> When you become an everyday creative person you instinctively solve problems more easily, see the world as a richer place, and enjoy life more. You get to use capabilities and skills that may be hidden under a barrel right now. If you're a writer or a would-be writer and begin to unleash your creativity, you write more deeply and more frequent-

ly. If a painter or a would-be painter, you paint more personally, passionately, and authentically. If you're self-employed, you see your options more quickly, and make them more fluidly. If you work in a large corporation, you become more self-directing, confident, and aware. Whatever you do, creativity helps you do it better; whatever details of life, you feel more alive. Creativity improves your work and enriches your life in general.

,

QUOTATIONS

"Of the truly creative no one is ever master; it must be left to go its own way."

Goethe

"Tis to create, and in creating live a being more intense, that we endow with what form our fancy, gaining as we give the life we image."

Byron

"Man's main task is to give birth to himself."

Eric Fromm, *Man for Himself*

"The most gifted members of the human species are at their creative best when they cannot have their way."

Eric Hoffer, *The Ordeal of Change*

"Men are like trees: each one must put forth the leaf that is created in him."

Henry Ward Beecher, *Proverbs from Plymouth Pulpit*

"Creativity varies inversely with the number of cooks involved in the broth."

Bernice Fitz-gibbon, *Macy's, Gimbel's and Me*

CHAPTER 1

PAINTERS / SCULPTORS

"In creating, the only hard thing is to begin; a grass blade's no easier to make than an oak."

James Russell Lowell, *A Fable for Critics*

LEONARDO DA VINCI (1452-1519) Painter, Sculptor, Engineer, Inventor

"Leonardo opened up vast areas of human knowledge and painted so superbly that for many people he represents the single universal example of Western man in his utmost accomplishment, Renaissance man in his utmost splendor."

Robert Payne, *Leonardo*

Leonardo da Vinci, born on April 15, 1452, is considered one of the great artists of all time. His best-known paintings are the *Mona Lisa* and *The Last Supper,* the most widely reproduced religious painting. He was born out of wedlock to Piero da Vinci, a legal notary, and Caterina, a peasant woman, in Vinci in the Republic of Florence, which was ruled by the Medici. Vinci is in the Arno River valley in Tuscany. The name da Vinci simply means "of Vinci."

Leonardo received an informal education in geometry, Latin, and mathematics. His early painting education was at the studio of the highly regarded Florentine painter, Andrea di Cione. He was apprenticed as a studio boy to Andrea del Verrocchio, the leading painter and sculptor in Florence. Leonardo was exposed to many technical skills, including drafting, chemistry, metalworking, and plaster casting, in addition to the artistic skills of drawing, modelling, painting and sculpture.

In 1472, twenty-year-old Leonardo qualified as a master in the Guild of St. Luke, a guild of artists. His father set him up in his own workshop, but he continued to do work for Verrocchio. From 1482 to 1499, Leonardo worked in Milan in the studio of Ludovico il Moro. He was commissioned to paint *Virgin on the Rocks* for the Confraternity of the Immaculate Conception and *The Last Supper* for the Monastery of Santa Maria delle Grazie.

From 1513 to 1516, during the time of Pope Leo X, Leonardo lived in the Vatican in Rome. Michelangelo and Raphael were also active there at the time. Leonardo, Michelangelo, and Raphael are considered the three giants of the Renaissance. However, they were not of the same generation. Leonardo was twenty-three years older than Michelangelo and thirty-one years older than Raphael. Raphael only lived to the age of thirty-seven. He died in 1420.

In October 1515, King Francis I of France recaptured Milan. That December, Leonardo was present at the meeting of Francis I and Pope Leo X in Bologna. Leonardo entered the service of King Francis I and was given the use of the manor house Clos Luce near the King's residence at the royal Chateau d'Ambroise. Francis became a close friend. Leonardo died at Clos Luce on May 2, 1519. Leonardo da Vinci was buried in the Chapel of Saint-Hubert in Chamboise in France.

After Leonardo's death, King Francis was quoted as saying: "There has never been another man born in the world who knew as much as Leonardo, not so much about painting, sculpture, and architecture, and he was a very great philosopher."

Leonardo had constantly experimented with new techniques. His designs were ingenious. They included the concepts of flying machines, solar power, an adding machine, and the catamaran hull for boats. He designed the first armored vehicle, or tank. It was round, with cannons sticking out around the circumference, and was mounted on wheels. One of his most unusual inventions was a suit for scuba diving. He was ahead of his time.

Although Leonardo was known for his many talents, it is as a painter that he is principally remembered. He liked to paint slowly, making changes as he went along. Fresco painting, painting on walls, was a multistep process beginning with an underpainting, the outline of a drawing, and then transferred to damp plaster. He experimented with many techniques and materials including the use of new colors and glazes. One of the problems he coped with was the humidity in the room in which he was working. He would touch up his work over long periods of time.

Leonardo began painting *Mona Lisa* between 1503 and 1506 while simultaneously working on *The Battle of Anghiari*. *Mona Lisa's* three-quarters pose, hint of a smile, and faded background became the classic portrait format. In *Mona Lisa,* Mary Rose Storey observed:

> The pose of the *Mona Lisa* was considered innovative in Leonardo's time and was widely imitated. It is a refined variation of the classical *contrapposto,* an Italian word often applied to the pose in which part of the body twists in a different direction from the rest.

Lisa, the model, was the twenty-five-year-old wife of Francescodel Giocondo, a Florentine silk merchant. Lisa had a charming smile but it was rarely seen. In order to encourage her to smile, Leonardo engaged people to provide music and students to amuse her while he painted.

In *Lives of the Artists,* Giorgio Vasari noted:

> In the normal course of events many men and women are born with remarkable talents, but occasionally, in a way that transcends nature, a single person is endowed by Heaven with beauty, grace, and talent in such abundance he leaves other men far behind. All his actions seem inspired and indeed everything he does clearly comes from God and not from human skill. Everyone acknowledged that this was true of Leonardo da Vinci, an artist of outstanding physical beauty, who displayed infinite grace in everything that he did and who cultivated his genius so brilliantly that all problems he studied he solved with ease.

MICHELANGELO (1475-1564) Sculptor, Artist, Architect, Poet, Engineer

"It is interesting to notice how some minds seem almost to create themselves, springing up under every disadvantage, and working their solitary but irresistible way through a thousand obstacles."

Washington Irving

Michelangelo was a talented man who lived in a time blessed with talent. Among his peers were Leonardo da Vinci and Raphael. In the opinion of Giorgio Vasari in his *Lives of the Most Excellent Sculptors, Painters, and Architects*: "The one genius who surpasses all others, both past and present, shedding his brilliance on all around him, is Michelangelo Buonarroti, the divine master not only in one art but in three [sculpture, painting, and architecture]."

In the sculptor Rodin's view, "Michelangelo is the last and the greatest of the Gothic artists. The soul turned in upon itself, suffering, distaste for life, struggle against the dominance of the matter—such are the elements of his inspiration." This observation was made about an individual who considered himself a sculptor, not a painter. In fact, he signed his name Michelangelo, sculptor.

Michelangelo didn't welcome the assignment by Pope Julius II to paint the ceiling of the Sistine Chapel. He was deeply involved in planning a mausoleum for the Pope, an ambitious project incorporating forty statues. The Pontiff decided that it wasn't wise to spend large sums on his own mausoleum while he was still alive.

Michelangelo begged the Pope, without success, for release from painting the Sistine ceiling. However, his resentment at being diverted from the sculpting of forty statues turned suddenly into feverish activity. He realized that he could paint his marble figures on the ceiling of the Sistine Chapel. He resolved to translate the statues that he wasn't permitted to sculpt into paintings.

Before he had chosen Michelangelo, the Pope had consulted with one of his advisors, Donati Bramante, on the advisability of Michelangelo's assignment to paint the Sistine ceiling. Bramante counseled against the assignment, expressing his concern about Michelangelo's limited experience in fresco painting and, in particular, his lack of experience in painting figures with foreshortening, a technique that makes them appear to project out of the surface and recede back from the surface. The figures are drawn in shortened view with outlines and shadows that to the eye are projected forward, even though they don't have the height or breadth that they appear to have. Bramante considered this a critical technique for work on ceilings because of the distance of the paintings from the viewer.

Michelangelo's working relationship with Bramante was strained for years after he heard of the advice Bramante had given the Pope. Michelangelo's reaction to that advice was one of the factors that ultimately motivated him to undertake the Sistine Chapel assignment.

The Pope, whose principal reputation had come from expanding the papal sphere of influence at the head of his army, had chosen Michelangelo, and that was who was going to do the job. Nevertheless, Pope Julius continued to browbeat Michelangelo as he worked on the ceiling; on one occasion he hit him with a cane and on another occasion threatened to throw him off the scaffold.

The Sistine Chapel had been built for papal ceremonies by Pope Sixtus IV, Pope Julius's uncle, between 1475 and 1481 and was dedicated to the Assumption of the Blessed Virgin Mary in August 1483. It is a rectangular building, approximately 132 feet by 45 feet, made of brick with travertine cornices and window frames. Frescoes on the walls depict the lives of Moses and Christ. Michelangelo modified the initial plans for the ceiling of the chapel. The religious community usually laid out the plan, and the artist conformed to it; rarely was an artist allowed such freedom.

On May 10, 1508, Michelangelo signed the contract to paint the ceiling. First he removed the scaffolding that had been erected by Bramante. Bramante had made holes in the ceiling from which the scaffolding was suspended by ropes. Michelangelo didn't want to work on swaying scaffolding, nor did he like the prospect of repairing the holes in the ceiling after his work was done. He rested the scaffolding on the projecting cornices and the tops of the columns that lined the walls. Bramante was impressed by this approach; he used it later during the construction of St. Peter's.

Michelangelo planned to paint scenes from Genesis, backward from The Flood to the Creation. He started with the nine central panels at the entrance and ended at the altar.

The Drunkenness of Noah

Noah, in a stupor, is reclining on the floor of his dwelling next to the wine jug, while his sons point to him. A man digging in the fields is behind him.

The Flood

As the waters rise, men and women, including some with children, are leaving the ark, seen in the background, to move to high ground and to a rocky promontory.

Noah's Sacrifice

Noah stands with his wife while his family prepares a burnt offering on the altar. Animals that have left the ark are standing at the left.

Temptation and Expulsion

A tree with the serpent coiled around it is in the center. Adam and Eve reaching for the apple are to the left of the tree and are seen again on the right being driven out of paradise.

The Creation of Eve

Adam is shown asleep leaning against the trunk of a tree. An astonished Eve is shown springing out of Adam's side as God approaches.

The Creation of Adam

Adam is depicted lying on the ground leaning on his right elbow while reaching with his left hand for the hand of God, who is borne by angels.

Congregation of the Waters

God is wafted by angels shrouded in a cloak over the surface of the sea as He stretches out His arms and blesses it.

Creation of the Sun and the Moon and the Plants
On the right, the Creator is rising as though borne on the wind and assigns the moon and the sun to their places. On the left, He is shown creating the fruits of the earth.

Separation of Light from Darkness
Michelangelo's depiction of Creation itself. The Creator is shown with his arms lifted high above his head creating the earth.

For the four corner spandrels (triangular spaces), Michelangelo planned scenes from the salvation of Israel: David and Goliath and Judith and Holofernes at the entrance end and The Crucifixion of Haman and The Brazen Serpent at the altar end of the Chapel. Along the sides and at the ends are twelve figures sitting on thrones: three lesser prophets, Joel, Jonah, and Zechariah; four major prophets, Daniel, Ezekiel, Isaiah, and Jeremiah; and five sibyls, the Cumean, Delphic, Erythraean, Libyan, and Persian.

Michelangelo was in trouble from the moment he started painting. He began with the central panel, The Flood. By January 1509, spots of mold appeared in the first third of the vault that Michelangelo had completed. Two factors contributed to the problem, which was caused by excess moisture. Not only had Rome had exceptionally wet weather during that fall and winter, but Michelangelo had used too much water in the plaster he had applied over the coarse base surface.

In fresco painting, a thin layer of smooth, wet plaster, the intonaco, is applied with a trowel on top of a rough layer of dry plaster, the arriccio. The artist doesn't have the luxury of touching up his work the following day, as with most other painting techniques. Pigments are added to the intonaco, which dries within the day, chemically bonding the pigment to the plaster. A hard, protective layer of calcium carbonate forms over the surface plaster as it dries. The only way the artist can touch up his work is to scrape away the previous day's work and redo it.

This early problem with mildew provided Michelangelo with an opportunity to go to Pope Julius and ask to be relieved of his assignment of painting the Sistine ceiling. He reminded the Pope again that he was a sculptor, not a painter. The Pope referred him to Giuliano da Sangallo, who identified the problem as excess moisture in the surface coat of plaster; Michelangelo continued with his work.

Initially, Michelangelo was provided with five young assistants from Florence who were familiar with the fresco technique. He sent one of them home in October 1508, and soon realized that this was a one-person job; he dispensed with the help of the other four assistants. During the four years of effort required to complete the ceiling, he worked long hours, didn't take the time or effort to eat properly, and didn't pay much attention to his clothing or his personal hygiene.

Many people question whether Michelangelo really painted while lying on his back for over four years. He drew a cartoon of himself painting while standing on the scaffolding. Apparently, his effort was a combination of lying and standing. Michelangelo described his discomfort:

> I have already developed a goiter . . . that pushes my belly under my chin. My beard points to heaven . . . and my brush continuously dripping onto my face turns it into a rich mosaic. My loins have penetrated my belly, my rump's a counterweight, and I walk around in vain, without seeing where I am going . . . Behind, my skin is shriveled from too much bending, and I am stretched like a Syrian bow.

The project experienced several delays. Michelangelo was ill in June 1509, and work was also stopped in February 1511, due to a delay in payment. The artist endured considerable physical and mental fatigue. In July 1512, he wrote, "I struggle more than any man ever has, in bad health and with the greatest labor, and still I remain patient in order to reach the desired goal."

Toward the end of his project, Michelangelo was working on low scaffolding painting Charon when he had a dizzy spell. Although he attempted to grab a railing, he fell onto the marble floor. His leg bled where he struck a piece of scaffolding as he fell. He refused to see a doctor until he developed a fever. The doctor cleansed the infected leg wound, and Michelangelo was back on the scaffolding within a week.

Finally, in October 1512, the ceiling was finished and was unveiled to the public. One contemporary present at the unveiling commented: "All Rome admired it and crowded to see it." Another viewer wrote, "It was such to make everyone speechless with astonishment." Later, upon seeing the ceiling of the Sistine Chapel for the first time, Goethe observed, "Its grandeur is beyond description . . . Anyone who has not seen the Sistine Chapel can have no idea of what a single man can achieve."

VINCENT VAN GOGH (1853-1890) Artist Who Sold Only One Painting in His Lifetime

"I should like to paint that which would appear after a century to the people living then as apparitions. So I do not endeavor to achieve this by a photographic resemblance, but by means of our impassioned expressions, using our knowledge of and our modern taste for color as a means of arriving at the expression and the intensification of the character."

Vincent Van Gogh, in a letter to his sister, Wil Van Gogh

Van Gogh sold only one painting in his lifetime. In 1890, the year of his death, *The Red Vineyard* sold for 400 francs (approximately eighty dollars) at the Brussels exhibition of Les Vingt, an organization of artists and authors. Another member of Les Vingt, painter Henry de Groux, would not permit his paintings to be displayed in the same exhibition as "the abominable pots of sunflowers." In 1987, one of Van Gogh's seven paintings of sunflowers was sold at an auction at Christie's in London for $39.9 million.

In *Makers of the Modern World*, Louis Untermeyer summarized Van Gogh's approach to painting:

> Vincent Van Gogh was only thirty-seven when he killed himself, and he had been a painter less than ten years. Yet in that decade he had crowded the time with some of the most passionate and personal canvasses ever conceived. His spirit struggling with agonized love and fear of life is shown as explicitly in those canvasses as in his revealing correspondence. Painting with him was a vehement confession, a tortured sacrament, rather than a source of pleasure. He combined beauty and squalor, exultation and misery, to turn despair into affirmative creation. "I want," he cried, "to paint humanity, humanity, humanity."
>
> There is drama in Van Gogh's very touch, the packed lines and turbulent colors mounting to a

blaze of rapture. Frenzied and tormented, Van Gogh never ceased to be concerned with the troubled human comedy; even in his paroxysms he responded to its moral force. Everything he did was another attempt to add mortal passion and pity to the immortal humanity of art.

At the age of twenty-seven, after unsuccessful careers as an art gallery manager and as a lay preacher, Van Gogh moved to the Hague to study with artist Anton Mauve, who was married to Van Gogh's cousin. Mauve was very helpful, particularly in assisting Van Gogh to get established in a studio and in teaching him oil techniques. Mauve gave Van Gogh an appreciation for color. However, Van Gogh did not accept critical advice well, and when Mauve suggested that he practice sketching with plaster statues, Van Gogh smashed the plaster casts; he said he wanted to draw life.

In the spring of 1882, Van Gogh completed his first large painting "The Potato Eaters," which is considered the precursor of Expressionism. Along with Paul Cézanne and Paul Gauguin, Van Gogh is revered as one of the founders of modern art.

In February 1886, Van Gogh moved to Paris, where his brother, Theo, was manager of an art gallery. Vincent enrolled at Cormon's studio, where he met Toulouse-Lautrec, who became his friend and a defender of his art. Through Theo, Vincent became familiar with the works of the Impressionists, such as Renoir and Manet. Pissarro had a definite influence on Van Gogh, particularly in the treatment of bright colors.

Van Gogh did not try to replicate on canvas the exact images that his eyes perceived. In his words: "Instead of trying to produce exactly what I have before my eyes, I use color more arbitrarily so as to express myself more forcibly. I should be in despair if my figures were 'correct.' My great longing is to learn to make those very corrections, those deviations, remodelings, changes of reality, that may become, yes, untruth—but more truth than the literal truth."

In Paris, Van Gogh awakened to the world of art. He visited the Louvre to see the old masters Rembrandt and Delacroix, and the art galleries to view the work of the Impressionists. He discovered the composition and color of Japanese prints, and he painted steadily; unfortunately, his work did not sell. He met many of the artists active in Paris, including Degas, Pissarro, and Gauguin, who was the one artist whom Van Gogh admired and respected; they became friends. Van Gogh frequented Père Tanguy's art supply shop as well as the Café Tambourin, a small restaurant where he hung his art on the walls and hoped that it would sell. He was finally in an environment in which he could mingle with other artists.

While living with his brother in Paris, Theo wrote to his mother, "There are two human beings in Vincent, the one extraordinarily gifted, sensitive, and gentle, the other selfish and insensitive. I am sure he is his own enemy, for he poisons not only the lives of others, but his own life, yet the seeds of greatness are in him too."

After two years, Van Gogh tired of the Paris scene. Many of the artists did not get along with one another. For example, Monet would not let his paintings hang in a gallery that included the works of Gauguin. Also, Van Gogh felt that he would experience brighter colors if he moved south; Toulouse-Lautrec encouraged him in this.

In February 1888, Van Gogh moved to Arles, an old Roman town in Provence. He made few friends and was lonely. He subsisted on a small allowance from Theo and was considered an oddity by the townspeople. He hoped that Gauguin would join him in Arles; he wanted to start a small artists' colony in southern France with himself and Gauguin as the nucleus.

Van Gogh was discouraged, but he persevered with his painting. Finally, in October 1888, Gauguin arrived in Arles and moved into a house with Van Gogh. Van Gogh was pleased to see him to relieve his loneliness. At this time, he viewed himself as a pupil of Gauguin; he was not aware that Gauguin was his inferior. Gauguin was impressed with the progress that Van Gogh had made in his art. They were different individuals. Gauguin was assertive, confident, and outgoing and had unusual tastes. His looks were striking, and he appealed to women.

Van Gogh, who was accustomed to living in poverty, did not possess much self-confidence; he was aware that his scruffy appearance tended to set him apart. Both Gauguin and Van Gogh viewed color as extremely important in their work, but they took different approaches to it. Van Gogh stressed primary colors and juxtaposed complementary ones, whereas Gauguin usually painted with the nonprimary colors and used related colors side by side, such as pink and orange, violet and purple.

Inevitably, differences of opinion arose between the two artists; Van Gogh described their arguments as "electric." Gauguin was critical of Van Gogh's work, and Van Gogh did not like to be criticized. They disagreed on who the great artists were. Van Gogh admired Daumier and Rousseau but did not care for the work of Ingres or Degas, whom Gauguin liked. One evening while they were drinking in a cafe, Van Gogh threw his drink at Gauguin. Gauguin took Van Gogh by the arm and led him home.

Van Gogh began to break down. Shortly after the scene in the cafe, Gauguin was walking near their yellow house on the Rue Lamartine when he heard someone behind him. He turned and saw Van Gogh with a open razor in his hand. When he asked Van Gogh what he was doing, Van Gogh turned and ran into the house without speaking. In his overwrought state, Van Gogh cut off the lower part of his right ear with the razor. He wrapped a towel around his ear to stop the bleeding, placed the severed portion of the ear in an envelope, and sent it to a young woman in return for teasing him about his big ears.

Gauguin had written earlier to Theo, who as a dealer was selling his art, that he and Van Gogh were incompatible and too different in temperament to live peacefully in Arles. Gauguin returned immediately to Paris after these incidents. Before he left, he sent a telegram to Theo suggesting that he come to Arles. Theo came and took his brother back to Paris. Van Gogh was treated at St. Paul's Hospital. His condition improved, and he returned home to Arles after a stay of two weeks. He started to paint again. His first painting was "Self-Portrait with Cut Ear."

However, the increased activity caused further attacks that were viewed more as a form of epilepsy than schizophrenia. After an especially bad attack, the townspeople asked him to leave Arles. His doctor recommended that he enter the asylum at Saint-Remy. He continued to paint after he moved there in May 1889.

Van Gogh accomplished some of his most notable work at Saint-Remy. Paintings of this period reflect his overexcited emotions, and he painted as though he were in a supercharged atmosphere. He increased his use of natural colors and captured the actual tones of the surrounding countryside. Although Van Gogh was technically under the care of a doctor, the treatment provided to patients at the asylum was minimal. Some of his paintings done at

Saint-Remy were "Yellow Wheat," "Starry Night," and a series of country scenes that he called "Impressions of Provence," which included works such as "Quarry Near Saint-Remy."

The duration of Van Gogh's attacks lengthened. After a year at Saint-Remy, Theo placed his brother under the care of Dr. Gachet at Auvers on the Oise River near Paris, where Theo and his wife, Joanna, could visit him. Dr. Gachet was a talented etcher as well as a connoisseur of art and a friend of Pissarro and Cézanne. Dr. Gachet realized that the best treatment for Van Gogh was his work. He encouraged Van Gogh to paint.

During the evening of July 27, 1890, Van Gogh wrote a letter to Theo:

> I shall always consider you to be something else than a simple dealer in Corots, that through my mediation you have your part in the actual production of certain canvasses, which will retain their calm even in catastrophe.

He did not finish the letter. He went for a walk in the fields, taking a revolver with him. After shooting himself, he stumbled back to the inn where he had a room. Theo was called immediately and came to Auvers to be with his brother. At age thirty-seven, Vincent Van Gogh passed away with his brother and lifelong friend, Theo, at his side.

Van Gogh did not begin his art career until he was twenty-seven years old. He was a productive artist for only ten years. However, he was a prolific painter and over 1,700 of his works have survived him. He painted in spurts of creativity in which he averaged a painting a day over a period of several weeks. He created over forty self-portraits, more than any of the masters except Rembrandt.

Van Gogh was right in thinking that "I cannot help it if my pictures do not sell. The time will come when people will see that they are worth more than the price of the paint and my own living—very meager, after all—that are put into them." In 1988, a picture of irises painted while he was in the asylum at Saint-Remy was sold for $53.3 million. In May 1990, his "Portrait of Dr. Gachet" was sold for $82.5 million.

PAUL GAUGUIN (1848-1903) Artist Who Emphasized the Primitive

"Different generations can find in Gauguin the examples and lessons which they demand of the past to guide them in the future. Gauguin's life was neither constant nor unified. It reflects struggles, continual waverings, and an opposition between the man and his work that make it one of the most dramatic of all time. It is, however, these contradictions and incessant conflicts between inclination and development that finally resolved the artist's life into a complete unity entirely dedicated to the fulfillment of personality. Continually, passionately pursuing his ideal and never wholly satisfied with his work, Gauguin was nevertheless sufficiently sure of his genius to sacrifice his whole existence to it."

Raymond Cogniat, *Gauguin*

Paul Gauguin was a stockbroker in Paris until he was thirty-five years old. Drawing and painting began as a hobby. By 1882, painting evenings and weekends in his spare time was no longer enough. He had a wife and four children when he began painting full time. In December 1882, a fifth child was born. Eventually, his wife moved with the children to Denmark, her native country, when it became apparent that Gauguin could not support them as an artist.

In *The Moon and Sixpence,* W. Somerset Maugham's protagonist, Strickland, a Gauguin-like artist, responds to the question, "What makes you think you have any talent?" with the reply "I've got to paint." Upon being questioned further and asked "Aren't you taking an awful chance?" Strickland again replies "I've got to paint." When Gauguin informed his wife that he had quit his job as a stockbroker, he told her, "From now on, I paint every day." He had to paint.

Unfortunately, Gauguin was never able to sell enough paintings during his lifetime to escape constant financial worry. He endured poverty and ill health but continued to paint. He is considered by art historians to have influenced the direction of modern painting more than any artist except Cézanne.

Paul Gauguin was born in Paris on June 7, 1848. His father, Clovis Gauguin, a political journalist from Orleans, died when Paul was very young. His mother, Aline Marie Chazal, the daughter of a Spanish-Peruvian nobleman, shared her father-in-law's home in Orleans with her brother-in-law. Paul attended the parochial school in Orleans and later attended the lycée.

At the age of seventeen, Gauguin shipped out as an apprentice on the *Luzitano,* a 1,200-ton sailing ship that carried passengers and cargo between Le Havre and Rio de Janeiro. After three years in the merchant service, he entered the French Navy and was assigned to the cruiser *Dessaid* patrolling the Cattegat. His mother died before he completed his military service in 1871.

Gauguin moved in with a friend of his mother, Gustav Arosa, in Paris. Gauguin's artistic interests were awakened while he lived with Arosa, who owned a substantial collection of contemporary artists and had painted reproductions of Courbet and Delacroix. Gauguin painted with the guidance of Arosa's daughter, Marguerite. Arosa arranged a job for him at Bertin's, a banking firm. Gauguin learned fast and was given the responsibility of closing the day's business for the bank on the Bourse. He made a good salary at Bertin's.

In 1873, Gauguin married Mette Sofie Gad of Copenhagen whom he had met in Paris while she was traveling with a friend. Mette, daughter of a magistrate, was a level-headed young woman who had been governess for the children of the Danish Prime Minister when she was seventeen.

Gauguin's co-worker and friend, Emile Schuffenecker, was also a part-time artist. They spent occasional evenings sketching at the Academie Colarassi. Gauguin began to collect Impressionist works, including paintings by Cézanne, Manet, Pissarro, Renoir, and Sisley.

One of Gauguin's favorite artists when he began to paint was Millet, who influenced some of his early works. Although Gauguin was to become the foremost colorist, his early paintings gave no indication of this direction. The artist who had the greatest influence on his early efforts was Camille Pissarro, who had worked in business until he was twenty-five.

Edouard Manet gave Gauguin early encouragement. When Gauguin told him that he was only an amateur who painted in his spare time, Manet responded, "Oh, the only amateurs are those who paint bad pictures." Gauguin contributed paintings to the Impressionist Exhibition; he received critical acclaim for his *Study of the Nude,* but not for his landscapes, which were considered too similar to Pissarro's.

In 1883, Gauguin resigned from Bertin's and painted full time. Mette, a very practical person, was astounded. She did not understand her husband's motivation; in fact, she never really fully reconciled herself to his decision. Even Pissarro was surprised at its abruptness.

In *Hommage a Gauguin,* Victor Segalen wrote about the influence of Pissarro on Gauguin:

> It was this master who taught him to choose the tones to put on his canvas: the elimination of waxy blacks, stuporous browns, earthy colors and thin ochres, and the naive resolution to stick to the three primaries and their immediate derivatives. Pissarro, a Dane born in the Antilles, forced by his family into business, who without instruction taught himself the elements of drawing . . . Far more than the division of colors, Pissarro first taught Gauguin how to get out of the clutches of one's family, how to avoid a commercial fate, with its ledgers of income and outgo and its balance sheets and banknotes: how not to become a businessman.

In early 1884, Gauguin, Mette, and the five children moved to Rouen, where they could live more cheaply and be closer to Pissarro. This did not work out because Gauguin was not able to sell his paintings. In August 1884, Mette returned to the relative security of Copenhagen. Gauguin joined the family there, and, partly to please his in-laws and partly for the income, became an agent for a manufacturer.

Gauguin's exhibition at the Society of Friends in Copenhagen was closed by the Academy. He was out of his element, and he offended Mette's family and friends. Mette taught French to young Danes who were preparing for foreign service. In June 1885,

Gauguin returned to Paris, where he experienced real poverty. Later in life, he said,

> I have known the direst poverty, I mean hunger and all the rest of it. This is nothing, or almost nothing. One gets used to it, and with a bit of will power, one laughs it down in the end. But there is another "suffering" which stimulates genius, although too much of it is liable to kill you . . . Having a great deal of conceit, I ended up with a great deal of energy and I DESIRED DESIRE.

In early 1886, Gauguin's works were displayed at the Eighth Impressionist Exhibition in Paris. His paintings were beginning to be more original and to look less like those of other Impressionists. Art critic Felix Fineon wrote a less than glowing review of his work: "Monsieur Gauguin's tones are very close to one another; hence the muffled harmony of his pictures."

In June 1886, Gauguin moved to Pont-Aven in Brittany, where he could live less expensively. His friend, Daniel de Monfried, thought that Gauguin went to Brittany to find "an atmosphere and environment different from our civilized milieu, so that, in his works, he could return to primitive art." This quest for primitive art was a lifelong search. Gauguin was looking for a pure cerebral art, such as the primitive art of Egypt. He met young artist Emile Bernard on this visit to Brittany. In the fall of 1886, Gauguin returned to Paris, where he met Vincent Van Gogh in Montmartre.

In his search for a more primitive way of life, Gauguin traveled to Panama. He worked for several months as a laborer on the Panama Canal and then moved to Martinique to escape the dysentery and fever associated with the Canal. In Martinique, some of the techniques that evolved over the remainder of his life began to take shape. His paintings showed the arrangement of substantial colors that became part of his mature works. Also, the works done at this time contain bands or contour lines, frequently blue, which framed the forms in the painting. In this, he was influenced by Emile Bernard.

In February 1888, Gauguin returned to Pont-Aven. In October of that year, he had a show at the branch of the Goupils Gallery run by Theo Van Gogh, Vincent's brother. Vincent Van Gogh had moved to Arles in southern France, where he hoped to establish an artists' colony with himself and Gauguin at its center. Theo Van Gogh convinced Gauguin to move to Arles, where he stayed with Van Gogh for two months at the end of 1888. The visit ended with Van Gogh threatening Gauguin with a razor. He caused no injury, but Van Gogh went home and cut off part of his right ear. Gauguin returned to Paris, and Van Gogh was placed in an asylum.

In early 1889, Gauguin returned to Brittany. He stayed in Poulder, a small fishing village more isolated than Pont-Aven, where his work departed even further from the Impressionists. He wrote to his friend Schuffenecker: "Do not copy nature too much. Art is an abstraction; draw it out of nature in a dream when you are thinking more about the act of creation than the result." His works "La Belle Angele" and "The Yellow Christ" were painted at this time. He said, "I love Brittany; there I find the wild and primitive. When my wooden shoes ring on the stony soil, I hear the muffled, dull and mighty tone I am seeking in painting."

In 1891, Gauguin moved to Tahiti. To raise money for the trip, he had a show of thirty paintings that earned him 9,860 francs. Octave Mirbeau wrote a commentary on the exhibit in the *Echo de Paris* making collectors aware that this was "a man fleeing from civilization, voluntarily seeking silence and oblivion in order to become more conscious of himself and better able to hear those inner voices which are stifled in the uproar of our passions and disputes."

Before leaving for Tahiti, Gauguin visited his family in Copenhagen. It was not a satisfactory visit; the younger children did not remember him, and they were all struck by the unusual way that he dressed. The visit was short.

Gauguin was given the official but unpaid mission to "study the customs and landscapes of the country" in Tahiti by the French Director of Fine Arts, Ary Renan. After his ship docked in Tahiti, Gauguin paid his respects to the Governor-General, who was impressed by the papers that Ary Renan had obtained from the Ministry of Public Instruction. Gauguin's initial impression of Papeete was: "Here was the Europe from which I had thought to escape, masquerading under the irritating form of colonial snobbery, childish imitation, grotesque to the point of caricature. That was not what I came here to seek."

Once Gauguin left Papeete and moved into the interior, he was more at ease with his decision to move to Tahiti and found something closer to what he had been seeking. In his manuscript, *Noanoa,* he described what he found in the interior: "I have all the joys of a free existence, animal and human. I have escaped from the artificial into the natural world. With the certainty of tomorrow as free and beautiful as today, peace descends upon me. I develop naturally and have no more vain cares." His paintings from his first stay on Tahiti include "When Are You To Be Married?" and "The Market."

After two years, Gauguin returned to Paris, where he exhibited his works at the Galerie Durand-Ruel without much success. Degas was the only painter who perceived Gauguin's large talent. His acceptance by the public was still in the future. He expressed his concern: "Oh, if the good public would learn to understand a little bit, how I would love it! When I see them examine one of my pictures and turn it upside down, I am terrified they may spoil it . . . And then someone in the crowd calls out to me, 'Why do you paint? For whom do you paint? For yourself alone?' That hits me. I crawl away ashamed."

Gauguin returned again to Pont-Aven to paint. In 1895, Gauguin visited his family in Copenhagen before leaving Paris for the last time. He returned to Tahiti, where he settled in a thatched hut surrounded by flowering shrubs at Punaauia. His art continued to evolve. Unfortunately, his health began to slip.

In 1897, Gauguin painted two of his better-known works, "Nevermore" and "Whence Come We? What Are We? Whither Go We?" He described his intent with "Nevermore": "I have tried to suggest a certain bygone barbaric luxury in a simple nude. The whole picture is bathed in deliberately somber colors. It is neither silk nor velvet nor batiste nor gold that creates this luxurious quality, but simply a richness of texture due to the hand of the artist. There is no fooling here . . . [but] the imagination of man alone with himself."

Gauguin was going through a particularly difficult time when he painted "Whence Come We? What Are We? Whither Go We?" He applied for a loan from the Bank of Tahiti to pay his living expenses. He received news of the death of his daughter, Aline, from pneumonia, and Mette stopped writing. He summed up his motivation to paint this work in a letter to a friend in July 1901: "I wanted to die and full of despair, I painted it at one go." It was a large work done on a piece of burlap measuring fourteen feet, nine inches by five feet, six inches. It is an example of symbolism; from left to right, it proceeds from birth, with several women near a baby, through representatives of adult life, to death depicted by older women on the right. The figure in the center of the work is plucking an apple from a tree.

Gauguin's health continued to decline. His eyesight worsened, and he developed eczema on his legs. In July 1901, he wrote to a friend, "I'm at the end of my rope . . . I'm going to make the final effort and am off next month to Fatu-Hiva in the Marquesas, an island still almost cannibalistic. I think that the savage element there, together with complete solitude, will revive the fire of enthusiasm before I die, give new life to my imagination, and bring my talents to a fitting conclusion."

In Paris, Gauguin's friend, Daniel de Monfried, continued to search for a market for his work. Ambroise Vollard, a dealer in Paris, was beginning to take an interest in his paintings and to find customers for them. Gauguin considered returning to France, but Monfried advised against it in December 1902: "You would do best not to come back . . . You now enjoy the immunity of the honored dead . . . Your name has passed into art history."

On May 8, 1903, Gauguin's native servant found him dead in bed. Interest in his work increased when news of his death reached France. Ambroise Vollard arranged a show in his memory. Public acceptance of his work was slow in coming, partly because the public did not understand it. Of his own work, Gauguin wrote, "The essential part of work is precisely that which is not expressed: it is implicit in the lines, without either colors or words, and has no material being."

Of his place in art history, Gauguin wrote, "You have known for a long time what I wanted to accomplish; the right to dare anything . . . The public owes me nothing, since my pictorial work is only 'relatively' good, but the painters who, today, are profiting from this freedom, do owe me something." Gauguin's niche in art history is difficult to evaluate because a considerable portion of his work was purchased by Russian collectors and for years could only be seen at the Hermitage in St. Petersburg and at the Public Museum in Moscow.

In 1988, Gauguin's work went on view in the West for the first time since 1906. The Paul Gauguin Retrospective, comprised of eleven paintings, was displayed at the National Gallery of Art in Washington and the Art Institute of Chicago; his paintings were shown at the Grand Palais in Paris the following year.

Gauguin has a reputation as a writer as well as a painter. Richard Breitell, an American curator who helped to organize the 1988-89 retrospective of Gauguin's works, commented that his writing was the "largest and most important body of texts, illustrated and otherwise, produced by any great artist in France since . . . Delacroix . . . That he has always been treated as a businessman-turned-artist rather than an artist shows the extent to which his literary achievement has been undervalued."

Gauguin was determined to make a mid-career change. He made a decision to do what he was created to do; this forced him to live in poverty and suffer from the rejection of his family. However, a case can be made that he rejected them. In her later years, Mette's views of her husband's actions mellowed. Shortly before she died, she gave Gauguin's letters to their youngest son, Paul (Pola), with the comment:

> Read them and they will give you a fairer estimate of your father; publish them if you think fit. He was a strong man both in his disposition and in his actions, without malice or suspicion. Perhaps he was rather inconsiderate in his candor and in acting according to his convictions, but he was always calm and consistent, without fanaticism. I could not understand his taking up art, though now I understand that he had a right to act as he did. But surely no one can be surprised that I refused to accompany him and bear him more children in an existence which to my mind was a mad and hopeless adventure.

Gauguin's accomplishments are more fully understood today than they were during his lifetime. He was determined to paint and, furthermore, to paint in a primitive style that the public did not understand. His place in art history confirms that he was right on both counts.

AMEDEO MODIGLIANI (1884-1920) Artist Who Would Only Paint

"For the distillation of Modigliani's quality as a man, when all is said, is found in the masterpieces he left behind him. They are more really himself than anything that has been recorded about the personality that produced them. Perhaps I have now got to the root of the matter. An artist should be judged not by his extravagances, intoxications, quarrels, vehement and silly letters, inability to be a bourgeois husband, lapses from being a 'perfect gentleman,' and so forth, but solely by the extent of his achievement. By these standards, Modigliani is among the immortals and requires no justification."

Douglas Goldring, *Artist Quarter*

The subjects of most of Modigliani's art were the human figure and face. He rarely painted landscapes or still lifes, and yet he was influenced by Cézanne. His work usually involved the single human form, in contrast with Cézanne's later paintings of multiple figures. The public was slow to gain an appreciation for Modigliani's distorted, elongated figures with tilted oval heads and long, pendulous noses. He varied his painting of eyes, from wide-open green eyes to lidded eyes that avoided eye contact.

Some of Modigliani's most notable works are his paintings of nude women. They are adult, erotic nudes in which physical realism is stressed, which was something that earlier artists either concealed or modified. The public in Paris during Modigliani's time was not ready for such openness in their art. That did not prevent Modigliani from providing it.

One catalog of Modigliani's works contains a list of 309 paintings dated from 1914 to 1920. It does not include the works destroyed by the artist. In his early years, he moved frequently. He was evicted for nonpayment of rent many times. On many of these occasions, he left hurriedly to escape arrest; many of his sketches and paintings were left behind and were destroyed by the enraged landlord. Estimates of his production during the years 1914-20 are as high as 450 paintings.

Amedeo Modigliani began to paint at age fourteen in his hometown of Leghorn, Italy, with the local painter, Guglielmo Micheli.

He left high school in 1899 to study painting full-time and enrolled in the Scuoli Di Nudo in Florence in May 1902. A year later, he moved to Venice, where he attended the Institute of Fine Arts for three years. In late 1905, Modigliani's mother visited him in Venice to give him money to travel to Paris.

In January 1906, Modigliani arrived in Paris to attend the Academie Colarossi. His "studio" in the *maquis* area of Paris was a rickety, run-down hut made of wood and corrugated steel. Louis Latourettes, a fellow artist, visited Modigliani in the *maquis* and said that he "had lots of promise but felt that, in general, the artist was rather uncertain of himself and fumbling for a road he had not found."

Modigliani agreed with him. He told Latourettes, "My damned Italian eyes are to blame. Somehow they can't get used to this Paris light . . . None of this stuff is any good. All junk." He told Latourettes that the only painters he admired were Pablo Picasso and Henri Rousseau. Since he wasn't able to approach their standards, he destroyed all of his paintings; he saved only a few drawings.

Modigliani received a small allowance from home, spent it as soon as he received it, and lived in poverty. He tried to sell his drawings in Montmartre and was continually looking for portrait customers. He found few customers, and, when he did, they paid him a nominal fee. It never occurred to him to do another type of work. His friend, Max Jacob, worked as an art critic and took part-time jobs to earn an income. Vlaminck worked nights in the market at Les Halles.

Picasso lived with an art colony in the Bateau-Lavoir, a large, dilapidated building at 13 Place Ravigon, where most of the artists did some type of odd jobs for spending money. Picasso did not need outside work; his art had been selling since his discovery by Gertrude Stein and her brother, Leo.

Modigliani frequently visited the Bateau-Lavoir, which came to be known as the birthplace of Cubism. The Bateau-Lavoir had been a habitat for artists and authors since the days of Gauguin. It was a ramshackle structure located on top of the Butte area of Montmartre, consisting of a rabbit warren of rooms.

Max Jacob gave the old factory its name because it reminded him of the washing boats or laundry barges that were tied up in the

Seine River. Both the Bateau-Lavoir and the laundry barges creaked in the wind, and both were entered from the top. The Bateau-Lavoir was entered from the third floor. Visitors had to walk down rickety stairs to a maze of hallways, which led to individual studios. Many artists, in addition to Picasso, lived and worked there.

The Bateau-Lavoir also contained small workshops for tailors and seamstresses. Modigliani was not a member of the inner group of artists at the Bateau-Lavoir because he was not a member of any school of artists; he did not join in the fashionable activity of rejecting the work of earlier painters.

The Lapin Agile (Agile Rabbit) was one of Modigliani's hangouts in the Montmartre area. It was a noisy, smoky place and the site of uninterrupted conversation, drinking, and entertainment. Some of the entertainment was provided by the owner, Frédéric Gérard (Frédé), who played the guitar and sang bawdy songs.

In addition to being an artists' haunt, the Lapin Agile was frequented by *apaches*, members of the Parisian underworld. They added to the atmosphere of the place; however, Frédé had to keep an old pistol handy to break up riots. Picasso and his fellow artists from the Bateau-Lavoir were regulars at the Lapin Agile.

Modigliani met Maurice Utrillo there. Utrillo was the son of Suzanne Valadon, who was once Renoir's model and was a talented artist herself. Utrillo, like Modigliani, had a drinking problem. He began drinking at an early age and would sell one of his drawings for a drink. Modigliani and Utrillo admired each other's work; when they met, they paid each other compliments. Each called the other the world's greatest painter. When the other disagreed, they argued at length before settling down and going to a bistro for several bottles of wine.

Modigliani considered Suzanne Valadon his "elected mother." He confided his sufferings to her. Occasionally, when he had too much to drink, he would run up the stairs to the apartment Suzanne shared with Monsieur Utter, tear off his clothes and enter the apartment stark naked, dancing in a wild manner. Suzanne and Utter would give him a bath and put him to bed. She did not think of Modigliani as a rowdy alcoholic, but as a gifted artist tormented by a touch of madness.

One morning Modigliani woke up in the bright sunlight and

was alarmed because he couldn't move. Two street cleaners were laughing at him. They helped him out of his predicament. Apparently, he had passed out in a bar the previous evening and had been carried out and jammed into a trash can while bent double. He could not stand when helped out of the trash bin because his circulation had been cut off, and his muscles ached. He laughed at his situation and took it as a joke. His only observation was, "A god in a dust bin!"

Dr. Alexandre, Modigliani's earliest patron in Paris, established a colony for artists where Modigliani worked briefly. In 1908, Dr. Alexandre convinced him to join the Société des Artistes Independents and to show his work at their salon that year.

Many of Modigliani's contemporaries had moderate success selling their art in the pre-World War I era. However, his work did not sell. In 1913, Modigliani became associated with Monsieur Cheron, an art dealer who was the son-in-law of one of the best-known art dealers in Paris. Cheron had been a bookmaker and wine merchant; he had no deep-seated love for art. In his opinion, an art dealer was a businessman. Cheron provided Modigliani with canvasses, paints, brushes, and a place to work in the basement of his shop on the Rue de la Boétie.

Modigliani produced one or two paintings a day for a louis, a gold coin worth twenty francs. Cheron also provided his young maid as a model and a bottle of cognac for Modigliani. Modigliani was locked in the basement as though he were a prisoner, and when he was done with his work he had to kick the door to be let out. The arrangement didn't last long.

Paul Guillaume, an intellectual who appreciated art, became interested in Modigliani when he left Cheron. Guillaume was a collector of African art who was interested in modern artists. Max Jacob introduced Modigliani to Guillaume. Jacob tried to arrange a sponsor for his friend similar to Gertrude Stein's sponsorship of Picasso. However, Guillaume was a very cautious, conservative individual who did not take substantial risks in advancing large amounts of money to unknown painters.

In 1916, Modigliani became associated with Leopold Zborowski, who was more a poor but determined art peddler than a professional dealer. Although he was considered an amateur in art circles, he worked hard for the artists he represented. He did more than anyone to make Modigliani's reputation as one of the modern masters.

Zborowski really cared for his artists as individuals. Frequently, he provided money to artists whose work he was trying to sell by skimping on living expenses for his family. Although Guillaume was probably the first serious dealer to represent Modigliani, he remained aloof and did not push hard to sell Modigliani's work. Zborowski pushed Modigliani's art relentlessly and became a friend, confidant, and advisor.

Zborowski convinced a gallery owner, Berthe Weill, to have a Modigliani show. The paintings were hung in her gallery on a Sunday, and a private showing was held the next day. A Modigliani nude, a painting of a long-haired woman with her head tilted, was displayed in the window and attracted a crowd immediately.

The office of the Division Police Commissioner was located across the street from Berthe's gallery. The Commissioner sent a policeman over with orders to remove the painting from the window. Berthe complied with the request, although the patrons at the private showing snickered because there were many more paintings of nudes inside the gallery.

The crowd outside became larger, and finally the same policeman returned and summoned Berthe to the Commissioner's office. The Commissioner, who had been told by the policeman that the paintings inside the gallery were as "bad" as the nude in the window, ordered Berthe to remove the nudes from her gallery. If she didn't, he would send policemen over to confiscate all of the paintings. The show, which had not yet officially opened to the public, was over. To compensate Zborowski for the disaster, Berthe bought two of the paintings. Also, two were sold at the truncated private showing. The incident brought Modigliani's name before the public.

World War I depressed the Paris art market, which delayed interest in Modigliani's art. Paris endured air raids. The Germans lobbed heavy shells into the city from three large railway cannons (big Berthas) 100 kilometers away. Panic spread through the city, and everyone who could afford to or who had relatives in the provinces left the city. Zborowski planned a trip to Nice, which he hoped was a better art market than the depressed Paris market. It wasn't, and a visit to Nice was not productive. Zborowski was unsuccessful in finding art buyers in the Nice-Cannes area. He also made a selling trip to Marseille without success.

Modigliani returned to Paris in May 1919. He continued to paint, but late in 1919 he began to cough and spit blood. He became weaker. On January 22, 1920, he lost consciousness and was taken to Charity Hospital in an ambulance. He never regained consciousness and died two days later of tuberculosis. On January 27, a cortege bore his body through the streets of Paris, and he was buried in Père-Lachaise Cemetery. An estimated 1,000 people attended his funeral, including most of his artist friends.

Recognition of Modigliani began after his death, when his work as an artist replaced the legend of Modigliani, the bohemian. He was always an individualist in his painting. The slow acceptance of his work is partially explained by his differences from other artists active in Paris at the time. He had considerable strengths as a draftsman when the Fauves school of artists gave color a dominant role in art. For example, Cézanne's goal was to attempt to present perspective by using color. After being influenced in his early work by the style of the 1890s, such as that of Toulouse-Lautrec, Modigliani matured as a painter at about the time the Cubists were emerging to the forefront of art in Paris. He was influenced by the distortions of Cézanne, the economy of Cubism, and the triangular shapes of African sculpture.

The market for Modigliani's work at the time of his death was a classic case of speculation in art. Interest in Modigliani's art increased significantly when he became seriously ill. Art speculators knew that the value of an artist's work increased sharply after his death. Leopold Zborowski, Modigliani's agent, was pressed to sell Modigliani's works within days of his death, but he held off. Before his death, Modigliani's paintings sold for 100-150 francs. Zborowski received an offer during his client's funeral procession of 40,000 francs for fifty paintings, or 800 francs each.

One dealer heard two days before Modigliani's death that he probably wouldn't recover. He hurried around Paris buying all of Modigliani's work that he could find. The dealer ran around saying, "Have I luck! Right up to his death watch, I still picked up some Modiglianis for nothing. It was about time."

The day after Modigliani's death, a customer in an art gallery in Paris asked for a Modigliani. The Swiss painter Fornerod said that the dealer went into his back room for a Modigliani marked 300 francs, added a zero, and sold the painting for 3,000 francs.

The paintings that Modigliani left at the Cité Falguiere studio were used by the landlord to reupholster his furniture. After Modigliani's death, when his paintings increased in value, the landlord disassembled the couch and chairs to sell Modigliani's works to a dealer for 10,000 francs. However, his wife had removed as much of the "dirty paint" as she could. The landlord became so furious about his lost windfall that he died of apoplexy.

In *Modigliani*, Pierre Sichel comments on Modigliani's life:

> Modi's art is the vindication of his life. He believed in himself and his art, and, truly, nothing else mattered. If he managed triumph only after his death, because he was his own worst enemy, it does not matter. How he lived his life does not matter; he did triumph—and so very few of us do.

Modigliani was motivated to create his style of art without public recognition or appreciation for his work in his lifetime. An example of the increase in value of Modigliani's paintings is "The Pretty Shopkeeper," which was sold for $12 million in November 1990 at an auction in Paris.

CHAPTER 2

SONGWRITERS / COMPOSERS

"Whatever you can do or dream you can do, begin it.
Boldness has genius, power, and magic in it. Begin it."

Goethe

CHARLES IVES (1874-1954) Composer and Musical Innovator

'Tis known by the name of perseverance in a good cause—and obstinacy in a bad one."

Lawrence Sterne, *Sermons*

Charles Ives is an excellent example of an individual who persevered in doing what he had to do. Composing music became a second career that paralleled his career in the insurance business. Most of his compositions were written in the twenty-year period between 1896 and 1916. Public recognition of his music didn't come for another half century, however. He knew that the music he was writing was revolutionary and wasn't liked by his friends or by the listening public. It was too full of dissonance and discord for the average ear. When asked by a friend why he didn't compose what people liked to hear, Ives replied, "I can't do it. I hear something else."

Ives is frequently compared with Bartok, Milhaud, Stravinsky, and Schoenberg. However, his pioneering predates all of theirs. For example, he used discords prior to Bartok; he composed polytonal music (music written in several keys simultaneously) before Milhaud; he utilized polyrhythms (a diverse set of rhythmic forms at the same time) earlier than Stravinsky; and he composed atonal music (music in no fixed key) that predated Schoenberg.

Henry Bellaman, the author of *King's Row,* who became familiar with Ives's work while lecturing in the South, was one of his early promoters. Bellaman arranged for "Concord Sonata" to be performed in New Orleans in October 1920. In January 1939, American pianist John Kirkpatrick played Ives's "Concord Sonata" at Town Hall, New York. It was performed again several weeks later to critical acclaim. Lawrence Gilman of the *Herald Tribune* declared that Ives was "the most original and extraordinary of American composers."

Most American composers were strongly influenced by European composers. Ives wasn't; he drew upon American subjects. His music was influenced by square dances, camp meetings, Fourth of July picnics, religious revival gatherings, rural and small town American settings, and the songs of America. American hymns, marches, and Stephen Foster's tunes are woven into many

46

of Ives's compositions.

Ives asked himself, "Why is it that I like to use these different things and try out other ways . . . which nobody has any pleasure in hearing, seeing and thinking about? Why do I like to do it? Is there some particular defect in me, or something worse that I'm afflicted with?"

During all the years when lack of recognition could have led to self-doubt, Ives persevered in writing the music that he felt he had to write. The support of his wife, Harmony Twitchell Ives, never flagged. In later years, he wrote, "She never once said: 'Now why don't you be good and write something the way they [his friends] like it?'—Never—she urged me on my way—to be myself! She gave me not only hope but a confidence that no one else since my father had given me."

Ives wrote his "First String Quartet" with four movements: "Chorale," "Prelude," "Offertory," and "Postlude," while in his sophomore year at Yale. He chose a technique in the quartet for which he later became known—the insertion of familiar melodies into his works. He incorporated the hymn "From Greenland's Icy Mountains" into the first movement of the quartet. Ives also wrote his "First Symphony," a remarkable accomplishment for an undergraduate, while at Yale. His music professor was highly critical of it and asked him to rewrite it using fewer keys. Ives preferred the less conventional version. Another of Ives's early, serious pieces was the "Prelude and Postlude for a Thanksgiving Service" for the organ, which he composed in 1897. His music professor disliked this work because it contained polytonal passages.

After graduating from Yale, Ives chose not to become a professional musician. In making this career decision, he was heavily influenced by his father's viewpoint on the subject. George Ives said:

> A man could keep his music interest stronger, cleaner, bigger, and freer if he didn't try to make a living out of it. Assuming a man lives by himself with no dependents, he might write music that no one would play prettily, listen to or buy. But—but if he had a nice wife and some nice children, how can he let the children starve on his dissonance? So

he has to weaken (and if he is a man, he SHOULD
weaken for his children), but his music more than
weakens—it goes "ta-ta" for money! Bad for him,
bad for music!

George Ives, a serious musician, had followed his own advice; he
worked for the Danbury Bank.

Charles Ives moved to New York City and went into the insurance business. During his early years in New York, he composed
evenings, weekends, and during vacations. Occasionally, he attended a concert at Carnegie Hall, but generally he didn't listen to other
composers' works. It took time away from the small amount of time
he had to compose. Also, he tended to carry the music he was composing in his head rather than write it down immediately. Attending
concerts and listening to the music of others confused him in his
own work.

In 1902, Ives completed his "Second Symphony" while living in
New York. He thought that it expressed the musical feelings around
Danbury, Connecticut, in the 1890s, that is, the music of the country folk. It includes melodic strains from "Columbia, the Gem of
the Ocean," "America, the Beautiful," "De Camptown Races," and
"Old Black Joe." Concurrently, he worked on his score for "Third
Symphony," although it wasn't completed until 1904. The inspiration for this work was provided by the camp meetings held in the
Danbury area. He drew upon hymns for a portion of this work,
including "O for a Thousand Tongues" and "Just as I am." It was
first conducted by Lou Harrison on April 5, 1946, forty-two years
after the score was completed.

During the years 1909-15, Ives wrote his "Concord Sonata,"
which is probably the best known of his works. It is a piano sonata
with four movements, each one named for Concord residents:
"Emerson," "Hawthorne," "The Alcotts," and "Thoreau." Ives
intended to express his emotional bond with the New England
Transcendentalists and the primacy of the spiritual and superindi-
vidual versus the material and the empirical. Ives wrote a booklet,
"Essays before a Sonata" to help explain it. It included a dedica-
tion: "These prefatory essays were written by the composer for
those who can't stand his music—and the music for those who
can't stand his essays; to those who can't stand either, the whole is

respectfully dedicated."

From 1903 to 1914, he worked on "Three Places in New England," with its movements, "Boston Common" (influenced by the St. Gaudens statue of Colonel Shaw and his African-American regiment); "Putnam's Camp" in Redding, Connecticut; and "The Housatonic at Stockbridge." This piece was inspired by three geographic settings in New England, rather than by hymns, marches, or folk songs, as were some of his earlier works. On January 10, 1931, it was heard for the first time, with Nicolas Slonimsky conducting the Boston Symphony Orchestra.

Ives's strong feelings for his style of music were demonstrated at this concert. Three American works were performed and all three were loudly hissed and booed, including Ives's "Three Places in New England." Ives remained silent while his work was booed. However, when the audience booed Carl Ruggles's "Men and Mountains," Ives couldn't contain himself any longer. He stood and shouted to the audience in general, "Don't be such a sissy! When you hear strong music like this, get up and try to use your ears like a man!"

In 1914, Ives completed his "Fourth Symphony," the last and most complicated of his symphonies. Its score was written for a huge orchestra with a brass band and a chorus. Twenty-seven different rhythms are played at the same time at one point in the symphony. Occasionally, it has required three conductors to conduct it. It includes portions of many hymns, including "The Sweet Bye and Bye," "Nearer My God to Thee," and "Watchman, Tell Us of the Night," as well as "Yankee Doodle" and "Turkey in the Straw." Its world premiere was on April 26, 1965, by the American Symphony Orchestra conducted by Leopold Stokowski and two assistants.

Ives was a promoter of concert music based on things American, not things European. A friend of Ives was asked by the French composer Vincent D'Indy, "Why don't your American composers inspire themselves by their own landscapes, their own legends and history, instead of leaning on the German walking stick?" That is precisely what Ives did. In referring to his dreams for the future, he said "we would rather believe . . . that the time is coming, but not in our lifetime, when music will develop possibilities inconceivable now—a language so transcendent, that its heights and depths will be common to all mankind. The future may not be with music itself, but rather . . . in the way it makes itself a part of the finer things humanity does and dreams of."

In 1946, Ives was elected to the National Institute of Arts and Letters, and his "Third Symphony," for which he won a Pulitzer Prize, was played for the first time—more than forty years after he wrote it. Leonard Bernstein and the New York Philharmonic performed the premier of Ives's "Second Symphony" in Carnegie Hall in 1951, almost fifty years after he composed it.

When Austrian composer Arnold Schoenberg died in 1951, a note was found among his papers:

> There is a great man living in this country—a
>   composer.
> He has solved the problem how to preserve
>   oneself and learn.
> He responds to negligence with contempt.
> He is not forced to accept praise or blame.
> His name is Ives.

GEORGE GERSHWIN (1898-1937) Popular Songwriter and Composer

"Just seven years tomorrow since George wrote 'Plenty O' Nuttin' and I took it down as he played it. My 'Porgy' lecture honestly wowed the people last night—the music is absolutely sure-fire in *any* group whatsoever. The whole audience left feeling proud that so important a work has been done in this country. And I left with a ghastly sense of the grayness of a world without George, a profound personal and universal sense of loss. For I believe his music is a force for strong Americanism, in the best sense, that it strikes a powerful blow against the evils that besiege us by giving people a magic lift and a strengthening touch . . . It's so positive and confident."

Kay Swift in a letter to Mary Lasker, 1942.

George Gershwin composed popular and classical music. His works in both genres are well-known. His best-known orchestral compositions include *Rhapsody in Blue* (1924), *An American in Paris* (1928), and the opera *Porgy and Bess* (1935).

Gershwin studied piano with Rubin Goldmark and composition with Henry Cowell. He began his career as a song plugger in Tin Pan Alley. Then he began to compose Broadway theater works with his brother, Ira, and Buddy DeSylva. He moved to Paris to study.

When Gershwin returned to New York City, he composed *Porgy and Bess*, working with Ira and DuBose Heyward. Initially a commercial failure, it is now one of the most important American operas of the twentieth century. Gershwin moved to Hollywood and composed many film scores until his death of a brain tumor in 1937.

George Gershwin was born Jacob Gershowitz, in Brooklyn, New York, on September 26, 1898, of Russian and Jewish heritage. George's father, Moishe Gershowitz, had worked as a leather cutter in St. Petersburg, Russia. Moishe fell in love with Roza Bruskins, daughter of a furrier. Born in Vilnius, Lithuania, Roza moved with her family to New York because of increasing anti-semitism in Russia. She changed her first name to Rose.

Moishe, faced with compulsory military service in Russia, followed Rose to New York. When he arrived in New York, Moishe Gershowitz changed his first name to Morris. He took a job as a foreman in a workshop. Morris and Rose were married on July 21, 1895. Gershowitz changed his name to Gershwin sometime between 1893 and 1895, perhaps when they were married.

The Gershwin's first child, Ira, was born on December 6, 1896. George Gershwin was born on September 26, 1898. Two more children were born to the family, Arthur in 1900 and Frances in 1906.

George's interest in music began at the age of ten when he heard a friend's violin recital. George's parents bought a piano so Ira could take piano lessons. However, to Ira's relief, it was brother George who took the lessons.

Charles Hambitzer taught Gershwin conventional piano techniques and acquainted him with the music of the European classical tradition. He encouraged Gershwin to attend orchestra concerts and, in effect, became his mentor. Later, Gershwin studied with the classical composer Rubin Goldmark and avant-garde composer-theorist Henry Cowell.

Gershwin left school at the age of fifteen and became a "song plugger" for a publishing firm in Tin Pan Alley. He published his first song at the age of seventeen and another one year later. He had his first national hit in 1919 with his song "Swanee," with lyrics by Irving Caesar. Performances by Al Jolson contributed to the popularity of the song.

In 1916, Gershwin began to work for the Aeolian Company, recording and arranging piano rolls. He produced hundreds of rolls under his name and assumed names. He also performed in vaudeville, providing piano accompaniment.

In the early 1920s, Gershwin collaborated with songwriter and music director William Daly on the Broadway musicals *Piccadilly to Broadway* (1920), *For Goodness' Sake* (1922), and *Our Nell* (1923). Gershwin also worked with Buddy DeSylva frequently. They wrote the one-act jazz opera *Blue Monday,* set in Harlem.

In 1924, Gershwin and his brother, Ira, collaborated on the musical comedy *Lady Be Good,* which included "Fascinating Rhythm" and "Oh, Lady, Be Good." They followed it with *Oh, Kay!* (1926), *Funny Face* (1927), and *Strike Up the Band* (1927). Next came *Show Girl* (1929), *Girl Crazy* (1930), which introduced "Embraceable

You" and "I Got Rhythm," and *Of Thee I Sing* (1931). *Of Thee I Sing* was the first musical comedy to win the Pulitzer Prize for drama.

In 1924, Gershwin composed *Rhapsody in Blue* for orchestra and piano, his first classical work. It was orchestrated by Ferde Grofe and introduced by Paul Whiteman's band in New York. In the mid-1920s, Gershwin moved to Paris, hoping to study with Nadia Boulanger and Maurice Ravel. Both turned him down, thinking that rigorous musical study would ruin his jazz-influenced style. In his rejection letter, Ravel asked, "Why become a second-rate Ravel when you're already a first-rate Gershwin?"

While in Paris, Gershwin wrote *An American in Paris,* which received mixed reviews at its premiere at Carnegie Hall on December 13, 1928. He returned to the United States and wrote his first opera, *Blue Monday,* a short one-act opera that was not a financial success.

In 1935, Gershwin wrote *Porgy and Bess,* based on the novel *Porgy* by DuBose Heyward, which he called a "folk opera." It received mixed reviews from music and drama critics. They had difficulty with it because it wasn't really an opera and it really wasn't a musical. It included "Summertime," "I Got Plenty o' Nuttin'." and "It Ain't Necessarily So."

Gershwin moved to Hollywood in 1936, where he wrote the music for the film *Shall We Dance,* starring Fred Astaire and Ginger Rodgers. His score, which combined ballet with jazz, was very popular.

Gershwin had a ten-year relationship with composer Kay Swift, whom he frequently consulted about his music. They never married. After Gershwin's death, Swift arranged some of his music, transcribed several of his recordings, and collaborated with his brother, Ira, on several songs.

Early in 1937, Gershwin began to complain of blinding headaches. On February 11, 1937, he performed his *Concerto in F* in a concert with the San Francisco Symphony Orchestra under the direction of Pierre Monteux. He suffered coordination problems and blackouts during the performance. He had been experiencing mood swings and could not eat without spilling his food. On July 9, he collapsed and was rushed to Cedars of Lebanon hospital, where he went into a coma.

It was determined that Gershwin had a brain tumor and that the need for surgery was immediate. He was operated on in the early hours of the 11th, but the operation was not successful. George Gershwin died on the morning of July 11, 1937, at the age of thirty-eight. He was buried at Westchester Hills Cemetery in Hastings-on-Hudson, New York.

One of the observations Gershwin made about his music was: "True music must reflect the thought and aspirations of the people and time. My people are Americans. My time is today."

COLE PORTER (1891-1964) Popular Songwriter and Composer

"As an undergraduate, you first won acclaim by writing the words and music to two of Yale's perennial football fight songs. Since then, you have achieved reputation as a towering figure in the American musical theater. Master of the deft phrase, the delectable rhymes, the distinctive melody, you are, in your own words and your own field, the top.

Confident that your graceful, impudent, inimical songs will be played and sung as long as footlights burn and curtains go up. Your alma mater confers upon you the degree of Doctor of Humane Letters."

Norman S. Buck, Provost, Yale University, 1960.

Cole Porter was born on June 9, 1891, to a wealthy family in Peru, Indiana. His maternal grandfather was a coal and timber speculator who expected his grandson to become a lawyer. Cole attended law school but knew that it wasn't for him. He wanted to write songs for the musical theater.

Porter's musical abilities weren't initially recognized. His success began in the 1920s, and by the 1930s he was one of the most popular songwriters on Broadway. Unlike George Gershwin and Richard Rodgers, Porter wrote the lyrics as well as the music.

In 1937, Porter had a very serious horseback riding accident that left him disabled and in constant pain. He continued to write songs but his shows of the 1940s did not measure up to those of the 1920s and 1930s. However, in 1948, he wrote what many consider his finest musical, *Kiss Me, Kate,* based on Shakespeare's *Taming of the Shrew.* It won the first Tony Award for Best Musical.

Among Porter's many musicals are *Anything Goes, Can-Can, Fifty Million Frenchmen,* and *Silk Stockings.* His many hit songs include "Begin the Beguine," "Night and Day," "What Is This Thing Called Love?," "You Do Something To Me," and "In the Still of the Night." Porter also composed scores for films from the 1930s to the 1950s, including *Born to Dance* (1936) with "You'd Be So Easy to Love," *Rosalie* (1937) with "In the Still of the Night," *High Society* (1956) with "True Love," and *Les Girls* (1957).

Porter was an only child born to Samuel Porter, a druggist, and Kate Cole Porter, the daughter of James Omar "J. O." Cole, "the richest man in Indiana." J. O. Cole dominated the family. Kate Porter strongly encouraged her son's musical training. He learned the violin at age six, the piano at eight, and with help from his mother wrote his first operetta at ten. Porter's father was a vocalist, a pianist, and an amateur poet. He may have been a minor influence on his son's talents in rhyme and meter. However, the father and son relationship was not close.

In 1905, Porter enrolled in Worchester Academy in Massachusetts. He was class valedictorian when he graduated in 1909, the year he entered Yale University. At Yale, he majored in English, minored in music, and also studied French. He was a member of Scroll and Key and Delta Kappa Epsilon fraternity and contributed to the humor magazine, *The Yale Record*. He was a member of the Wiffenpoofs singing group. In his senior year, Porter was elected president of the Yale Glee Club and was its main soloist.

Porter wrote 300 songs at Yale, including student songs, such as "Eli Yale" and "Bulldog":
:

> Bull Dog! Bull Dog! Bow, wow, wow
> Eli Yale
> Bull Dog! Bull Dog! Bow, wow, wow
> Our team can never fail.

They are still sung at Yale today.

Porter also wrote music for his fraternity, the Yale Dramat (the Yale dramatic society), and while attending Law School at Harvard University. He enrolled in Harvard Law School in 1913 but soon switched to the Music School, where he studied harmony and counterpoint with Pietro Yon. J. O. Cole was not told of this move.

Porter's first song on Broadway was "Esmeralda" from *Hands Up* in 1915. This first success was followed by the failure of his first Broadway show in 1916, *See America First,* a "patriotic comic opera." It folded after two weeks.

In 1917, when the United States entered World War I, Porter moved to Paris. He joined the French Foreign Legion, served in North Africa, transferred to the French Officers' School at

Fontainebleau, and taught gunnery to U.S. soldiers. After the war, Porter leased a luxury apartment in Paris, where he hosted lavish parties known for "much gay and bisexual activity, Italian nobility, cross-dressing, and international musicians."

In 1918, Porter met Linda Lee Thomas, a wealthy divorcee eight years his senior. Linda was beautiful and had many social connections. They had mutual interests, including a love of travel. Linda became Porter's companion and confidant.

They were married in 1919, even though Linda was aware of Porter's homosexuality. Linda was provided with continued social status; Porter was provided with a heterosexual image at a time when homosexuality was not acknowledged in public. They were very devoted to each other and remained married until her death in 1954.

Porter enrolled at the Schola Cantorum in Paris to study orchestration and counterpoint with Vincent d'Indy. In 1919, Porter had his first big hit, "Old Fashioned Garden." The following year he contributed several songs to *A Night Out.* Porter had little success with his songwriting in the 1920s. The poor public response to his work hurt him. He came very close to giving up songwriting as a career.

In 1928, at the age of thirty-six, Porter reentered the Broadway scene with his first real hit musical, *Paris,* which included the songs "Let's Misbehave" and "Let's Do It." His revue *Wake Up and Dream* ran for 263 performances in London and then moved to New York, where it ran for 136 performances, being shortened by the Wall Street crash of 1929. Nevertheless, its song "What Is This Thing Called Love?" became extremely popular.

In 1929, Porter wrote the music for *Fifty Million Frenchmen,* which included "You Do Something To Me" and "You've Got That Thing." It was doing poorly at the box office until Irving Berlin placed an advertisement in the newspaper observing: "The best musical comedy I've heard in years . . . One of the best collections of song numbers that I have ever listened to."

In 1930, Porter's *The New Yorker* was popular, particularly the song "Love for Sale." Porter's next success was Fred Astaire's last stage show, *Gay Divorce* in 1932, with Porter's best-known song, *"Night and Day."*

Anything Goes was an instant hit in 1934 with its "I Get a Kick Out of You," "All Through the Night," "You're the Top," and "Blow, Gabriel, Blow." It was the first of five Porter shows starring Ethel Merman. In 1935 came *Jubilee,* with "Begin the Beguine" and "Just One of Those Things."

On October 24, 1937, Porter was riding at Piping Rock Club at Locust Valley, when his horse rolled on him and crushed his legs. He became a cripple and was in constant pain for the rest of his life. Linda hurried home from Paris to be with him at the hospital for seven months and afterwards, when he was allowed to return home to the Waldorf Towers.

In 1939, with increased unrest in Europe, Linda closed their house in Paris and purchased a home in the Berkshire Mountains, near Williamstown, Massachusetts. Porter spent time in Hollywood, New York, and their home in Williamstown. Porter continued to write songs for Hollywood movies, including *You'll Never Get Rich* with Fred Astaire and Rita Hayworth. He cooperated with the production of *Night and Day,* the somewhat fictional biography of Cole Porter starring Cary Grant. It was popular principally due to Porter's songs.

In 1948, *Kiss Me, Kate*, Porter's most successful show, was staged, running 1,077 performances in New York and 400 in London. It included "So In Love," "Too Darn Hot," and "Always True to You (In My Fashion)." His *Can-Can* in 1952 was a hit, followed by another success, *Silk Stockings,* his last original Broadway production, in 1955. He wrote the score for *High Society,* including "True Love," in 1956 and some of the songs for *Les Girls* in 1957.

Porter's mother died in 1952, and Linda died in 1954 from emphysema. In 1958, after thirty-four operations, Porter's right leg had to be amputated and replaced with an artificial leg. He never wrote another song. He spent the remaining six years of his life in seclusion. Cole Porter died on October 15, 1964, of kidney failure in Santa Monica, California, at the age of seventy-three.

ALEC WILDER (1907-1980) Popular Songwriter and Composer

"Alec Wilder's music is a unique blend of American musical traditions—among them jazz and the American popular song—and basic 'classical' European forms and techniques. As such, it fiercely resists all labeling. Although it pained Alec that his music was not more widely accepted by either jazz or classical performers, undeterred he wrote a great deal of music of remarkable originality in many forms: sonatas, suites, concertos, operas, ballets, art songs, woodwind quartets, brass quintets, jazz suites—and hundreds of popular songs.

"Many times his music wasn't jazz enough for the 'jazzers,' or 'highbrow,' 'classical,' or 'avant-garde' enough for the classical establishment. In essence, Wilder's music was so unique in its originality that it didn't fit in any of the preordained musical slots and stylistic pigeon-holes. His music was never out of vogue because, in effect, it was never in vogue; its non-stereotypical specialness virtually precluding widespread acceptance."

> Gunther Schuller, Loonis McGlohon, and Robert Levy,
> "A Short Biography"

Alec Wilder's grandfather, Samuel Wilder, made the family fortune in banking and real estate in Rochester, New York. He was the principal owner of Corinthian Hall, where the Swedish nightingale, Jenny Lind, gave her first Rochester performance. Alec's father, George, Samuel's second son, was also a successful Rochester banker. Alec's mother was Lillian Chew Wilder, daughter of Alexander Lafayette Chew and Sarah Prouty Chew of Geneva, New York. The Marquis de Lafayette was Alexander Chew's godfather.

Alec Wilder was born on February 16, 1907. He had an older brother, George, and an older sister, Helen, with whom he was close. Helen introduced him to music by singing the music of Jerome Kern to him. When Wilder was three years old, his father died. By the time he was a teenager, he knew that he did not want to be a banker like his grandfather and his father: "I wanted no part of it . . . for my family was virtually littered with bankers, nor was I inclined to be friendly with the sons and daughters of the conventional families of my family's world."

The Wilder family moved frequently. Wilder attended three private schools: Saint Paul's in Garden City, Long Island, Lawrenceville in New Jersey, and the Collegiate School in Manhattan, where they lived from 1921 until 1924. His first visit to the theater was to see *Shuffle Along,* Eubie Blake's all-black show.

In his late teens, Wilder toured Europe and became interested by music in Venice and Florence. He composed his first piano piece while in Italy and wrote to a friend:

> Something keeps shouting at me to look deeper and deeper into music. I've heard no music but that of countless people singing in the streets. Yet, I've started buying stacks of music; in fact I've even rented a piano. I don't know about music, don't play worth a damn nor read well, but ever since you took me to that concert at Carnegie Hall and I heard "L'Apres-Midi d'un Faune" I've got the bug. I've even written a piece of music that's not just a tune. I don't think it's good, but it is something which I wrote. And it's the first one.

When Wilder returned to New York, he wrote some popular tunes and then, at the suggestion of his friend, tried a cantata based on one of Kipling's poems.

In 1926, Wilder returned to Rochester for the first time since his family had moved to Garden City during World War I. He had decided on a career in music; however, he did not enroll at the Eastman School of Music. Instead, he took private lessons from two faculty members. He studied counterpoint with Herbert Inch, who later won the Prix de Rome, and composition with Edward Royce, son of Harvard University logician Josiah Royce.

Wilder was impressed with the Eastman School. He noted: "It's the wild, free, searching, roaring world of young people who know what they want . . . and my God, how they love music." He met french horn player John Barrows, oboist Mitch Miller, violist Joe

Schiff, and tenor Frank Baker. Wilder was becoming immersed in music: "Music, its sounds, rhythms, patterns and unverbal implications, directions and secret affirmations had always fascinated me. The more I heard, the more I learned, the more dedicated I became to trying to speak its language."

Wilder's favorite composer was Bach. He was also influenced by Mussorgsky, Debussy, and Ravel. Although Howard Hanson was the director of the Eastman School at the time, he and Wilder were too dissimilar to become close. Hanson composed large works in the romantic tradition. His favorite composers were Beethoven, Handel, and Scriabin. Hanson was an autocratic leader; Wilder had little respect for authority. Nevertheless, Hanson said of Wilder's compositions, "His music—intimate, appealing, and very well done—had great charm."

In 1928, Wilder composed eight songs for voice and orchestra based on poems by James Stephens and the song "Annabelle Lee," using text from Edgar Allan Poe. The following year, he composed one of his first works for orchestra, "Symphonic Piece." Also, in his student days, he composed popular songs with a particular singer in mind, e.g. Mildred Bailey, Ethel Waters, and Bing Crosby. "Mildred wound up singing some, Ethel Waters none, and, at the end of his career, Crosby a few."

During his time at the Eastman School, Wilder wrote the revue *Haywire*. His friend, Eastman student Mitch Miller, commented: "He was a very complicated man. I forced him to face his own talent. I got him to write *Haywire*." Although two other students wrote some of the lyrics and one or two of the musical numbers were interpolated, it was loaded with his wit and essentially was a Wilder show.

While in Rochester, Wilder became close with his mentor and father figure, James Sibley Watson, Jr., grandson of Western Union co-founder Hiram Sibley. According to Desmond Stone in *Alec Wilder in Spite of Himself,* Watson was "a true Renaissance figure: physician, major influence in American literature in the 1920s, translator of French poetry [such as Rimbaud], pioneer in radiology and in amateur filmmaking, artist, flyer, expert marksman, inventor, millionaire philanthropist."

In association with Melville Webber, Watson produced two American cinematic landmarks: *The Fall of the House of Usher* in

1929 and *Lot in Sodom* in 1932. In the opinion of James Card, previously film archivist at the International Museum of Photography. "Watson produced avant-garde films long before there were avant-garde films." Watson provided Wilder with an introduction to filmmaking and film scoring.

Another of Wilder's close friends in Rochester was photographer Louis Ouzer. Later, Ouzer was known for his portraits of Marian Anderson, Louis Armstrong, Vladimir Horowitz, Isaac Stern, and other musicians who performed at the Eastman Theatre. He also used his talent in photography to document social change. He was particularly sympathetic to the cause of civil rights for African Americans.

In 1930, Wilder had his first success in writing popular songs: "All the King's Men" written with Eddie Brandt for *Three's a Crowd,* a Broadway revue starring Fred Allen, Libby Holman, and Clifton Webb. By the mid-1930s, Wilder's friends from the Eastman School, Mitch Miller and John Barrows, had moved from Rochester. By this time, Wilder had spent (and given away) his inheritance except for a small quarterly allowance from a family trust fund.

Wilder returned to New York City and lived at the Algonquin Hotel, which would be his home for four decades. As noted by biographer Desmond Stone, in later years Wilder observed:

> I have been coming here since I was a child, and there are still people on the staff who have been here as long as I have. They take care of me. They send out my laundry without my having to fill out a laundry slip, they hang a few suits for me when I'm away, they forward my mail, and they shepherded me through my drinking days . . . I got into a cab to go uptown to a restaurant, and when I got there I simply couldn't move. I told the driver to take me back to the Algonquin, and whoever was on the door sized up the situation immediately. A bellman appeared, and he and the doorman made one of those four-handed seats, got me onto it, and whisked me up to my room.

An anecdote about Wilder's drinking relates that on one occasion while in his cups at the Algonquin's Blue Bar, he asked Benny Goodman to step outside and take his glasses off. Wilder did not remember the incident the next morning. The story is unlikely. One of Wilder's friends described him as a "great walk-away artist."

Wilder was influenced by the music of Harold Arlen, Jerome Kern, and Vincent Youmans. Wilder's friend, Mitch Miller, obtained a position for him as staff arranger for the *Ford Hour* on radio, but Wilder could not tolerate the lack of freedom that he encountered. Miller also encouraged Wilder to write the woodwind octets that were recorded by the Alec Wilder Octet and introduced him to people in musical circles.

In 1939, Wilder met William Engvick, who became one of his lyricists. Their first collaboration was in revising *Ladies and Gents,* on which Engvick had worked previously.

Wilder met Frank Sinatra when the young singer performed at the Paramount Theatre in New York in the 1940s. In 1945, Mitch Miller talked with Sinatra about performing some of Wilder's orchestral pieces. Sinatra, who had not conducted before, recorded a suite of six numbers mixing classical music, jazz, and pop, *Frank Sinatra Conducts the Music of Alec Wilder,* for Columbia Records. Sinatra observed that Wilder's music "helped my own musical conceptions to reach a higher plane than would have been possible without him."

During the 1940s, Wilder composed many of his best-known popular songs, including "Who Can I Turn To?" (1940); "It's So Peaceful in the Country" (1941), which he wrote for Mildred Bailey; "I'll Be Around" (1942); "While We're Young" (1943); "Trouble Is a Man" (1944); and "Where Is the One?" (1948).

Wilder had the highest regard for cabaret singer Mabel Mercer, whom he considered "the guardian of the tenuous dreams created by the writers of songs." Wilder wrote many songs for her, including "Did You Ever Cross Over to Snedden's?," "Goodbye, John," and "Is It Always Like This?" Mercer and Wilder were friends for forty years.

Wilder had successes but never the big one. His lyricist, William Engvick, identified the problem: "Wilder's unusual and, for the time, difficult arrangements and his oddly shaped, under-stated and unpredictable melodies caused much antagonism (as they still do) and his progress was difficult. This was complicated by a totally uncommercial dignity and a trenchant wit which left his antagonists sneering, unaware that they were bleeding internally."

Wilder hurt himself by refusing to promote his own works. At times, he was stubborn; he lost the opportunity to write the score for *Peter Pan* for Mary Martin because he did not want to work with Martin's lyricist. He turned down a man who called him to ask if he would do the score for a ballet because "I didn't like the sound of his voice." The ballet was *Fancy Free,* which established Leonard Bernstein's stage reputation. Wilder described his view of this behavior: "I blame no one but myself for the minimal success I have known. I have had to pay this price for keeping myself whole."

In the late 1940s, Wilder wrote his first opera, *The Impossible Forest.* Dancer Gene Kelly had recommended that Wilder compose the music. The libretto was written by Marshall Barer, who wrote *Once Upon a Mattress* with Mary Rodgers. Scenery and costume designer Lemuel Ayers, who had done *Kiss Me Kate,* was signed up, and Jerome Robbins was interested in staging the opera and doing the choreography. Henry Fonda considered starring in it. Unfortunately, sufficient funding could not be raised.

Wilder composed a second opera, *The Wind Blows Free,* with playwright and lyricist Arnold Sundgaard that suffered the same fate, insufficient funding. In Sundgaard's opinion, "The songs worked fine, but not the play itself." Two of Wilder's songs survived on their own. He went back to writing popular songs, some of which, such as "While We're Young,*"* were sung by Peggy Lee.

Wilder and Engvick were invited to Hollywood by Twentieth Century Fox to write the songs for *Daddy Long Legs.* After writing fifteen songs, they were told that the script was not ready and that they would have to wait until it was. Even though he would be retained on salary, Wilder decided to return to New York. Fox sold the rights to the movie and when *Daddy Long Legs* was finally filmed with Fred Astaire and Leslie Caron, the music of Johnny Mercer (who later wrote lyrics for Wilder) was used instead. The original songs remained out of the public domain.

Wilder developed a friendship with Judy Holliday. Her reputation had been made when she was asked, on short notice, to fill in for Jean Arthur, who had become ill while starring in Garson Kanin's hit comedy, *Born Yesterday.* In 1958, Holliday made a record album for Columbia Records, *Trouble Is a Man.* She chose songs by Berlin, Bernstein, Wilder, and others. She opened the album with the title song by Wilder. It was thought that Wilder had an idealized love for Holliday, whose personality he considered a "sometime, someplace woman, girl, female."

With the introduction of rock and roll in the 1950s and 1960s, interest in popular music waned. Wilder's old friend from the Eastman School, John Barrows, turned him toward concert music and introduced him to many musicians. Wilder's first efforts were two sonatas for horn and piano and *Suite for French Horn and Piano.* He composed for instruments that had been ignored by composers over the years, including the tuba, marimba, guitar, baritone saxophone, and harp.

In 1959, Wilder wrote *Sonata No. 1 for Tuba and Piano.* Only two solos had been written for tuba previously, one by Vaughan Williams and the other by Hindemith. Next he composed *Effie Suite* for tuba, about the experiences of an elephant named Effie. These were followed by *Sonata for Bass Trombone and Piano; Concerto for Oboe, String Orchestra, and Percussion; Jazz Suite for Four Horns; Concerto No. 1 for Horn and Chamber Orchestra;* and *Suite No. 1 for Horn, Tuba, and Piano.*

Wilder also wrote many children's pieces, some by himself and some with Engvick or Sundgaard. In 1954, Wilder wrote, with lyrics by Marshall Barer, *A Child's Introduction to the Orchestra,* which Mitch Miller conducted with the Golden Symphony and the Sandpiper Chorus. In 1965, *Lullabies and Night Songs,* an illustrated collection of children's songs by Wilder and Engvick, was published by Harper & Row.

Wilder teamed with his third lyricist, Loonis McGlohon, on *Land of Oz,* an outdoor version of *The Wizard of Oz* staged on top of Beech Mountain in western North Carolina. It was the first of many successful collaborations with McGlohon. One of the finest was "Blackberry Winter." McGlohon was a composer as well as a lyricist. As a pianist, he had accompanied Eileen Farrell, Judy Garland, Maxine Sullivan, and Maxine VerPlanck. Buffalo native Harold Arlen gave them permission to use "Over the Rainbow" for

Land of Oz, and Wilder composed many new numbers.

In 1968, Wilder began to work on *American Popular Song: The Great Innovators, 1900-1950,* edited by James Maher, who also wrote the Introduction. The book, a distillation of a half-century of popular songwriting, was published by Oxford University Press in 1972 to critical acclaim. None of Wilder's works are included in the book, but 800 others are examined. In 1973, the book won the Deems Taylor ASCAP Award and a National Book Award nomination.

When Maher visited Wilder in Manhattan to begin their collaboration, Wilder invited him up to his room at the Algonquin Hotel. Maher, who assumed that he was being invited to a suite of rooms, observed: "This was the suite of Alec Wilder! No books, no records—no room, for that matter. There was a second chair, a side chair, but I couldn't see it because there was an opened suitcase on it. Tobacco, some shirts, a bobble bird, a jar of special honey, some airmail writing pads, and similar odds and ends lay on top of the dresser." Nevertheless, as soon as he and Maher began to discuss the book, Wilder knew that he had found the organized collaborator that he needed.

It was important to Wilder that he could be packed and out of his room in twenty minutes. One of his pastimes was riding the railroad—not to any particular destination. Biographer Desmond Stone quoted Wilder:

> Years ago, I'd check out when I had a little money and get on a train, and I'd stay on trains for weeks at a time. I'd travel the main trunks, and I'd transfer and take all the spurs. I loved sitting in a junction in the back of the beyond on a hot day and reading a long novel and listening to the chatter between the baggage man and the conductor. I loved talking with the engineer when he oiled his engine. Can you imagine nattering with a man fueling a jet?

Wilder's persona evolved into that of a rumpled professor of English Literature. In 1974, Whitney Balliett described Wilder in his *New Yorker* profile, "The President of the Derriére-garde":

Wilder is is a tall man with a big head and small feet. He was wearing a sports jacket, gray slacks, and loafers, and they had a resigned look of functional clothes. He has a long, handsome face and receding gray hair that flows out the back of his head, giving the impression that he is in constant motion. His eyebrows are heavy and curved, and when he has finished making a point—often punctuated by his slamming his fist down on the nearest piece of furniture—they shoot up and the corners of his mouth shoot down.

He has piercing, deep-set eyes cushioned by dark, doomsday pouches—diamonds resting on velvet. His face is heavily wrinkled—not with the soft, oh-I-am-growing-old lines but with strong, heavy weather ones. He has a loud baritone voice, and he talks rapidly. When he is agitated, his words roll like cannonballs around the room. He laughs a lot and he swears a lot, in an old-fashioned, Mark Twain manner, and when he is seated, he leans forward, like a figurehead breasting a flood tide. A small, serene mustache marks the eye of the hurricane.

On one occasion, a visitor to the Algonquin Hotel asked the doorman if he had seen Wilder. The doorman replied that you don't see Mr. Wilder, you hear him.

In 1975, Wilder was commissioned by the New York State Arts Council to compose an orchestral piece. *Entertainment No. 6* was first performed in 1977 by the Rochester Philharmonic Orchestra. That year and the following year, he completed many more instrumental compositions, including *Brass Quintet No. 6, Concerto for Flute and Chamber Orchestra, Sextet for Marimba and Wind Quintet, Suite for Flute and Marimba, Woodwind Quintet No. 13, Brass Quintet No. 7, Suite for Flute and Strings, Suite for Horn and Tuba,* and *Suite for Trumpet and Marimba.* Interest in these pieces was limited, but they pleased the musicians for whom they were written.

By 1978, Wilder knew that his health was slipping. In November that year in Gainesville, Florida, the life-long smoker had a cancerous lung removed. He recovered slowly, but eventually he began to compose again. Two of his last collaborations with McGlohon were "A Long Night" and "South to a Warmer Place," which subsequently were recorded by Sinatra. By December 1980, Wilder was short of breath and hallucinating.

Wilder's friend Louis Ouzer told another Rochester friend, lawyer and jazz program host Thomas Hampson, about their mutual friend's condition. Hampson flew to Gainesville to find that Wilder's condition was deteriorating rapidly. Hampson updated his friend's will and was appointed executor. Wilder died early in the morning of December 24.

Wilder was buried in St. Agnes Cemetery in Avon, New York, near the plot where his friend, Father Henry Atwell, previously pastor of St. Agnes Church, had been buried. Wilder had requested that there be no funeral, no religious service, and no notice in the newspapers of his death.

Hampson notified friends that he had arranged for a modest gravestone and a short burial ceremony: "I intend to honor Alec's request that there be no religious service, but a number of his friends said that they wanted to be present, and I certainly think that they should be permitted to do so."

Mitch Miller and long-time friend jazz pianist Marian McPartland, for whom Wilder had written a dozen pieces, were among those who attended the burial ceremony. Loonis McGlohon paid tribute to his collaborator: "Letters from strangers never went unanswered, even when they came from, in your words, people who lived in old soldiers' homes who thought that you were Thornton's brother . . . You were a soft touch, Alec. As long as people believed in something, you couldn't say no." The ceremony was concluded by a trumpet playing "It's So Peaceful in the Country" and by old friend Louis Ouzer blowing a string of bubbles, something that Wilder and his friends, including Marian McPartland, had enjoyed doing, over the grave.

Wilder's own observation on his music was: "My life's work is accepted in large measure only by the old and the young. The middle-aged self-proclaimed musical elite dismiss it as traditional, and therefore suspect." In 1983, Alec Wilder was inducted into the Songwriters' Hall of Fame, and, in 1991, the Alec Wilder Reading Room in the Sibley Music Library was dedicated at the Eastman School of Music.

BETTY COMDEN (1917-2006) *& ADOLPH GREEN* (1914-2002) Songwriters / Playwrights

"Perhaps the greatest wonder is the joint career of Betty Comden and Adolph Green, merry-andrews and collaborators extraordinary. For twenty-two years, Comden and Green have amicably and successfully collaborated as performers with other performers; as lyricists with several different composers, choreographers, and librettists; as librettists with a half-dozen directors and producers, as authors with a swarm of temperamental stars; and, needless to say, with each other. It is a record of harmony unique in the theater."

Peter Lyon in "The Antic Arts: Two Minds That Beat As One," *Holiday* magazine, December 30, 1961.

Betty Comden and Adolph Green collaborated on films, musicals, and revues for over fifty years. Neither wrote a libretto, lyric, or screenplay without the other. They thought as one person, and one was rarely mentioned without the other. In fact, they were treated as one person in their contracts. After over fifty years of collaboration, they had the ability to speak virtually as one person. One started a sentence, and the other finished it.

They seldom disagreed about their work. Their main personal difference was about being on time. Betty was always on time, and Adolph was usually late, although he became more punctual as he grew older. Betty was calm and under control, in contrast to Adolph, who was always restless and moving around. Betty had a vivid imagination, a strong sense of humor, and a sharp wit, which she rarely used to be unkind. Adolph, who also had a brilliant imagination, had an encyclopedic mind and a zany, unpredictable sense of humor. Their personal strengths were amazingly complementary. They accomplished together what they couldn't have done alone.

Betty Comden and Adolph Green are known as the prolific librettists / lyricists for many Broadway musicals, including *On the Town, Wonderful Town, Bells Are Ringing, Do Re Mi, Fade Out—Fade In, Hallelujah,* and *Applause.* They are also known for writing screenplays and lyrics for movies, including *On the Town, Singin' in the Rain,* and *The Band Wagon.* They were the recipients of the Writers Guild Award for *On the Town,* 1949; *Singin' in the*

Rain, 1952; and *Bells Are Ringing,* 1960.

Betty Comden and Adolph Green began their collaboration in the late 1930s. Their first joint effort was in preparing material for the Revuers, a quintet of comedians and singers with whom they performed at the Village Vanguard. They looked for material for their act and were told that they would have to pay royalties, which they couldn't afford. Betty and Adolph began to write all of the material for their acts, including music, lyrics, and skits.

Comden and Green worked every day, usually in Betty's apartment. Initially, Adolph described their methods: "Sometimes when you're on a project, you go all day and all evening. Sometimes you just work only a short time. It depends on what stage the project is in."

Writer Peter Lyon captured their different natures:

> Betty Comden and Adolph Green present an odd contrast . . . She is carefully composed; he is tense, as though he had been wound up too tight. Her voice is soft and pitched low; his rises, excited and extravagant. She is murmurous; he is clamorous. Her manner is tentative and seems almost apologetic; his is offhand and abrupt. In repose, her mouth curves down, her expression sad and her face quite beautiful; even if his face were ever in repose, the same could scarcely be said of it.

> And yet, as they speak, the dissimilarities blur. Each refers to the other with a glance, with a grimace; each sets the other to chuckling; they are constantly attuned, it is clear, to the same wavelength.

Betty said that "Adolph and I have lots of old, outdated references and phrases we have mutually piled up over the years. There is a kind of radar between us, knowing what the other is thinking based on stuff we have both read or shared." Betty told a story about their being on the same wavelength that occurred on Adolph's thirty-third birthday. She met him in midtown Manhattan and noticed that he was subdued and even somewhat gloomy. She thought that he was probably depressed because he was thirty-three-years old and felt that he hadn't accomplished as much as he should've by this time.

Betty knew of a book, *At Thirty-three,* by Eva LeGalienne, the founder of the Civic Repertory Theatre, about her life up to that age. It wasn't a best-seller, but Betty, knowing that Adolph was a voracious reader, figured that he had probably read it. She turned to him and said, "Eva LeGalienne?" He nodded his head in agreement and continued walking. He knew exactly what she meant by the question. Anyone overhearing the interchange wouldn't have had an inkling of its meaning.

In *Off Stage,* Betty describes Adolph: "The mythic character of my life, my partner, Adolph Green, it seems to me must have sprung full-blown from his own head. There is no other head quite capable of having done the job. Only his head has the antic, manic imagination and offbeat creative erudite plos childlike originality to conceive of such a person." She gave a lengthy example of how her collaborator creates, along with the comment, "I can just hear his head making him up":

> "How's about I jump out like this . . . tall, blond, grand, and NAH!" The head shakes with fierce rejection. "How's about medium, dark, Hungarian, with a Hapsburg jaw and lots of assorted teeth . . . and I'll study music and literature and the cinema and . . . NAH!" Again the head shakes violently. "I'll just absorb it all, sort of osmosis-wise, simply by listening and reading and watching and just being, and I'll store it away in here along with stuff like the succession of the heavyweight boxing champions of the world, the famous old Yankee lineups, the great comic strips, and vaudeville acts and songs like 'I Wish That I Was Born in Borneo,' . . . and my body will be like Michelangelo's David and . . . NAH!"

> "Who needs it? . . . It will be spare and strong with a well-turned leg—two of them, in fact—and they will be able to lift me into the air like Nureyev, and

I will have an easy rhythmic saunter like—dare I say it? What the hell!—like Astaire, so that some critic one day will write of me, 'A dancer of rare comedic grace,' and somewhere early on I'll meet a girl and we'll be on the same wavelength, and we will have a big career together with nary a thought of romance, let alone marriage."

"And I'll have a nice voice like Placido, and . . . NAH, PLEASE! but it will be loud, very loud, but sometimes surprisingly tender and good on ballads, and I'll know acres and acres of poetry and miles and miles and miles of art, and I'll know every piece of music ever written, and I'll be able to sing it, replicating a full orchestra if need be, and I'll know the director and stars and cast, down to the last extra, of every movie ever made."

"And, listen, so I may get depressed once in a while *(once in a while!!!???)*, but here comes the best part: I'll be funny. I'll be able to make people laugh. I'll be witty. I'll say things in an unexpected way, spontaneously juxtaposing odd thoughts and words, giving them a kind of surreal twist, and . . . and . . . NAH! that's not the best part. The best part is I'll marry the most beautiful, gifted girl in Jersey City and all the rest of the world and have two smashing children . . . And wow! No one will believe such a creature could exist, but I *will!!!* I *will!!!* Here I come, ready or not!!!!!!!!!"

Comden and Green placed considerable emphasis on structure in writing the story for a musical or a screenplay. Adolph observed that "What we find most effective is structuring the book as much as we can before writing any songs. The more structure you have, the better off you are, and the more tightly the plot will mesh." They were extremely successful in incorporating the songs into the storyline, something that was not emphasized until they did it. Two of their early successes at doing this were *Singin' in the Rain* and

The Band Wagon.

According to Betty: "That doesn't mean that you don't start working on the score before the book is written. People like Leonard Bernstein, Jule Styne, Cy Coleman are dramatists, and they always write for the theater, for situation and character. It's collaborative, flexible." Comden and Green remembered vividly the constantly changing approach used in creating *On the Town*. "Sometimes Leonard [Bernstein] had some melody that he decided should be used, and we put words to it. Other times we came with a full lyric, and he'd work on it. Still other times we'd have an idea and start working on it together. And we'd use patterns of other songs and start putting a few lines of lyric to them, just to get a start."

Comden and Green always used experiences from their own lives in their work. Early in their careers, they went to Hollywood, and the movie for which they were to write the screenplay was cancelled. They weren't able to find other work in Hollywood. Betty returned to New York first, and then Adolph returned because his mother was ill. Betty met him at Grand Central Station carrying a sign that read "The Adolph Green Fan Club" when he returned.

They used that idea in *The Band Wagon*, when Fred Astaire, playing an actor whose career was fading, walked slowly and dejectedly up the railroad station ramp singing "By Myself." He was met by two friends, played by Oscar Levant and Nanette Fabray, carrying "fan club" signs that cheered him up.

One of their hit songs was "Just in Time" from *Bells Are Ringing*, which starred Judy Holliday. Jule Styne wrote a simple melody for which no lyrics were written for several months. They referred to it as "Da-Da-Da." Finally, they found a situation in the storyline that provided them with the title, "Just In Time." Their creative process encompassed many variations on a theme. They were pragmatic. If it worked, they used it.

Another technique they employed was to listen to the audience. Betty observed: "You listen to what they're saying, not necessarily to the critics. We like the idea of going out of town. You have to listen to the audience, plus keep in mind what your own intention was."

On occasion, the collaborators encountered "second act trouble." Adolph commented on that phenomenon: "That's probably because the story isn't spreading itself out in inevitable fashion, which is what you strive for. Very often the problems are in the first act. The second act has to play off whatever you've set up in the first."

Because they were so successful, the impression is sometimes given that it was an easy road. Adolph described the creative process as "agony." He explained their way of generating an idea. "Just read, think, kick around things, meet every day and stare at each other and say no to something for a year, then suddenly say, 'Let's try it.' Sometimes other people you're involved with get enthusiasm and pull you along, and suddenly you say, 'Well, this can work.'"

Comden and Green always collaborated with each other. In careers that spanned over fifty-five years, neither of them worked with another collaborator. They were once asked if either of them had ever considered working on their own. They both quickly responded: "Never! Unthinkable!"

Betty summed up the reasons for their success:

> We write with humor about basically serious things. We like to think we're expressing something of ourselves, something of what we feel is important in the world today. At the same time, we try to help audiences feel the way they should when they leave the theater—that is, glad to be alive. That windows have been opened, fresh air has been let in, and they're leaving as happy people.

They certainly accomplished their goal of making people— thousands of people— happy. It is difficult to imagine what the world of the Broadway musical and musical films would be like without the contributions of Comden and Green.

Betty Comden was born Betty Cohen on May 3, 1917, in Brooklyn, New York, to Leo and Rebecca Sadvoransky Cohen. Her first acting experience came at the age of eleven when she was cast as Rebecca in Sir Walter Scott's *Ivanhoe* in the seventh grade at the Brooklyn Ethical Culture School. After graduating from Erasmus Hall High School, she majored in drama at New York University.

She graduated with a B.S. degree in drama in 1938 and began acting in theater groups.

Adolph Green was born on December 2, 1914, in the Bronx, New York, to Daniel and Helen Weiss Green. In grammar school, he wrote poetry and acted in plays. He grew up loving music, and, although he did not receive formal training in music, he developed an encyclopedic musical memory. In 1934, he graduated from DeWitt Clinton High School and attended college, but he didn't complete the courses required for a degree. During the day, he worked as a runner on Wall Street and then as an installer for a carpet company; in the evenings, he participated in little theater groups.

Comden and Green met through a mutual friend while Betty was at New York University. Their paths crossed again while they were acting in the theater. Their first break came during the summer of 1938 when Judy Tuvim, later Judy Holliday, saw Green perform and was impressed with his energy and humor.

Holliday met Max Gordon, the proprietor of the Village Vanguard, and asked him to consider hiring a group that did songs and skits. Holliday asked Green if they could get a group together, and, when Green saw Comden at an audition, he asked her if she would be interested. They both knew an actor who was looking for a job, and five of them, including Judy Holliday, formed a group called "The Revuers."

Initially, each member of the group earned $5.00 for one show a week. They couldn't afford to pay royalties for outside material, so they wrote their own—skits, music, and lyrics. The five performers met to "brainstorm," and Betty recorded the ideas that were generated. When they identified a good idea, they improvised on it. It was a cooperative effort, and no one kept a record of who contributed what. Their shows were humorous, satirical skits about the social mores of the 1930s. Eventually, they did two shows, five nights a week. A favorable review by Dick Manson of the *New York Post* increased their audience significantly.

In November 1939, The Revuers performed at the Rainbow Room on the top floor of Rockefeller Plaza. They did their well-developed impersonations of Noel Coward, Joan Crawford, Queen Victoria, and Oscar Wilde, as well as sketches of Broadway, Hollywood, and the New York World's Fair. Patrons at the

Rainbow Room were conservative, and what worked at the Village Vanguard didn't work there. They received respectable reviews, but they thought that they had "bombed."

In October 1940, The Revuers performed five times a day for three weeks at Radio City Music Hall. In December, they returned to the Village Vanguard. They were disappointed, because it seemed that they were back where they started. The following year they toured the country as far west as St. Louis.

In 1942, Irving Caesar, the lyricist who wrote "Swanee" and "Tea for Two" cast The Revuers in a musical called *My Dear Public*. The play had a short run in New York, so The Revuers returned to the nightclub circuit. They had a long engagement at the Blue Angel, Max Gordon's cabaret on the east side of Manhattan, and then went on a road tour, which included an engagement at the Blackstone Hotel in Chicago.

On January 4, 1942, Betty Comden married Siegfried Schutzman, who subsequently changed his name to Steven Kyle. He was an artist about to enter the U.S. Army. Later, they had two children; Susanna was born in 1949, and Alan was born in 1953. Their friend Leonard Bernstein wrote "Anniversary for Susanna Kyle" to celebrate the birth of their first child.

During the summer of 1942, The Revuers went to Los Angeles, where Hollywood agent Kurt Frings had obtained roles for them in the film version of the popular radio show, *Duffy's Tavern*. However, upon their arrival in Hollywood, they were told that the film had been cancelled.

The Revuers obtained an engagement at the Trocadero night club; they opened to rave reviews. Agents offered Judy Holliday movie contracts, but none of the other members of The Revuers received any offers. Holliday didn't want to accept a contract with Twentieth Century Fox unless the other members of The Revuers were included. Comden and Green told her that she would be foolish not to take the studio's offer.

On completion of their engagement at the Trocadero, Comden returned to New York, where her husband was on leave from the Army. She planned to return to Hollywood when Kyle's furlough was over, but Adolph called her to tell her that he was coming to New York to visit his mother who was ill. Temporarily, they were unemployed.

Comden and Green, without the rest of The Revuers, returned to perform at Max Gordon's Blue Angel in Manhattan. From this point onward in their careers, they continued to perform but became more creators than performers. In between performances at the Blue Angel, they were visited by Leonard Bernstein, Paul Feigay, and Oliver Smith. The three men were motivated by the success of the ballet, *Fancy Free,* which Bernstein and Jerome Robbins had presented with the Ballet Theatre.

Oliver Smith, who had designed the set for the ballet, and Paul Feigay wanted to produce a musical about three sailors on leave in New York; the ballet version had premiered at the Metropolitan Opera House on April 18, 1944, to rave reviews. They asked Betty and Adolph to write the script and the lyrics for the musical. During the summer that year, Comden and Green wrote the libretto and the lyrics while Bernstein wrote the music.

Comden and Green wrote lively parts for themselves into the script of *On the Town.* They had to audition, but they were chosen for the parts. Adolph was one of the three sailors, Ozzie, and Betty played Claire de Loone, an anthropologist. Claire is fascinated by Ozzie because, in her opinion, his appearance is that of a prehistoric man. The storyline is about three sailors pursuing "Miss Turnstiles," whose picture they had seen on a poster in a subway train. The success of the musical was virtually assured when George Abbot agreed to direct the play. He was the only one of the creators of the musical who was over thirty years old.

The team that created *On the Town,* except Bernstein, who was not available, immediately started work on another musical. Morton Gould wrote the music for *Billion Dollar Baby,* which opened at the Alvin Theatre on December 21, 1945. The musical, which starred Joan McCracken, was about the roaring twenties. It was only moderately successful, but Comden and Green now had two successful plays to their credit. They wanted to return to Hollywood to work on a film.

Metro-Goldwyn-Mayer gave them an offer to write a screenplay based on the Broadway musical about college life, *Good News,* working with the producer Arthur Freed. Initially, Comden and Green weren't enthusiastic about the project, which was a revision of a 1930 film. They wrote a new screenplay that incorporated most of the songs from the original script. However, they added to the original lyrics and wrote a catchy song, "The French Lesson," about the subject that the football hero was flunking. June Allyson, Peter Lawford, and Joan McCracken starred in the film. *Good News* was considered to be the best college-theme musical produced in the 1940s.

Comden's and Green's second screenplay was *The Barkleys of Broadway,* starring Fred Astaire and Ginger Rogers. It was about a married couple, an acting and dancing team, who danced well together but whose off-stage relationship was stormy. It was one of the top-rated films of 1949, and it received a nomination for a Screenwriters Guild Award.

Comden's and Green's next Hollywood project was to write the lyrics for four songs for *Take Me Out to the Ball Game,* starring Gene Kelly and Frank Sinatra. The story was written by Gene Kelly and his assistant and friend, Stanley Donen. Gene Kelly was one of the few people in Hollywood that Betty and Adolph knew when they moved west. They had met Kelly in 1939 when they had performed at the Westport Country Playhouse. *Take Me Out to the Ball Game,* which was released in 1949, was another successful movie.

Comden's and Green's greatest success in 1949 was the movie made from their Broadway musical, *On The Town,* which was co-directed by Gene Kelly and Stanley Donen. The producer, Arthur Freed, considered Bernstein's music to be too avant-garde, so he asked Roger Edens to write the music and Comden and Green to write the lyrics for eight new songs.

Only four songs of Bernstein's original Broadway score were used in the film. The three sailors on the town were played by Gene Kelly, Frank Sinatra, and Jules Munshin, the same trio from *Take Me Out to the Ball Game. On The Town*, which premiered at Radio City Music Hall on December 30, 1949, earned Comden and Green a Screenwriters Guild Award.

In the summer of 1937, Green had played the Pirate King in *the Pirates of Penzance* at Camp Onata, a boys' summer camp near Pittsfield, Massachusetts. The music counselor that summer was a young Harvard music student, Leonard Bernstein. Bernstein sat down at the piano and played a practical joke on Green. He mentioned that he was going to play a Shostakovich prelude. Green asked, "Which one?" Bernstein responded, "This one," but instead he played a series of dissonances. Green told him that it wasn't any of Shostakovich's preludes. Bernstein laughed; he had played the trick many times before, and the listeners always had claimed to recognize the music.

They both possessed a knowledge of music and a sense of humor, and they became close friends. Bernstein's younger brother, Burton, wrote that Green was "capable of performing—a capella and with every orchestral instrument outrageously imitated—just about any symphonic work, classical or modern, down to the last cymbal crash."

In June 1939, Leonard Bernstein graduated from Harvard University and moved to New York to look for a job. He shared an apartment in Greenwich Village with Green and occasionally filled in as the pianist for The Revuers. Frequently, Bernstein played the piano at the parties that he and Green attended. At one of these parties, Betty Comden met Bernstein. She went home, awakened her mother from a sound sleep, and told her, "I met a real genius tonight."

Bernstein discussed his future with Dimitri Mitropoulos, who told him that he had all the necessary skills to be a conductor. Bernstein applied to the Julliard School in September and was told that no more applications were being accepted. He enrolled at the Curtis Institute in Philadelphia and was on his way to becoming famous.

In 1942, The Revuers were cast in a musical called *My Dear Public,* which played in Philadelphia before opening in New York. Leonard Bernstein had completed his conductor training at the Curtis Institute but was unable to find a steady job so he hung out with the cast of *My Dear Public.* Bernstein impressed Irving Caesar, who had done the casting for the play. He compared the young man to George Gershwin. Caesar found Bernstein a job in New York making piano arrangements for a music publishing company.

The following year, Artur Rodzinski was appointed conductor of the New York Philharmonic and appointed Bernstein his assistant. On November 14, 1943, Bruno Walter, the guest conductor, was ill, and Maestro Rodzinski was snowed in at his Stockbridge farm. Twenty-five-year-old Bernstein conducted the New York Philharmonic that evening and made the most of the opportunity.

The performance was broadcast nationally on radio, and Bernstein woke up the next morning a famous man. However, he and Comden and Green continued to collaborate on musicals.

In June 1944, Bernstein entered the hospital to have an operation for a deviated septum to relieve his chronic sinus problems. At the same time, Adolph had his enlarged tonsils removed. They were operated on the same day by the same doctor and shared a hospital room, so that they could continue to work on the musical, *On the Town*. As they recuperated, Betty worked with them in their room. When friends visited they became a bit rowdy, which irritated the hospital staff. One nurse upset by Bernstein's antics commented, "He may be God's gift to music, but I'd hate to tell you where he gives me a pain."

In August, Bernstein accompanied the Ballet Theatre to California to conduct *Fancy Free*. He composed the music for *On the Town* en route and while he was in California. He wrote the first major number, "New York, New York," as the train sped across the flat farmland of Nebraska. *On the Town* was completed that autumn and opened at the Adelphi Theatre on December 28, 1944. Critics praised the book by the young writing team, Comden and Green, and called the work "fresh." In particular, they liked the integration of the storyline with the choreography and the songs. Comden and Green maintained their friendship and collaboration with Leonard Bernstein over the years.

In 1951, Comden and Green received an urgent call from Metro-Goldwyn-Mayer to return to Hollywood to write an original story, screenplay, and lyrics for a new musical film. The screenplay was about the transition from silent movies to the talkies. The lead character, who began his career in vaudeville, was to be shown making the successful transition from silent films.

They were to work for producer Arthur Freed in the Thalberg Administration Building. At their first meeting with Freed, they were told that they had been assigned to write the story and screenplay, but that the songs used would be ones already written by lyricist Arthur Freed (the producer) and composer Nacio Herb Brown. The movie was to be called *Singin' in the Rain*.

Comden and Green erupted. They had been told that they were to write the lyrics, and, furthermore, their previous agent had told them that their contract stated that they were to create the lyrics unless the music was written by Irving Berlin, Cole Porter, or Richard Rodgers and Oscar Hammerstein. They stomped off the job and threatened to return to New York. They accused Freed of breaking his promises; the strained relations continued for two weeks.

Finally, their new agent, Irving Lazar, suggested that they read their contract. The clause about Berlin, Porter, and Rodgers and Hammerstein wasn't there. Lazar told them "anyone can write lyrics for your picture: Berlin, Porter, Rodgers and Hammerstein, Freed, Karloff, Lugosi, Johnny Weissmuller—you name it. My suggestion is you write 'Singin' in the Rain' at the top of a page, followed by 'Fade-in,' and don't stop until you come to 'That's All, Folks.'"

Roger Edens, the associate producer and music director, played the songs as the collaborators searched for a storyline. Initially, they had difficulty coming up with a usable plot. For example, the song, "The Wedding of the Painted Doll," might have suggested a story about a painted doll who got married. Many of the songs are now well-known, including "Broadway Melody," "Fit as a Fiddle," "You Were Meant for Me," and the title song, "Singin' in the Rain." The only song in the movie for which Comden and Green wrote the lyrics was "Moses Supposes His Toes-es Are Roses."

They also had difficulty deciding on the time period in which the movie should be set. Many of these songs had been written between 1929 and 1931 for the first musical movies made. Instead of placing the story in contemporary times or a period like the gay nineties, they decided to use the time during which the songs were written.

Knowing who would play the lead was important, because that would affect the storyline. Initially, Howard Keel was considered for the role. Freed wanted Gene Kelly for the starring role, but Kelly was busy filming *An American in Paris*. Because of the delays in getting started on the story and screenplay, Gene Kelly became available. Kelly was so enthusiastic about the plans for *Singin' in the Rain* that he agreed to co-direct the film with Stanley Donen.

After the first month of planning the screenplay, Comden and Green had three possible openings:

- the premiére of an important silent movie in New York
- an action sequence from the silent movie being pre-
  miéred in New York, with the star meeting a girl in
  New York, losing her, and returning to Hollywood

- an interview for a magazine, with the star in
  Hollywood relating a fantasized life story.

Comden and Green couldn't decide which opening to use. The work just wasn't moving along smoothly; they were depressed. They seriously considered returning the money that MGM had given them, packing up, and returning to Manhattan.

About that time, Betty's husband, Steve Kyle, arrived from New York. He wasn't surprised to see them slumped over in near despair. He had seen them this way before on earlier projects that weren't going well. Steve wasn't a writer; he was an artist with a successful merchandising business. However, they frequently used him as a sounding board, and he had been a valuable source of ideas. He laughed when he read the material. They asked him which opening they should use; he suggested that they use all three openings.

Steve's suggestion resulted in the realization that all of the action could take place on Hollywood Boulevard instead of on Fifth Avenue in New York. The change wasn't significant; however, Comden observed:

> It seems pitifully obvious now, bordering on the moronic, but at the time we felt like [Jean Francois] Champollion deciphering the Rosetta Stone. From here on, the gates were open and the writing of the screenplay gushed in a relatively exuberant flow. We tapped the roots of our memories and experiences without editing ourselves when our ideas got wild, satirical, and extravagantly nonsensical. To our gratified surprise, not only did Roger seem delighted with it all, but Arthur, to whom we read each section as we completed it, gave his happy approval.

The final approval was given by Dore Schary, who had recently replaced L. B. Mayer as head of MGM.

Meetings began with Gene Kelly and Stanley Donen in which they applied their skills in integrating the various elements of the musical. Comden and Green realized that the success of the film was to a large extent due to what they referred to as the "four-way mental radar" among them. Kelly and Donen were professionals who excelled at the execution of the performance while sustaining a light, carefree air.

They all knew from their first reading that the musical involved a scene that took place in the rain. What none of them realized was that "here Gene Kelly performs the most notable solo musical number of his career," or, in other words, "miracle happens here." The song, "The Wedding of the Painted Doll," was replaced with "Make 'Em Laugh," in which Donald O'Connor pulled out all the stops and did a classic, upbeat vaudeville / clown number.

Comden and Green returned to New York after completing the screenplay for *Singin' in the Rain* to write sketches and lyrics for *Two on the Aisle*. They were in Philadelphia, helping to whip that revue into shape prior to playing on Broadway, when they received an urgent call from Kelly and Donen. They were asked to drop everything and write a romantic scene in an empty sound stage where Kelly would sing one song and do one dance with Debbie Reynolds. This was to replace a lengthy love scene in which Kelly and Reynolds danced and did a medley of songs involving multiple sets.

Comden and Green unplugged themselves from a frantic effort to finish *Two on the Aisle* and projected themselves back to the atmosphere of *Singin' in the Rain*. Their efforts clicked, and the movie was wildly successful. It is consistently rated as one of the ten best musical films; in one rating, it is considered to be third best. Critic Pauline Kael wrote: "This exuberant and malicious satire of Hollywood in the late twenties is perhaps the most enjoyable of all movie musicals—just about the best Hollywood musical of all time."

Comden and Green won their second Screenwriters Guild Award for the movie, which opened at Radio City Music Hall on March 27, 1952. The film in which the writers of the screenplay almost gave up and went home—not once, but twice—turned out to be one of the best ever.

After finally completing work on *Singin' in the Rain,* Comden and Green returned to New York to finish revising the skits and the lyrics for the revue *Two on the Aisle,* which starred Bert Lahr and Delores Gray. Lahr, who was a talented comedian, is remembered mainly for his role as the Cowardly Lion in *The Wizard of Oz*. Delores Gray, an accomplished singer and comedienne, had her first success starring in the role of Annie Oakley in *Annie Get Your Gun* in London. *Two on the Aisle* was the first of many musicals in which Comden and Green collaborated with composer Jule Styne.

Their next screenplay was *The Band Wagon,* which starred Fred Astaire and was directed by Vincent Minnelli. The movie was based on the 1931 Broadway revue starring Fred Astaire and his sister, Adele. It was about a film star whose career was fading being invited to New York by friends, a writing team much like Comden and Green, to star in a Broadway musical. The film, which received an Academy Award nomination, debuted at Radio City Music Hall in July 1953.

Comden's and Green's next musical, *Wonderful Town,* opened at the Winter Garden Theatre on February 25, 1953, to rave reviews. It was based on the 1940 play, *My Sister Eileen,* which, in turn, was based on Ruth McKenney's stories about herself and her lively sister in New York in the 1930s. Rosalind Russell starred as Ruth, as she had in the 1940 movie version.

Comden and Green were pleased to be working again with their friend, Leonard Bernstein, who wrote the music for the play. George Abbott directed the musical, which won a Tony Award for Outstanding Musical of the Year. Rosalind Russell won the award for Outstanding Musical Actress and Comden and Green won a Donaldson Award for *Wonderful Town,* which played for 559 performances.

In May 1956, Comden and Green reviewed the first draft of *Bells Are Ringing* with Judy Holliday and enticed her to star in the play. The story was about a switchboard operator at an answering service who takes a personal interest in the service's customers. The music was written by Jule Styne, and the musical was directed by Jerome Robbins. It opened at the Shubert Theatre on November 29, 1956, and ran for 924 performances. Judy Holliday won a 1957 Tony Award for her role.

Phyllis Newman met Adolph Green when she was Judy Holliday's understudy in *Bells Are Ringing.* Adolph visited the theater frequently because he was a friend of both Judy Holliday and the leading man, Sydney Chaplin, the son of Charlie Chaplin. Phyllis was attracted to Adolph, but she was intimidated by "his age, his reputation as an intellectual, his success, and, most of all, by his mind-boggling eccentricity." In her book, *Just in Time,* Phyllis commented about Adolph: "He always looks suspicious and guilty, as though he has just done something he shouldn't have. He rarely looks you straight in the eye. He seems to be hiding something, but I have never found out what it is."

Adolph and Phyllis dated, and she was intimidated again—this time by his famous friends, such as Lauren Bacall and Leonard Bernstein. She realized that she was in love with Adolph after seeing him and Betty perform in *A Party With Betty Comden and Adolph Green* at the Westport Playhouse in Connecticut. Phyllis and Adolph were married on January 31, 1960.

Work on the film version of *Bells Are Ringing* began on October 6, 1959. Judy Holliday reprised her role as the switchboard operator; Vincent Minnelli directed. The movie opened at Radio City Music Hall on June 23, 1960. Betty and Adolph won their third Screenwriters Guild Award for the screenplay.

Also that year, Comden and Green wrote the lyrics for *Do Re Mi,* a musical based on the novella by Garson Kanin. Jule Styne wrote the music. Phil Silvers starred as Hubie Cram, a nobody with aspirations of fame and fortune. Comedienne Nancy Walker contributed a memorable performance as Mrs. Cram. The play opened on December 26, 1960, at the St. James Theatre and ran for over 400 performances. The song, "Make Someone Happy" by Comden, Green, and Styne, was the hit song from the musical.

Comden's and Green's hit of the 1970s was *Applause,* which opened at the Palace Theatre on March 30, 1970 with Lauren Bacall in the leading role. They wrote the book; the music was by Charles Strouse and the lyrics were by Lee Adams. When Bacall was asked by the producers about Comden and Green doing the book she hesitated because they were good friends, and she didn't want to mix friendship and career. She ultimately agreed because "they were so smart and funny, and talented."

Applause was based on the film *All About Eve,* which starred Anne Baxter and Bette Davis. The musical won the Tony Award for Best Musical in 1970, and Bacall won the Award for Best Actress in a Musical. Comden, Green, Adams, and Strouse all won Tony Awards that year. *Applause* ran for 840 performances on Broadway.

On March 17, 1980, Betty and Adolph were voted into the

Songwriters Hall of Fame. In 1981, they were selected by drama critics and editors for entrance into the Theatre Hall of Fame. Requirements for membership are a Broadway career of at least twenty-five years and more than five major credits. They continued to write plays and lyrics into the 1990s, in addition to teaching at New York University's Tisch School of the Arts.

On May 29, 1991, Betty and Adolph were presented with the Johnny Mercer Award for Lifetime Achievement by the Songwriters Hall of Fame. On December 8, 1991, the collaborators were awarded the Kennedy Center Honors for Lifetime Achievement in the Performing Arts, a fine capstone for their careers.

CHAPTER 3

AUTHORS / POETS

"If I bind the future I bind my will. If I bind my will I strangle creation."

George Bernard Shaw, *Back to Methuselah*

JOHN MILTON (1608-1674) Author of *Paradise Lost*

"Yet I argue not
Against heaven's hand or will,
　　nor bate a jot
Of heart and hope; but still bear up
　　and steer
Right onward."

Milton, *Sonnet XXII*

John Milton is considered the foremost English dramatic poet, with the possible exception of Spenser. Shakespeare was a larger literary figure than Milton, but most of his work was for the stage. Milton wrote epics that are now appreciated principally by the academic community. His own life was an epic. He had been imprisoned and had faced a possible death sentence for his support of the Lord Protector, Lord Cromwell, during the Reformation. Milton lost his sight at the age of forty-three; however, he wasn't deterred from writing a major work in his later years that he knew he was destined to write. Writing a magnum opus was his reason for being.

Milton's blindness has caused much speculation. Possible diagnoses include glaucoma, paralysis of the optic nerves, and detached retinas. Sight in his left eye was nearly gone by early 1650; he became totally blind during the winter of 1651-52, with his great work still unwritten. When his vision began to fail, his doctor advised him to spare his eyesight by writing less. He responded, "The choice lay before me between dereliction of a supreme duty and loss of eyesight . . . I could but obey the inward monitor that spoke to me from above . . . If my affliction is incurable, I prepare and compose myself accordingly." Milton said, "It is not so wretched to be blind as it is not to be capable of enduring blindness."

James II, when he was Duke of York, visited Milton and told him that his blindness was punishment from above for writing a justification of the execution of Charles I. Milton replied, "If Your Highness thinks that misfortunes are indexes of the wrath of heaven, what must you think of your father's tragical end? I have only lost my eyes—he lost his head."

Milton's attitude toward his affliction is summed up in the following autobiographical sonnet:

> When I consider how my light is spent
> Ere half my days in this dark world and wide,
> And that one talent which is death to hide
> Lodged with me useless, though my soul more bent
> To serve wherewith my Maker, and present
> My true account, lest He returning chide;
> "Doth God exact day-labor, light denied?"
> I fondly ask. But patience, to prevent
> That murmur, soon replies, "God doth not need
> Either man's work or his own gifts. Who best
> Bear his mild yoke, they serve Him best. His state
> Is kingly: thousands at his bidding speed,
> And post o'er land and ocean without rest;
> They also serve who only stand and wait."

Milton's life was difficult; he was dependent upon amanuenses to whom he dictated. He relied heavily on his three daughters, who had been taught to pronounce six languages to read to their father. Unfortunately, they didn't understand what they were reading. The older daughters, Anne and Mary, considered the task drudgery and, according to biographer Edward Phillips, were "condemned to a trial of patience almost beyond endurance." The youngest daughter, Deborah, was the only one who willingly helped her father.

Milton was in his fifties when he began his epic work, *Paradise Lost*. Earlier, he had considered an English theme for his great work, such as the legend of King Arthur and the Knights of the Round Table. In 1640, when he was in his early thirties, he had approximately one hundred biblical and historical themes for plays that he documented in the *Cambridge Manuscript*.

Eventually, he rejected the subject of a narrative poem of heroes for that of a moral saga describing, on a grand scale, the battle between Good and Evil. He envisioned a battle fought by angels and demons for the benefit of humanity.

In the first part of the *Paradise Lost*, Milton describes an unsuccessful rebellion in heaven, after which Satan, Beelzebub, Moloch,

Mammon, and a host of lesser angels are expelled from heaven and sent to hell. The principal source for his work is the Bible, including the Apocrypha. Milton deals with the fall of man in the second part of the narrative. He discusses the temptation in which Eve sins by the weakness of reason and Adam sins through the weakness of will, their expulsion from Paradise, and Christ's intercession for all mankind.

Milton's next work was *Paradise Regained*, in which he describes the temptation of Christ in the wilderness. He describes Christ's resistance to temptation in winning back for mankind that which was lost by Adam's sins. Satan is a much diminished figure in *Paradise Regained*, compared with his almost heroic proportions in the first two books of *Paradise Lost*. Critics don't consider *Paradise Regained* to be on the same level as *Paradise Lost*.

Milton's last work was *Samson Agonistes*, a story about the last years of Samson's life, done in the style of a Greek tragedy. Milton describes Samson's betrayal by the untrustworthy Delilah and how a human sinner is regenerated after reaching the depths of despair. Milton published *Samson Agonistes* in 1667, the same year that he published the less popular *Paradise Regained*.

When he was twenty-one, Milton had set a goal to write a major epic for the ages, and he refused to let the loss of his sight keep him from his goal. He persevered until, late in life, he accomplished his reason for being. Milton had a profound impact on later poets. The Miltonic form of the sonnet was used by Coleridge, Keats, and Wordsworth.

A. E. Housman gave Milton a rich tribute: "The dignity, the sanity, the unfaltering elevation of style, the just subordination of detail, the due adoption of means to ends, the high respect of the craftsman for his craft and for himself, which ennoble Virgil and the great Greeks, are all to be found in Milton and nowhere else are they in English literature to be found."

SIR WALTER SCOTT (1771-1832) Modern Historical Novel Pioneer

"Great works are performed not by strength but by perseverance."

Samuel Johnson, *Rasselas VIII*

Walter Scott was born on August 15, 1771, in Edinburgh, Scotland. He was named for his father, a lawyer (advocate) who was Writer to the Signet, a Scottish legal office. Scott's mother was Anne Rutherford, the oldest daughter of Dr. John Rutherford, a professor of medicine at Edinburgh University and a pioneer in medical education.

Young Walter lost partial use of his right leg at the age of one and a half, possibly due to poliomyelitis. He never let his lameness restrict him. To strengthen his leg, he took extensive walks around the Scottish countryside meeting many people and listening to their stories, many of which he incorporated into his historical novels.

After graduating from Edinburgh University, Scott was apprenticed to his father for five years of training in the law. His father had many clients in the highlands around Perth as well as in many of the border towns. On trips for his father, he became familiar with the area around Loch Katrine and the sites associated with the Jacobite rebellion of 1745. He listened to many stories told by those who had survived the battles of that disruptive era. Many of these stories were the basis for the *Waverly* novels, considered by many his best work.

In 1802, Scott wrote *The Minstrelsy of the Scottish Border*, the work that established his reputation as a writer. His next significant work was *Lay of the Last Minstrel* in 1805. The outstanding success of this book caused Scott to view writing as his primary effort, although he continued to practice law. He published his narrative poem, *Marmion*, in 1808 and *The Lady of the Lake* two years later.

In 1811, Scott purchased the property that was to grow into his baronial estate, Abbotsford. Many of his best works were written at Abbotsford, including *Guy Mannering, Kenilworth, Ivanhoe, Rob Roy*, and *Heart of Midlothian*.

Sir Walter Scott displayed notable creativity during his lifetime including writing fourteen novels in one six-year period. His perseverance and drive were shown during the last years of his life. 1825 was a year of speculation in the money markets, and the speculative boom extended into 1826. Both Scott's Edinburgh publisher, Archibald Constable, and his printer, Ballantyne and Company, failed due to careless business practices. These failures were caused by Robinson of Hurst, Robinson, and Company, Constable's London agent, who speculated in hops with disastrous results and was unable to meet his financial obligations.

Scott, a part owner of Ballantyne and Company, was personally responsible for only a part of the debt incurred by them. However, he refused to declare bankruptcy and was determined to pay off the total debt. Many of Scott's friends offered to give him financial assistance, but he replied, "No, this right hand shall work it off." He paid off a substantial portion of the debt in his lifetime, but at significant cost to his physical well-being. When royalties from his published works after his death are taken into account, he accomplished his objective of paying off all of the debts.

Scott neglected the business side of the literary profession. He enjoyed writing but paid little attention to the publishing and printing side of his endeavors. The Ballantyne brothers didn't follow sound business practices. Scott, as well as James and John Ballantyne, withdrew money from the business occasionally, but Scott was kept in ignorance of the balance sheet.

In the years before the financial difficulties, Scott borrowed money to expand his estate on bills drawn by James Ballantyne and Company on Constable and Company. These bills were then discounted by the banks. Scott provided security to Constable and Company by giving Ballantyne and Company counter bills for the equivalent sums. These counter bills remained with Constable as a precautionary measure.

However, the original bills were never discharged, and the banks renewed the bills when requested; the unredeemed debt increased with each renewal. Faced with ruin, Constable raised money on the counter bills that were supposed to be kept for security and not for circulation. Therefore, Scott was liable not only for the original bills dishonored by Constable, but also for the counter bills dishonored by Ballantyne. In effect, he paid twice for the money he borrowed.

Scott explained to his son, Walter, that he had "left bonds in their hands which should have been paid off by them many years since but which not very fairly they kept up by paying the interest regularly, so that I never knew of their existence." The total debt was £130,000.

By the time of Scott's death, he had paid off £70,000 of the encumbrance. Part of the earnings from the copyrights on Scott's works was applied to the debt after his death, and, by 1847, his estate was free of all debts. Although he didn't live to see it, the work of his pen ultimately did accomplish his goal.

In February 1830, Scott had the first of several strokes that caused temporary paralysis and loss of speech. He recovered and continued to write, ignoring his doctor's recommendation to rest. Scott was unwavering in working toward his goal, even when he was in severe pain. As the result of his strokes, however, he wasn't in full command of his faculties.

Scott's works extended from narrative poetry to romantic novels to biography and history. His productivity was legendary. He wrote twenty-six novels in seventeen years while also working as an advocate. The novels for which he is best known include *Waverley, Guy Mannering, Rob Roy, The Heart of Midlothian, Kenilworth, Quentin Durward, The Talisman*, and *Ivanhoe*. He is remembered for saying: "Time and I against any two." Scott knew that he had the creativity to accomplish virtually anything that he set out to do. He was nearly right; he paid off much of the debt within his lifetime.

ELIZABETH BARRETT BROWNING (1806-1861) Poet
Who Overcame Illness

> "How do I love thee? Let me count the ways.
> I love thee to the depth and breadth and height
> My soul can reach, when feeling out of sight
> For the ends of Being and ideal Grace.
> I love thee to the level of every day's
> Most quiet need, by sun and candlelight.
> I love thee freely, as men strive for Right;
> I love thee purely, as men turn from Praise.
> I love thee with the passion put to use
> In my old griefs, and with my childhood's faith.
> I lived with a love I seemed to lose
> With my lost saints,—I love thee with the breath,
> Smiles, tears, of all my life!—and, if God chooses,
> I shall love thee better after death."

Elizabeth Barrett Browning, *Sonnets from the Portuguese*

Elizabeth Barrett's reputation as a poet exceeded that of Robert Browning when they met. She was an invalid who rarely left her room in her parents' home. Initially, they corresponded, and then Robert arranged their meeting through a mutual friend. Each had a strong respect for the other's poetry, and they found that they had much in common emotionally.

Elizabeth's father had forbidden his children, both sons and daughters, to marry. Since Elizabeth was chronically ill, she wasn't concerned about this parental edict until she met Robert. Her health improved as their love for each other developed.

Elizabeth and Robert were married secretly, eloped, and moved to Italy. Elizabeth was disowned by her father, but she had a small annuity on which to live. Robert's income was not sufficient to support them. They remained deeply in love and had an idyllic marriage. They had no serious arguments, and each was strongly supportive of the other's writing. In her opinion, she had not begun to live until she met Robert. Ultimately, with her advice and editing, Robert's poetry gained a wider acceptance than his earlier works, and her poetry was also improved by his advice and suggestions.

Elizabeth's story cannot be told without also telling the story of Robert.

Elizabeth Barrett, the oldest child of Edward Moulton Barrett and Mary Graham-Clarke Barrett, was born on March 6, 1806, in Durham, England. Edward Barrett was a wealthy merchant whose family owned a plantation in Jamaica. Elizabeth received no formal education, but she read widely and, to a large extent, was self-educated. She learned Greek by participating in her brother Edward's lessons. Her first poems, including "The Battle of Marathon," were published when she was thirteen. Her father paid for a private printing of her early poems.

In 1832, the Barrett family moved to Devon and three years later moved to London. In 1838, they moved into 50 Wimpole Street, which was popularized in Rudolf Besier's play, *The Barretts of Wimpole Street*. She published *The Seraphim and Other Poems* that year and suffered a serious health problem that affected her respiratory system, which may have involved abscesses in the lungs. Her health deteriorated to the point that she was considered an invalid.

For health reasons, she was sent to Torquay, where her brother, Edward, drowned. Elizabeth and Edward had been close. Because he had accompanied her to Torquay, she considered herself at least partially responsible for his death. In 1841, she returned to London as a complete invalid. She spent her days reclining on a sofa and rarely left her room. She received few visitors and did not envision much of a future for herself. However, she wrote many letters and stayed current in the literary world by corresponding with scholars and writers of the day.

In 1844, her reputation as a poet was enhanced by the publication of her new book of poems, which included "A Drama of Exile" (about the exile of Adam and Eve from Paradise), twenty-eight sonnets, some romantic ballads, and miscellaneous other poems. These poems elevated her standing with the critics and brought her to the attention of a fellow poet, Robert Browning.

Robert Browning, oldest child of Robert Browning, Sr., and Sarah Weidemann Browning, was born at Camberwell, England, on May 7, 1812. Robert's sister, Sarianna, was born two years later. Robert Browning, Sr. was a bibliophile and scholar who worked for the Bank of England for fifty years. Young Robert grew up in a home with thousands of books. He attended private schools in his neighborhood, but most of his education was received at home with his father serving as one of his tutors. His education was almost exclusively literary and musical.

Father and son were very close throughout their lives. Robert was also close with his mother, even to the extent of sharing illnesses with her when he was growing up. He frequently displayed his temper as a young man; his tolerant parents provided an environment that was "sheltered, enclosed, dependent." He lived at home until he married at the age of thirty-three.

When he was sixteen, Robert attended classes in Greek at London University and decided that writing poetry was his life's work. The generous father was willing to finance his son's writing. Robert was never bothered by financial problems; he was grateful to his father for his support.

When he was twenty-one, Robert published, anonymously, "Pauline, a Fragment of a Confession." Mr. W. J. Fox of *The Monthly Repository* gave it a favorable review, but it was not well-received by other critics. In later years, Robert was ashamed of this early work and destroyed all copies that he could find. At this stage of his development as a poet, he was strongly influenced by Shelley.

For the next twelve years, Robert was a prolific author, writing "Paracelsus," "Sordello," "Pippa Passes," "Bells and Pomegranates," and five plays—*King Victor and King Charles, The Return of the Druses, Columbe's Birthday, Strafford,* and *A Blot in the 'Scutcheon.* The last two had very short runs on the stage, and the other dramas were not produced. He was not considered a successful playwright.

Robert had a full social life, and he had many literary friends including John Forster, literary critic of *The Examiner.* Initially, Forster was the only critic to perceive the merit of "Paracelsus." Thomas Carlyle became a lifelong friend. Robert had many women friends but no close attachments with women. That was about to change.

Elizabeth was ambitious and wanted to break out of the shell that her illness had imposed on her. She did not think of love and sexual passion, but she wanted to find another person with whom she could share poetic passion. When she read "Paracelsus," she suspected that Robert Browning might be that poet. Most of what she knew of Robert was from his poetry and her interpretation of it. She knew a few facts about Robert, the man, from her distant cousin, John Kenyon.

In late December 1844, Robert returned from a trip to Italy and read Elizabeth Barrett's collection of poems, which had been published the preceding August. He admired her poetry and heard more about her from his friend and her cousin, John Kenyon. Robert wrote to Elizabeth to tell her how much he enjoyed her poetry.

In his first letter to her, Robert said, "I love your verses with all my heart, dear Miss Barrett." He did not attempt to analyze her poetry; he said that "into me it has gone, and part of me it has become, this great living poetry of yours, not a flower of which but took root and grew . . . I do, as I say, love these books with all my heart—and I love you too."

Elizabeth replied that she was delighted with "the sympathy of a poet, and such a poet!" She asked him for criticisms of her writing and offered some comments on his efforts: "'Misty' is an infamous word for your kind of obscurity. You are never misty—not even in 'Sordello'—never vague. Your graver cuts deep sharp lines, always—and there is an extra-distinctness in your images and thoughts, from the midst of which, crossing each other infinitely, the general significance seems to escape."

They corresponded frequently. Over 600 of their letters survive, providing a wealth of personal information for biographers. In one of her letters to him, she offers her views on writing: "Like to write? Of course, of course I do. I seem to live while I write—it is life, for me. Why, what is to live? Not to eat and drink and breathe—but to feel the life in you down all the fibers of being, passionately and joyfully. And thus, one lives in composition surely—not always—but when the wheel goes round and the process is uninterrupted."

Initially, their letters were about their craft, but soon the relationship deepened. On May 20, 1845, they met for the first time. After that meeting, Robert wrote to her, concluding his letter: "I am proud and happy in your friendship—now and forever. May God bless you!" He followed that letter with one declaring his love. He was moving too fast for her. She responded, "You do not know what pain you give me by speaking so wildly . . . you have said some intemperate things . . . fancies—which you will not say over again, nor unsay, but forget at once." He replied that she had misunderstood him; she accepted his explanation.

Robert's letters give the impression of a man attempting to control an overwhelming emotion. Her letters in response provide a recurring theme; she is unworthy, and she fears that she will encumber him because her poor health will limit his social activity.

Elizabeth had another problem in addition to her health concerns. Her autocratic father refused to allow any of his children, either sons or daughters, to marry. No rational explanation exists for this behavior. Several biographers have conjectured that some Negro blood had entered into the family genealogy in Jamaica, and that Barrett did not want to pass it on to subsequent generations of the family.

Elizabeth, the oldest child in the family, had been left a modest legacy on which she could live. Her sisters, Henrietta and Arabel, did not have a comparable annual stipend. They were entirely dependent on their father for support, or on a husband if they chose to go against their father's wishes and marry. Henrietta married, but Arabel remained single and was always financially dependent upon her father.

Elizabeth held Robert off. She viewed him as the giver and herself as the taker; she felt that she was not good enough for him. Ultimately, Elizabeth and Robert acknowledged to each other that they were very much in love; they began to plan their marriage.

They planned to be married in secret and then wait for a time when her father was away to leave for a honeymoon in Italy. Elizabeth told her sisters of her plans, but would not allow them to attend the wedding ceremony because it would upset their father. She did not tell her brothers or most of her close friends about her wedding plans.

The deception during the two months before their wedding upset Elizabeth. She was not used to being devious. "I am so nervous that my own footsteps startle me . . . To hear the voice of my father and meet his eyes makes me shrink back—to talk to my brothers leaves my nerves trembling."

They were married in St. Marylebone parish church on September 12, 1846. Elizabeth lived another week in her father's house before embarking for France en route to Italy. She said, "I did hate so, to have to take off the ring."

On September 19, accompanied by her maid, the Brownings left for Italy. Elizabeth had almost fifteen years of happy married life and creative professional life ahead of her. She gave birth to a son in 1849, and in 1861, after a flurry of loving kisses, died peacefully in Robert's arms.

Their letters provide a comprehensive look at the complexity of their relationship. They even corresponded when Robert was away on a short trip, for example, to find a place to stay for the summer away from the heat of Florence. Both correspondents were able to express their feelings superbly in writing. When Elizabeth died, Robert exclaimed, "How strange it will be to have no more letters."

While living at the Casa Guidi in Florence after the birth of their son, Weidemann ("Pen"), Elizabeth showed Robert the poems that she had written during their courtship but had never let him read. She had traced their courtship from hesitation, doubt, and reservation to the happiness of reciprocated love. They were personal poems, and she suspected that he would object to their being published.

To the contrary, Robert considered them among the best sonnets in the English language. "When Robert saw them he was much touched and pleased—and thinking highly of the poetry he did not let . . . could not consent, he said, that they should be lost to my volumes [of 1850] and so we agreed to slip them in under some sort of veil, and after much consideration chose the 'Portuguese.'" The collection of forty-three sonnets was entitled *Sonnets from the Portuguese*.

Robert completed two volumes of poetry entitled *Men and Women* while living in Florence. At the same time, Elizabeth worked on *Aurora Leigh*, a novel in verse that she described as "the novel or romance I have been hankering after for so long." She described it to her brother, George, as "beyond question my best work."

In Elizabeth's verse novel, Aurora Leigh is born in Italy to an English father and an Italian mother, from whom she is orphaned at the age of thirteen. A disciplinarian aunt in England, who raised her, wants her to marry her cousin, but Aurora wants to become a poet. Her cousin proposes to a poor girl who jilts him. She uses an intricate plot to tell her "thoroughly modern" story. Elizabeth addresses the question in her work of whether women can be happy with just their art or if they need men to feel fulfilled.

Elizabeth told her sister Arabel, "Robert and I work every day—he has a large volume of short poems which will be completed by the spring—and I have some four thousand, five hundred lines of mine—I am afraid six thousand lines will not finish it." To protect their work schedule, they did not receive visitors before three o'clock. Elizabeth wrote in the drawing room, and Robert worked in the sitting room. The doors to the dining room in between these two rooms remained closed. She wrote in an armchair with her feet raised; he worked at a desk.

Although Elizabeth and Robert edited each other's completed work, they did not review each other's daily effort nor did they discuss their work every day. Elizabeth, in particular, had strong feelings about this. She thought that no matter how close two people are to each other, that closeness should not extend to their work. She said, "An artist must, I fancy, either find or make solitude to work in, if it is to be good work at all." Until her work was completed, she kept the details to herself.

The Brownings visited London to oversee the printing of Robert's *Men and Women*. Elizabeth pitched in and read the proofs as they came off the press. The effort was very exhausting for her, but she was convinced that this work would enhance her husband's reputation. Her own effort to complete *Aurora Leigh* was postponed.

Men and Women was successful initially; the first edition sold out immediately, and American publishers requested the rights to reprint it. Elizabeth had helped Robert to be clearer in expressing his artistic feelings. Critics were no longer calling his work obscure. Elizabeth had also helped him to think less of financial concerns and to place more emphasis on writing poems. She considered *Men and Women* a brilliant collection and hoped that his genius would be acclaimed by his peers.

As soon as Elizabeth had completed *Aurora Leigh*, Robert made arrangements to have it published; in effect, he acted as her business manager. Both Elizabeth and Robert read the proofs and prepared the manuscript for the press. He discontinued the promotion of his last collection and postponed work on his next book of poems. Sales of *Men and Women* began to slip; it could have used additional promotion.

Robert took drawing and sculpting lessons in Florence. While they lived in Italy, he was not as dedicated to writing as Elizabeth was. During their fifteen-year marriage, his poetic output was not nearly as great as hers. Before their marriage, he had lived at home where his sister and his parents had ministered to his needs. He had no responsibilities that diverted him from writing. After he was married, he had to look after Elizabeth, whose health continued to be delicate.

Their son, Robert Weidemann Browning ("Pen"), was born on March 9, 1849. Elizabeth wrote poetry while she was pregnant; she completed the first part of "Casa Guidi Windows" during this time. Early in their marriage, Robert learned from Elizabeth; her reputation was greater than his at that stage of their careers. She encouraged him to concentrate on dramatic monologues in poetry and to give up playwriting. She was concerned that he was not measuring up to his potential because of his reduced productivity. He was not concerned; he looked upon it as a temporary condition.

After the birth of their son, Robert began work on a long double poem entitled "Christmas Eve and Easter Day." Elizabeth was a strong influence on the choice of a theme for this work. She suggested that he write from the heart, not the head, and that he convey his own thoughts using a minimum of dramatic devices. She encouraged him to write about his hopes and fears, particularly those of a religious nature, in his poetry.

On January 1, 1852, Elizabeth was pleased to hear that Robert had made a New Year's resolution to write a poem every day. He began with "Love Among the Ruins," "Women and Roses," and "Childe Rolande." However, his writing was not sustained. They were staying in Paris at the time, and he resumed his contacts with society. Elizabeth encouraged this, even though she was unable to accompany him. However, she experienced social activity vicariously through him and stayed current with the Paris social scene.

Attending social events provided an outlet for Robert at a time when Elizabeth's poor health restricted her mobility. However, talk continued to be an important factor in the couple's relationship. They knew that as long as they could be together and communicate freely, Elizabeth's delicate health would not ruin their marriage. This openness extended to instances of minor disagreement.

Elizabeth wrote to Robert's sister, Sarianna, that "the peculiarity of our relation is that even when he's displeased with me, he thinks out loud and can't stop himself."

The Brownings' marriage was solid and enduring. The few disagreements that they had involved viewing some of their friends from different perspectives. Elizabeth could learn from Robert about the nature of people, but she tended to stay with her own evaluation of friends.

Their principal difference of opinion was Elizabeth's belief in spiritualism and in communicating with the dead in seances. They attended sessions with the seer Daniel Douglas Home. Robert remained unconvinced of the value of seances; he wrote a spoof of spiritualism entitled "Mr. Sludge, the Medium."

Elizabeth and Robert retained their own identities. They thought independently and were exciting conversationalists. Neither tried to convert the other to their image of an ideal partner in marriage. Robert wrote to his brother-in-law George, "I shall only say that Ba [Elizabeth] and I know each other for a time and, I dare trust, eternity — We differ . . . as to spirit-rapping, we quarrel sometimes about politics, and estimate people's characters with enormous difference, but, in the main, we know each other, I say."

Elizabeth's health deteriorated during the last three years of her life. When she seemed to be slipping away, the doctor was summoned. She appeared to be sleeping; Robert whispered in her ear, "Do you know me?" She murmured, "My Robert — my heavens, my beloved!" She kissed him repeatedly and said, "Our lives are held by God." He laid her head on the pillow. She tried to kiss him again but could no longer reach him, so she kissed her own hand and extended it to him. Robert asked, "Are you comfortable?" She responded, "Beautiful."

She began to fall asleep again, and Robert realized that she should not be in a reclining position when a cough was coming. He raised her up to ease the cough. She began to cough up phlegm but then stopped. Robert was not sure if she had fainted or fallen asleep. He saw her brow contract as though in pain and then relax. She looked very young. Their servant Annunciata, who realized that she was dead, said in Italian, "Her last gesture a kiss, her last thought of love."

Robert's friends expected him to break down completely after the loss of one so close. However, he remained in control, partly because Elizabeth had died so peacefully in his arms. Robert knew that his friends felt sorry for him in his loss. He was extremely grateful for the fifteen years that he and Elizabeth had together. He knew that she had more to give, but he appreciated the rare union that they had.

Friends were also concerned about Pen, who had been as close to his mother as a son and a mother can be. He, too, held up well and, in fact, was a consolation to his father. Robert told his sister, Sarianna, that Pen was "perfect to me."

Elizabeth's place in literary history was summarized by essayist and poet Alice Meynell:

> The place of Elizabeth Barrett Browning in English literature is high, if not on the summits. She had an original genius, a great heart, and an intellect that was, if not great, exceedingly active. She seldom has composure or repose, but it is not true that her poetry is purely emotional. It is full of abundant, and often overabundant thoughts.
>
> It is intellectually restless . . . she "dashed" not by reason of feminine weakness, but as it were to prove her possession of masculine strength. Her gentler work, as in the *Sonnets from the Portuguese*, is beyond praise. There is in her poetic personality a glory of righteousness, of spirituality, and of ardor that makes her name a splendid one in the history of incomparable literature.

Although Elizabeth was only fifty-five when she died, she had accomplished the goal that she had set as a young girl: to produce lasting poetry that made a significant contribution to her era. She influenced other poets, including Emily Dickinson, even before she died.

Elizabeth was not sure that marriage was for her; she knew that the goals of husband, home, and children, by themselves, were not enough. To have found Robert to love and to have her love reciprocated was more that she had hoped for. Having a son at the age of forty-three added to her joy. She never stopped appreciating her good fortune to be poet, wife, and mother. Her remaining goal was for Robert to make the mark in poetry of which she knew he was capable.

Robert and Pen left Florence on July 27, 1861. In September, they arrived in London, where Robert lived for the next twenty-eight years. He visited Italy, but he never returned to Florence. Initially, he was lonely, but eventually he resumed his literary connections in society. He published *Dramatis Personae* in 1864, which led to his being lionized. In 1867, Oxford University awarded him a Master of Arts degree "by diploma" and Balliol College elected him an honorary Fellow.

The Ring and the Book, generally regarded as his masterpiece, was published in four volumes in 1868-69. Elizabeth's dreams were at last realized when he was hailed as "a great dramatic poet." In *The Ring and the Book*, which was based on Guido Franceschini's court case in Florence, Browning told the story of a gruesome murder twelve times. He versified the arguments of the counsels for the prosecution and the defense as well as the gossip of busybodies. The story was told with the detail of a court recorder.

In 1881, the Browning Society was formed by Dr. Furnival and Miss E. H. Hickey. Browning received additional honors: a LL.D degree from Cambridge University in 1879, the D.C.L. from Oxford University in 1882, and a LL.D degree from Edinburgh University in 1884. In 1886, he became foreign correspondent to the Royal Academy.

During his twenty-eight-year widowhood, privacy was important to him. He destroyed all of the letters of his youth and all of the letters to his family. He could not destroy his wife's letters to him, nor could he destroy his letters to her. However, he was not sure what to do with them. He left them to his son to decide; Pen published them in 1899. Robert never ceased promoting Elizabeth's work. He realized that part of his popularity was because he was the widower of Elizabeth Barrett Browning.

Robert died on December 12, 1889, while visiting Pen in Venice. His body was transported to London for burial in Westminster Abbey. It was proposed that Elizabeth's body be disinterred from the cemetery in Florence and buried alongside her husband. However, Pen decided that her grave should not be disturbed.

EMILY DICKINSON (1830-1886) Poet and Recluse

> "I'm nobody! Who are you?
> Are you nobody, too?
> Then there's a pair of us—don't tell!
> They'd banish us, you know!
>
> How dreary to be somebody!
> How public, like a frog,
> To tell your name the livelong day
> To an admiring bog!"
>
> Emily Dickinson

Emily Dickinson spent her days as a recluse in her parents' home writing poetry. By the late 1860s, she had discontinued virtually all contact with the outside world, except for a small group of relatives and friends. Her mentor, Thomas Wentworth Higginson, observed upon meeting her, "She was much too enigmatical a being for me to solve in an hour's interview, and an instinct told me that the slightest attempt at cross-examination would make her withdraw into her shell; I could only sit still and watch, as one does in the woods."

During her lifetime, Dickinson published only seven poems, all anonymously. After her death in 1886, Lavinia Dickinson found 900 of her sister's poems in a locked trunk in her bedroom. Later, 875 additional poems were discovered. Dickinson's highly crafted and usually short poems were written in a conversational idiom about a wide variety of topics. She was a pioneer in the use of rhyme and measured poetic patterns; she was an original and is considered a founder of modern American poetry.

Louis Untermeyer summarized Dickinson's poetry in *Makers of the Modern World:*

> She wrote both as a bereaved woman and a happy, irresponsible child. Often, indeed, her writing is almost too coy for comfort. There is, at times, an embarrassing affectation, a willing naiveté, as though she were determined to be not only a child but a spoiled child—a child who patronizes the

universe and is arch with its Creator. But the pertness suddenly turns to pure perception, and the teasing is forgotten in revelation.

There is no way of analyzing her unique blend of whimsicality and wisdom, of solving her trick of turning what seems to be cryptic *non sequiturs* into crystal epigrams, no way of measuring her deceptive simplicity and her startling depths. The mystery of Emily Dickinson is not the way she lived but the way she wrote, a mystery which enabled a New England recluse to charge the literature of her country with poems she never cared to publish.

Emily Dickinson was born to Edward Dickinson and Emily Norcross Dickinson on December 10, 1830, in Amherst, Massachusetts. She was a middle child; her brother Austin was two years older, and her sister Lavinia was two years younger. Emily was born in a large, brick house called the Homestead, built by her grandfather, Samuel Dickinson, a founder of Amherst College. Samuel, a successful lawyer, was such a strong supporter of the College that he spent his savings on the struggling school in its early days. After finishing college and entering law practice, Emily's father supported his parents and his siblings.

Edward was a strict disciplinarian with his children. Emily's view of him was that his "heart was pure and terrible, and I think no other like it exists." Nevertheless, he believed in education and ensured that his daughters were well educated. Emily's mother was a literate woman; however, Emily once said of her: "Mother does not care for thought." Later in life, Emily told her mentor that she "never had a mother." Like his father, Edward was the treasurer of Amherst College. He also served as a member of the Massachusetts General Court and as U.S. Congressman for two terms.

As a member of a religious Congregationalist family, Emily was discouraged from reading fiction in her adolescent years; nevertheless, she was allowed to read the novels of Nathaniel Hawthorne, Charles Dickens, and Sir Walter Scott. She also read the works of Ralph Waldo Emerson, Henry Wadsworth Longfellow, Henry David Thoreau, and British women writers, including the Bronté sisters, Elizabeth Barrett Browning, and George Eliot.

After attending Amherst Academy, Emily enrolled at the Mt. Holyoke Female Seminary established by Mary Lyon, who had been a student of Edward Hitchcock, the president of Amherst College. The program at Mt. Holyoke was a combination of academic courses and religious services. Students were encouraged to "convert" to committed Christianity. Emily's religious beliefs were continually questioned, and she was admonished daily to save her soul. She hesitated to convert because "it is hard for me to give up the world." She left Mt. Holyoke after one year because of the religious pressures and homesickness.

When she returned home, Dickinson found that many of her friends had left Amherst. She became a good friend of Susan Gilbert, who later became her sister-in-law. Dickinson was close with her sister, Lavinia, throughout their lifetimes. In 1850, following a religious revival near Amherst, Susan Gilbert as well as Dickinson's brother, Austin, and sister, Lavinia, converted. Dickinson's hesitancy about religion remained; she did not convert. She expressed her feeling in verse:

> I shall know why—when Time is over—
> And I have ceased to wonder why—
> Christ will explain each separate anguish
> In the fair schoolroom in the sky—
> He will tell me what "Peter" promised—
> And I—for wonder at his woe—
> I shall forget the drop of anguish
> That scalds me now—that scalds me now.

In 1850, Austin went to Cambridge for four years to attend Harvard Law School. Dickinson wrote to him almost every day. She wrote poetry throughout the 1850s. Her first two published poems were valentines, printed in the *Amherst College Indicator* and the *Springfield Republican*. Both poems were published anonymously.

Dickinson was encouraged in her writing by Benjamin Newton, a clerk in her father's law office from 1847 to 1849. He was a prolific reader nine years her senior, who helped her with her evolving style. She wrote to Susan, "I have found a beautiful new friend." It is probable that they were just friends; however, some biographers consider Newton Dickinson's first love interest. Three years after meeting Dickinson, Newton married a woman twelve years older than he. He died of tuberculosis in 1853.

Dickinson's friendship with Susan Gilbert was enhanced by their mutual interest in literature. Susan was also well educated. She and Dickinson were a good intellectual match; however, their relationship was sometimes strained. In 1856, Susan and Austin Dickinson were married and moved into their home, Evergreen, next door to the Homestead. Susan was loved by the Dickinson family; nevertheless, the relationship between Susan and Lavinia was occasionally tense.

Emily Dickinson rarely left Amherst, but in 1855 she visited Philadelphia and Washington, D.C. with her father. In Philadelphia, she met Charles Wadsworth, a young minister with personal magnetism. Many of Dickinson's biographers think she had a romantic relationship with Wadsworth, a married man. In 1862, Wadsworth received a call from Calvary Church in San Francisco and moved there. Dickinson expressed her feelings in a sad poem:

> I cannot live with You—
> It would be Life—
> And Life is over there—
> Behind the Shelf
>
> ....
> So we must keep apart—
> You there—I—here—
> With just the Door ajar
> That Oceans are—and Prayer—
> And that White Sustenance—
> Despair—

Wadsworth visited Amherst twice, in 1860 and 1880; he and Dickinson corresponded regularly.

In 1860-61, Dickinson wrote moving letters to her "Master":

> I am older—tonight, Master—but the love is the
> same—so are the moon and the crescent. If it had

been God's will that I might breathe where you breathed—and find the place—myself—at night— if I [can] never forget that I am not with you—and that sorrow and frost are nearer than I . . . I want to see you more—Sir—than all I wish in this world— and the wish—altered a little—will be my only one—for the skies.

Dickinson wrote one of her more passionate love poems in 1861:

> Wild Nights—Wild Nights!
> Were I with thee
> Wild Nights should be
> Our luxury!
> Futile—the Winds—
> To a Heart in port
> Done with the Compass—
> Done with the Chart!
> Rowing in Eden—
> Ah, the Sea!
> Might I but moor—Tonight
> In Thee!

She did not date her poems. Thankfully, her handwriting changed over the years; handwriting analysis was helpful in assigning an approximate date to her work.

Martha Dickinson Bianchi, Dickinson's niece, thought that Wadsworth was her aunt's "fate," and that they had fallen in love at first sight. Dickinson destroyed most of her correspondence before she died; however, three letters addressed to her "Master" were found among her papers, which caused much speculation. Wadsworth died in 1882. Dickinson wrote a poem that biographers speculate refers to the deaths of Newton and Wadsworth:

> My life closed twice before its close;
>   It yet remains to see
> If immortality unveil
>   A third event to me,
> So huge, so hopeless to conceive,

As these that twice befell.
Parting is all we know of heaven,
And all we need of hell.

Late in the 1850s, Dickinson began to withdraw increasingly from society. As she retreated from society, her output of poetry increased significantly. However, her brother and sister-in-law were very active socially, and Dickinson met many famous people at Evergreen, the house next door. In 1857, Ralph Waldo Emerson stayed at Evergreen during a series of lectures at Amherst College, and Austin and Susan also hosted Harriet Beecher Stowe, author of *Uncle Tom's Cabin*, and Samuel Bowles, editor of the Springfield *Republican*. Bowles, an ambitious, charismatic man, published several of Dickinson's poems in the 1850s.

In 1860, Dickinson stopped attending church. She commented that some people kept the Sabbath by going to church, but that she kept it by staying at home.

In the early 1860s, Dickinson's eyesight began to fail. Her vision was blurred, and her eyes were extremely sensitive to light. She visited ophthalmologists in Boston and was advised to use her eyes less, a heart-rending prescription for a person like her. Worried that her ailment might be progressive, she stepped up her production of poems. Fortunately, her eyesight improved during the late 1860s.

Dickinson had a high regard for the literary opinions of her sister-in-law, Susan. She sent 267 poems over the years to her, soliciting suggestions for improvement. Susan did not always respond, causing some friction between the two women. In 1861, Susan had her first child, Edward; raising a family put increased demands on her time.

Dickinson responded to an essay in the newspaper, "Letter to a Young Contributor," by Thomas Wentworth Higginson, who became her mentor. She sent four poems to him and asked for his advice, and then didn't take it. He asked her to visit him in Boston so that he could introduce her to his literary friends. She didn't make the trip to Boston, but she invited him to Amherst. After corresponding for eight years, he finally visited her at her home.

When Higginson entered the house, Dickinson presented him with two lilies and said, "These are my introduction. Forgive me if

I am frightened; I never see strangers and hardly know what to say." He remembered that, "She talked soon and henceforward continuously for her own relief, and wholly without watching its effect on her hearer." She told Higginson, "If I read a book [and] it makes my whole body so cold no fire can ever warm me, I know that is poetry. If I feel physically as if the top of my head were taken off, I know that is poetry. These are the only ways I know it." Higginson admitted, "I never was with anyone who drained my nerve power so much. Without touching her, she drew from me. I am glad not to live near her."

Initially, Dickinson was too obscure for him to understand her well. She experimented with meter and rhyme, including eye rhymes: words that are spelled similarly but do not rhyme, such as sword and word. However, she was meticulous in her choice of words. Although Higginson encouraged her, she never sought publication of her poems.

As Dickinson's poetry became more profound, she socialized less and less. During the 1860s, she was a prolific writer of poetry. She wrote her poems on large sheets of paper and organized them into small bundles by folding the sheets and sewing the pages together. Thirty-nine of these packets, containing a total of 811 poems, were found after her death.

By 1869, Dickinson rarely ventured out of the house. She said, "I do not cross my father's ground to any house or town." Lavinia commented on the family's spheres of activity: "Emily had to think—she was the only one of us who had that to do . . . Father believed; and mother loved; and Austin had Amherst: and I had the family to keep track of."

Friends admired Dickinson's work and suggested that she publish her poems; she resisted. One was her childhood friend, Helen Fiske, who married E. B. Hunt and was widowed during the Civil War. She then married W. S. Jackson, and as Helen Hunt Jackson became the best-known woman poet in America at the time. In particular, she wanted Dickinson to publish the following poem:

> Success is counted sweetest
> By those who ne'er succeed.
> To comprehend a nectar
> Requires sorest need.

Not one of all the purple Host
Who took the Flag today
Can tell the definition
So plain of Victory

As he defeated—dying
On whose forbidden ear
The distant strains of triumph
Break, agonizing clear!

The poem was published with the title "Success" in *A Masque of Poets* anthology in 1878.

Dickinson's third romance was with Judge Otis Phillips Lord, a friend of her father, nineteen years her senior. Lord was an Amherst alumnus who returned regularly for reunions and visited the Homestead, even after Edward's death. Friendship evolved into romance. One year after the death of Lord's wife, Dickinson wrote in one surviving letter, "I confess that I love him—I rejoice that I love him—I thank the Maker of Heaven and Earth—that gave him me to love." It is not known whether he ever proposed to her. He passed away in 1884.

Dickinson's reputation as an eccentric grew. Mabel Loomis Todd, who was married to an Amherst professor, moved to town in the fall of 1881 and wrote to her parents about the "nun of Amherst": "I must tell you about the character of Amherst; it is a lady whom the people call the 'Myth.' She is a sister of Mr. Dickinson and seems to be the climax of all the family oddity. She has not been out of her own house in fifteen years, except once to see a new church, when she crept out at night and viewed it by moonlight." Mabel Loomis Todd first listened to Dickinson's poems at Evergreen and thought that they were "full of power."

Dickinson had a reputation for remaining behind half-closed doors instead of mixing with visitors to the Homestead. In her later years, she always wore white. She liked children, but would not go outside to talk with them. She lowered candy and cookies to them in a basket from her bedroom window.

Mabel Loomis Todd and her husband, David Peck Todd, socialized with Austin and Susan Dickinson as well as with Lavinia

Dickinson. Shortly after her first visit to Evergreen, Loomis Todd and Austin Dickinson began a love affair that continued until he died in 1895. They made no attempt to hide their emotions.

In the spring of 1884, Dickinson became ill with the kidney disease that ultimately caused her death. On May 13, 1886, she went into a coma; she died two days later. Her obituary appeared in the *Springfield Republican*: "Very few in the village, except among the older inhabitants, knew Miss Emily personally, although the facts of her seclusion and her intellectual brilliancy were familiar Amherst traditions . . . As she passed on in life, her sensitive nature shrank from much personal contact with the world, and more and more turned to her own large wealth of individual resources for companionship."

Shortly after Dickinson's death, Lavinia Dickinson discovered her sister's poems. In 1890, the first edition of *Emily Dickinson's Poems* was published. William Dean Howells, America's dean of letters at the time, praised the volume as a "distinctive addition" to the country's literature. During her later years, Dickinson wrote her poems on scraps of paper and the flaps of envelopes as thoughts occurred to her. This made editing her work extremely difficult. In 1891, Loomis Todd and Higginson edited a second volume of Dickinson's poetry, and, in 1893, Loomis Todd published another volume of Dickinson's poetry.

After Austin Dickinson died in 1895, Lavinia Dickinson, who had been working with Loomis Todd editing her sister's poems, decided that she no longer wanted Loomis Todd to edit the remaining poems. Tension had built up over the more than ten-year duration of Loomis Todd's affair with Austin Dickinson. Loomis Todd put the poems that she had been editing in the attic of her house, where they stayed for thirty years.

In 1914, Martha Dickinson Bianchi, Dickinson's niece, published 143 of her aunt's unpublished poems. In 1930, Millicent Todd Bingham, Loomis Todd's daughter, and Alfred Leete Hampson edited and published *Further Poems of Emily Dickinson*. Subsequent collections were published in 1935 and 1945. In 1955, *The Poems of Emily Dickinson*, all 1,775 original poems in three volumes, was published.

The principal insight into Dickinson's inner life is in her poetry, not her biographies. She provided at least a limited view of her thoughts about her verse:

> This is my letter to the World
> That never wrote to Me—
> The simple News that Nature told—
> With tender Majesty
> Her Message is committed
> To Hands I cannot see—
> For love of Her—Sweet countrymen—
> Judge tenderly—of Me.

GEORGE BERNARD SHAW (1856-1950) Playwright and Critic

"When I was young I observed that nine out of every ten things I did were failures, so I did ten times more work."

George Bernard Shaw

In 1879 at the age of twenty-three, George Bernard Shaw began his career by writing a novel. His first novel entitled (as Shaw observed, "with merciless fitness"), *Immaturity*, was written in his spare time while working for the Edison Telephone Company. After Shaw had worked six months, Edison was bought out by the Bell Telephone Company, and Shaw quit his job to prepare himself for his life's work — writing. He virtually lived at the British Museum, educating himself while his mother supported him. He didn't require much support since he ate little and wore the same suit for years.

His next novel, *The Irrational Knot*, was the first of Shaw's treatments of marriage and the relationships between men and women. His third novel was *Love Among the Artists*, which, despite its title, wasn't a spicy story. Shaw's fourth novel was *Cashel Byron's Profession*, a story about prizefighting, which was against the law in England at the time. It was the most readable of Shaw's novels and was the first one to be published when it appeared in 1884 in *Today*, a Socialist magazine with a small circulation. He received no money for his story, but he had the satisfaction of seeing his work in print.

In 1901, Shaw looked back on this experience and commented, "I never think of *Cashel Byron's Profession* without a shudder at the narrowness of my escape from being a successful novelist at the age of twenty-six. At that moment an adventurous publisher might have ruined me."

Shaw's next novel was *An Unsocial Socialist*. His last attempt at writing a novel was no more successful than his previous four attempts. He wrote several pages of a sixth novel before deciding that fiction writing wasn't his forte. However, fiction writing was part of his apprenticeship in learning the writing craft. This apprenticeship lasted fifteen years, until he became a successful playwright in 1894. Many of the characters and situations from his unsuccessful novels were translated into similar characters and situations in his successful plays. Of his attempts at writing fiction, he observed, "Fifty or sixty refusals without a single acceptance forced me into a fierce self-sufficiency. I became undiscourageable, acquiring a superhuman insensitivity to praise or blame which has become useful at times since."

Shaw's next literary effort was writing short stories, including "The Brand of Cain," which was rejected by many editors. One editor suggested changes and offered to reread it. Upon its return, Shaw reread it and sent the editor a note admitting that "the failure of the story is more than you suppose."

Shaw submitted an essay entitled "Exhausted Arts" to John Morley, editor of the *Pall Mall Gazette*. Morley suggested that Shaw give up writing: "It is a precarious, dependent, and unsatisfactory profession, excepting for very few who have the knack or manage to persuade people that they have it." Shaw's response began with "Thank you very much for your attempt to befriend me" and concluded with "Should you ever require anything particularly unpleasant written about anybody, pray remember, Yours Faithfully, G. B. Shaw."

In September 1882, Shaw heard the American economist and Socialist, Henry George, speak in London about his doctrine of the Single Tax. In *Progress and Poverty*, George proposed that governments should use just one tax, a tax on land. Shortly after that lecture, Shaw continued his self-education at the British Museum by reading Karl Marx's *Das Kapital*. Shaw didn't agree with Marx's advocation of a class struggle leading to a violent revolution, but he agreed with Marx's proposal to nationalize all forms of capital, including land. In 1884, Shaw joined a socialist group called the Fabian Society, which was named for the Roman statesman Quintus Fabius Maximus. Fabius was called "the delayer" because he advocated guerrilla action in fighting Hannibal instead of head-on battle.

The Fabians believed in equal distribution of wealth and revolution through controlled change by vote, rather than by war. Shaw was an active member of the society, writing pamphlets, appeals, and magazine and newspaper articles. He became an experienced public speaker and gave over 2,000 speeches on the street, in Hyde

Park, and in halls, such as Albert Hall. Shaw's writing and speech-making for Socialist causes were significant components of his journalistic apprenticeship and journeymanship and were important facets of his development as an author.

In 1885, Shaw undertook some "paid journalism," such as book reviews, occasional news items, and reviews of art exhibits, concerts, and plays. He became an art critic through William Archer, drama critic for the *World*, whom Shaw met at his "university," the British Museum. Although Archer was a drama critic, he was also expected to write art reviews. He didn't feel well prepared, so Shaw accompanied him to art exhibits and contributed heavily to Archer's reviews. Initially, Shaw was hesitant to accept pay for his contributions, but ultimately he agreed. From then on, he supported himself and provided support for his mother.

Shaw's resignation as art critic for the *World* was due to a change in ownership. The new owner asked Shaw to write favorably of her friend's art and when Shaw refused, she changed his copy. He left the *World* to write music reviews for the *Star*. He was well prepared for his position as music critic, since he was from a musical family. His mother was a mezzo-soprano, and his sister, Lucinda, was also a professional singer. Shaw had been immersed in music since his infancy. He wrote using the pen name "Corno di Bassetto," the Italian name for the bassett horn, which hadn't been popular since Mozart's time. Shaw used humor heavily in his musical reviews. While serving as music critic for the *Star*, he wrote a book of music criticism entitled *The Perfect Wagnerite,* in which he reviewed Richard Wagner's *The Ring of the Nibelungs*. He presented Wagner in a very favorable light at a time when Wagner wasn't popular.

In 1894, Shaw became more interested in the theater, and he began to review plays for the *Saturday Review*. He was an early promoter of the Norwegian playwright Henrik Ibsen. Shaw wrote a book explaining twelve of Ibsen's plays, from *Brand* to *Hedda Gabler*, to the British public, who found them unusual and offensive.

While serving as art critic for the *World*, William Archer suggested that Shaw write a play. Shaw knew he would have difficulty inventing the plot, but he was willing to describe the scenes, delineate the characters, and write the dialogue. Shaw and Archer decided to collaborate; Archer would supply the plot. The collaboration wasn't a success. In fact, Shaw wasn't the kind of individual to use someone else's viewpoint or contribution. Shaw set the manuscript aside for seven years. In 1892, he finished the play, *Widowers' Houses*, which was his first to be published. It was a satirical play in which rich widowers take advantage of the poor.

In 1893, Shaw made his second attempt as a playwright: *The Philanderer: A Topical Comedy*. He described his views on the institution of marriage, which were derived from Ibsen's plays, including *A Doll's House* and *Hedda Gabler*. In particular, Shaw agreed with Ibsen's views on the ascent of the New Woman and the superiority of individual morality over institutional morality as represented by marriage. *The Philanderer* was a better play than *Widowers' Houses*. Shaw's improved skills as a playwright are evident; the characters are described more clearly, and the dialogue is improved significantly. Nevertheless, the response to this play was lukewarm, and it wasn't performed until 1907.

Shaw's next play was *Mrs. Warren's Profession*, in which Mrs. Warren lived comfortably from her income as an owner of a syndicate of bordellos and sent her daughter to Cambridge University. The plot includes a description her daughter's reaction on discovering the source of her mother's income. Her mother leads her to believe that the string of houses of prostitution is no longer operating. The mother / daughter relationship is changed dramatically when the daughter finds that her mother has deceived her.

The play was controversial, and Shaw received unrelenting abuse from the reviewers and the public. They strongly objected to it even though Shaw made no attempt to pass judgment on prostitutes, and the play had no bordello scenes. Shaw was unsuccessful in defending himself by explaining that he was merely trying to describe the economic side of the profession.

By the age of thirty-seven, Shaw had experienced a notable lack of success in his last eight attempts as an author, including five novels and three plays. Although there were times when he was discouraged, he never considered giving up his goal. He observed, "Man is a creature of habit. You cannot write three plays and stop."

His next two plays, written in 1894, were *Arms and the Man* and *Candida*. Later, he published his first seven plays in two volumes, *Plays Unpleasant* and *Plays Pleasant*. *The Philanderer* and *Mrs. Warren's Profession* were plays in which Shaw was influenced by the reality of Ibsen; they were included in *Plays Unpleasant*.

Arms and the Man and *Candida* were included in *Plays Pleasant*, because Shaw took a different playwriting approach beginning with these two plays. He realized that the playreading and playgoing public didn't need or want the heavy doses of reality he was providing. His new approach focused on the contrast between perceived truth and truth itself. It included the portrayal of people who, when stripped to the basics, were better people than they appeared to be.

The Devil's Disciple was the most important of Shaw's next plays. Its success in the United States in 1897, the year after it was written, permitted Shaw to improve his lifestyle. The play earned Shaw ten percent of the gross of £25,000 from its run of sixty-seven performances in Albany and New York. Shaw resigned his position as a critic and seriously considered marriage. In June 1897, he married Charlotte Payne-Townsend, a wealthy Irish heiress, who was a fellow member of the Fabian society.

Shaw began to receive recognition as a playwright. *Caesar and Cleopatra* in 1898 was followed by *Captain Brassbound's Conversion* in 1899. One of his best known plays, *Man and Superman*, was written in 1903. John Tanner, Don Juan Tenorio anglicized, is credited with being the author of "The Revolutionist's Handbook and Pocket Companion," a handbook with over 200 maxims on a variety of subjects. From the mouth of John Tanner, many sayings are attributed to Shaw, e.g. "Marriage is popular because it combines the maximum of temptation with the maximum of opportunity."

Before becoming a successful playwright, Shaw struggled for fifteen years, nine of which he was dependent upon his mother for support. Later, he commented on his struggle: "The spontaneous recognition of really original work begins with a mere handful of people and propagates itself so slowly that it has become commonplace to say that genius demanding bread is given a stone until after its possessor's death. The remedy for this is sedulous advertisement. Accordingly, I advertised myself so well that I found myself while still in middle life almost as legendary as the Flying Dutchman."

Shaw claimed that he had fifteen reputations: art critic, music critic, literature critic, drama critic, novelist, dramatist, economist, funny man, street-corner agitator, Shelleyan atheist, Fabian Socialist, vegetarian, humanitarian, preacher, and philosopher. He was all of these things, but to become a successful dramatist—second only to Shakespeare in the opinion of many—he was a creator.

CHAPTER 4

INVENTORS / RESEARCHERS

"For good and evil, man is a free creative spirit. This produces the very queer world we live in, a world in continuous creation and therefore continuous change and insecurity."

Joyce Cary, *Writers at Work*

THOMAS EDISON (1847-1931) Inventor Extraordinaire

"From eighteen to twenty hours a day for the last seven months, I have worked on the single word 'specia.' I said to the phonograph, 'specia, specia, specia,' but the instrument replied 'pecia, pecia, pecia.' It was enough to drive one mad. But I held firm, and I have succeeded."

Thomas Alva Edison

Thomas Edison was a determined individual throughout his career as an inventor. He conducted thousands of experiments in which he considered many alternatives until he found one that suited his needs. Even if he had not found the material or approach for which he was looking, he was eliminating the alternatives that would not work well or were not practical. Of many examples of Edison's creativity, two notable ones are his efforts to develop the phonograph and his struggle to find a practical filament for the light bulb.

While attempting to improve the transmitter used with Alexander Graham Bell's telephone, Edison had his first thoughts about inventing a device for recording the human voice. His challenge was to find a material to improve the operation of the transmitter used to transmit voice over telephone lines. He tried hundreds of materials before arriving at the choice of carbon as the optimum transmitter material.

Edison made a sketch of a device that he felt could be used to record and play back the sound of the human voice. He asked one of his associates to make a model from the sketch. The device consisted of a long, narrow cylinder on a shaft that was turned by a hand crank. A thin metal disk picked up the voice sound waves. A similar approach was used to receive sound waves in the telephone. Turning the crank caused the cylinder to rotate and a pin to move along the axis of the cylinder.

The pin in the center of the disk made a groove that modeled the voice pattern on tinfoil wrapped around the cylinder. Another pin used with a second disk picked up the voice pattern and converted it into vibrations that generated the sound. The quality of sound that this first phonograph reproduced was poor. However, Edison had proved that the voice could be recorded and then played back. He set this invention aside and went on to other things.

Ten years later, Edison decided that he should do something to improve the fidelity of the sound of his phonograph. Its principal shortcomings were in reproducing the sibilants (hissing sounds) and the higher tones of musical notes. Edison noted that, in order to overcome the defects in his phonograph design, "I worked over one year, twenty hours a day, Sundays and all to get the word 'specia' perfectly recorded and reproduced on the phonograph. When this was done, I knew everything else could be done—which was a fact."

A second example of Edison's resolve was his search for a practical filament material for the electric lightbulb. Electric light had been around for a long time. The first electric arc light had been developed by the English scientist, Sir Humphrey Davy, and had been improved upon by Jablochkoff, a Russian engineer. However, their arc lights generated a very glaring light and radiated considerable heat. The initial arc lamp burned for only a few minutes before the filament burned out. Improvements had been made that allowed the filament to last several hours.

Edison's challenge was to find a filament material that would heat up from the low currents and high voltages used at the time. Filaments burned out quickly when in contact with oxygen. He had to find a way to minimize the amount of oxygen in contact with the filament. In his search for a filament material, he needed a substance with a high melting point that would last considerably longer than a few hours.

The first material that Edison tried was carbon. His first carbon filaments were carbonized strips of paper. These filaments burned out in eight minutes. His next series of experiments were with threads of rare metals. He tried barium, platinum, rhodium, ruthenium, titanium, and zirconium. Of these materials, platinum worked the best. He used a double spiral of platinum for his filament. Next he investigated the problem of minimizing the amount of oxygen in contact with the filament. He asked his glass blower to make some enclosed, pear-shaped bulbs.

Edison searched for the best air pump that he could obtain. He ordered a new pump, called the Sprengel pump, and borrowed one from Princeton University until his was available. His first experiment with a pear-shaped bulb using the Sprengel pump to form a partial vacuum inside the bulb was a success. The platinum filament provided five times more footcandles of light than previous experiments. However, platinum was a rare metal and was expensive. He considered using tungsten, the material used in lightbulbs today, but, unfortunately, he did not have the delicate tools required to work with it.

Edison persisted in his search for an improved filament. He experimented with various grasses, linen thread, and wood splinters. He even tried a red hair from a man's beard. His goal was to make a light bulb for fifty cents or less. He had moderate success in an experiment with a bamboo filament. He was sufficiently hopeful that bamboo was a practical filament material that he sent out three men to obtain bamboo samples for him. One went to China and Japan. A second searched across South America. The third traveled to Ceylon (Sri Lanka), India, and Burma looking for bamboo samples. Edison tried over 1,600 different materials in his search for an optimum material for his filament.

On October 21, 1879, Edison used a filament made of carbonized thread. In that experiment, the light bulb burned for thirteen and a half hours. The next day he used a different type of cotton thread, which had also been carbonized. That filament burned for forty hours. Edison and his assistants were jubilant. If they could make a filament that would burn for forty hours, they could make one that would last for a multiple of forty hours.

Edison filed the patent for his invention on November 1, 1879. Later, he was able to make a filament by carbonizing a thread of cellulose extruded from a die. This filament burned longer than the carbonized cotton filament. Also, he found that he could make a filament from carbonized cardboard that would burn for 160 hours.

On New Year's Eve 1879, 3,000 people, most of whom were from New York and Philadelphia, came to Edison's laboratory in Menlo Park, New Jersey. They were transported to Menlo Park by the Pennsylvania Railroad to witness their first view of Edison's incandescent light and to celebrate with him. Newspapers, including the New York *Herald*, gave Edison widespread coverage; the age of the electric light had begun.

ORVILLE WRIGHT (1871-1948) & *WILBUR WRIGHT* (1867-1912) Pioneers of Flight

"Vacillating people seldom succeed. They seldom win the respect of their fellows. Successful men and women are very careful in reaching decisions and very persistent and determined in action later."

L. C. Elliott

In 1903, the year of the Wright brothers' successful flight, Professor of Astronomy Simon Newcomb said, "Human flight is not only impossible but illogical." He added that if a flyer managed to get an engine-powered aircraft in the air, he would crash and lose his life: "Once he slackens his speed, down he begins to fall. Once he stops, he falls a dead mass." However, the Wright brothers persevered and succeeded where others had failed "by dauntless resolution and unconquerable faith."

Wilbur Wright, born on April 16, 1867, near Millville, Indiana, and Orville Wright, born on August 19, 1871, in Dayton, Ohio, were two of seven children of Milton Wright, a bishop of the United Brethren Church, and Susan Koerner Wright. Neither Wilbur nor Orville graduated from high school. Wilbur did not graduate because his family moved from Indiana to Ohio before he finished his senior year, and Orville took advanced college preparatory courses in his junior year that prevented him from graduating with his class.

Wilbur and Orville were excellent students who took advantage of an extensive family library to expand their knowledge through comprehensive private study. They excelled in mathematics and science and benefited from growing up in an inquiring, well-educated family. In December 1892, they opened their first shop to sell and repair bicycles. In 1895, they began to design and build their own because of increased competition in the sale and repair of bicycles.

Wilbur and Orville worked extremely well as a team, and it is unlikely that either would have achieved the success individually that they experienced together. Wilbur noted: "from the time we were little children my brother Orville and myself lived together, played together, worked together and, in fact, thought together. We usually owned all of our toys in common and talked over our thoughts and aspirations so that nearly everything that was done in our lives has been the result of conversations, suggestions, and discussions between us."

In August 1896, while Orville was seriously ill with typhoid fever, Wilbur read about the death of German aviation pioneer Otto Lilienthal, whose back was broken when his kite stalled in a gust of wind and fell fifty feet. Lilienthal had added to the body of aeronautical knowledge, but his means of controlling the craft was limited—the pilot shifted his weight to control the kite. On May 30, 1899, Wilbur wrote to the Smithsonian Institution requesting information about human flight: "My observations . . . have . . . convinced me that human flight is possible and practicable." He intended to "begin a systematic study of the subject in preparation for practical work." The Smithsonian's suggested reading list included *The Aeronautical Annual* for 1895, 1896, and 1897, edited by James Means; *Experiments in Aerodynamics* by Samuel Langley; and *Progress in Flying Machines* by Octave Chanute.

To test their ideas about control systems, Wilbur built a small two-winged kite with a wingspan of five feet and a chord (wing width) of thirteen inches. It used a "canard" configuration with the stabilizing surface (elevator) ahead of the wings. With this kite, they tested their concept of "wing warping" to control the craft's roll motion in the air, which in modern aircraft is accomplished by ailerons in the wings. Wilbur demonstrated the concept with an empty cardboard box that had held a bicycle inner tube. The box retained its lateral stiffness when he twisted it. He showed Orville how the idea could be applied to biplane wings.

In August 1900, Wilbur and Orville constructed their first full-sized glider capable of manned flight. The metal struts, wing ribs, and metal fittings were made in Dayton. French sateen fabric was used to cover the ash and spruce frame.

Wilbur asked Octave Chanute and the National Weather Bureau for recommendations on a site for test flights. Wilbur selected Kitty Hawk, North Carolina, because of its fifteen-to-twenty-mile-per-hour winds, its lack of hills and trees, and its sandy surface. He traveled to Kitty Hawk ahead of Orville and stayed with the Tate family until he selected a site and pitched a tent. Orville arrived in September to build their experimental glider.

Wilbur had planned to buy eighteen-foot lengths of spruce en route for use as spars, but the longest he could find were sixteen-foot lengths. They modified their kite's wingspan and used a smaller wing surface area, 165 square feet instead of 200, than they had planned. Wooden bows added to the wing tips increased the wingspan to 17 1/2 feet; wing chord was five feet. The total weight of the craft was fifty-two pounds. Fabric on the 1900 glider was not sealed or varnished as it had been on the 1899 kite.

In October, they flew the tethered glider with a man on board. Young Tom Tate, the landlord's son, did most of the piloting because he weighed less than Wilbur or Orville. The brothers also flew the glider as an unmanned kite using lines to the ground to control it. In addition, they tried flying it with a fifty-pound ballast. After several days of tests, the glider was caught in a gust of wind and severely damaged. They considered giving up, but instead they spent the next three days repairing it.

Wilbur and Orville moved the glider to Kill Devil Hills, four miles away, to take advantage of higher winds. On October 20, when Wilbur flew the craft, he became the first of the brothers to experience free flight. Wilbur conducted flights of 300 to 400 feet distance over a duration of fifteen to twenty seconds. The Wrights were disappointed with the lift of the glider, but they realized it was at least partially due to the reduced wing area. After completing the trials, they gave the glider to the Tate family to use for materials and left for Dayton on October 23 with plans to build another glider at Kitty Hawk the following summer.

The 1901 glider was a biplane with a wingspan of twenty-two feet, a chord of seven feet, and a wing area of 290 square feet. The camber (curvature) of the wing was increased. The ninety-eight pound craft was the largest anyone had flown until that time. In Dayton, they hired a machinist, Charlie Taylor, who later designed and built the engine for their 1903 aircraft. In July 1901, Wilbur and Orville traveled to Kitty Hawk, where they constructed a sixteen-foot by twenty-five-foot hangar for their glider.

Wilbur conducted the test flights. The lift and the speed of the new glider were disappointing. Control of pitch was not as responsive as they had hoped, and Wilbur experienced stalls in which the forward stabilizer assisted him in making a safe landing. The brothers sharpened the leading edge of the wing to decrease wind resistance, but the change improved lift and speed only slightly. In August, Wilbur made flights of thirteen seconds or more over distances up to 389 feet.

The wing warping mechanism worked well, but they experienced a reversal in the roll motion of the glider that they could not explain. On one flight, Wilbur was distracted when this occurred, and he did not respond quickly to the controls. He dropped onto the sand abruptly and suffered a black eye and a bruised nose. Soon afterward, they returned to Dayton. On the trip back to Dayton, Wilbur told Orville that "men would not fly for fifty years."

The brothers expanded their shop by adding a band saw and a drill press powered by a one-cylinder engine. Charlie Taylor, whose assistance was essential to their experiments, designed and manufactured their first internal combustion engine. With a machinist like Taylor and the additional equipment, the Wrights were now able to make both bicycle and airplane parts of increased complexity.

Octave Chanute invited the brothers to present a summary of their work to the Western Society of Engineers in Chicago. On September 18, 1901, Wilbur "arrayed in Orv's shirt, cuffs, cuff links, and overcoat" (Orville was a natty dresser, Wilbur a casual dresser) presented his paper, "Some Aeronautical Experiments." The paper was well-received; it became the state-of-the-art reference for aeronautical experimenters.

Wilbur and Orville built a small wind tunnel to check the coefficients required to design their aircraft. The results were so useful that they built a larger wind tunnel, a wooden box measuring sixteen-inches square by six-feet long with a glass observation window on top. They worked for a month to ensure that the thirty-mile-per-hour wind flowed through the tunnel without turbulence. It was not the first wind tunnel, but the discipline they used to apply aerodynamic data directly to the design of aircraft was new. They collected data for a variety of wing configurations to use in lift and drag formulae.

Wilbur and Orville found that the Smeaton coefficient, a factor used in their aerodynamic formula, was off by fifty percent. In addition to studying lift and drag, they also studied the aspect ratio, the ratio of the wingspan to the wing chord. The brothers learned that long, narrow wings produce more lift than short, wide wings with the same wing area.

In December, they discontinued their experiments and returned to the bicycle business that financed their experiments. Chanute offered to ask Andrew Carnegie to provide financial support for their aeronautical work. However, the Wrights did not want to be indebted to anyone; they chose to finance their own experimental work.

Wilbur and Orville designed the 1902 glider with a wingspan of thirty-two feet and a wing chord of five feet (compared with the 1901 wingspan of twenty-two feet and a chord of seven feet), which doubled the aspect ratio. In February 1902, they added a fixed rudder to address the problem of the reversal of the direction of a roll when the wing warping mechanism was applied.

When Wilbur and Orville arrived in Kitty Hawk, they found that high winds and wind-driven sand had virtually destroyed their hangar. They rebuilt a sturdier and more comfortable structure. On September 19, the 1902 glider with 305 square feet of wing area was ready for its first test. The new glider had a forward elevator of fifteen square feet and a longer, narrower rudder than the 1901 glider and weighed almost 120 pounds. The first tests were unmanned; they made fifty tests covering distances of under 200 feet during the first two days.

In the first manned flights, Wilbur encountered crosswinds that affected the lateral stability more severely than on previous models. The brothers addressed the problem by adjusting the wing trusses and causing the tips of the wings to droop about four inches. A crosswind could not catch a wingtip as easily as before. Orville began to make flights at this point. On one of his early attempts, he lost control at an altitude of thirty feet, with disastrous results for the glider. Fortunately, Orville was unhurt. The craft was rebuilt.

The reversal of the roll motion when the wing warping mechanism was applied, the cause of Orville's crash, was a recurring problem. It is now called a tailspin. In the middle of the night, Orville thought of a solution to the problem. In the morning, he suggested to Wilbur that they install a movable rudder to compensate for the sudden change in direction. Wilbur agreed with the solution but suggested that the rudder control be coupled with the wing warping control because the pilot already had enough on his mind.

Evolution of the controls of Wright airplanes was now complete. Three-axis motion could now be controlled; that is, the pilot could regulate pitch, roll, and yaw. The Wright Brothers had invented the first truly controllable aircraft and were ready for powered flight. On October 28, they went home to Dayton.

The Wright's first patent, which they had filed at the end of 1902, was denied because it lacked clarity. Even though they had hired a patent attorney to help them, they were not granted a patent until May 1906. It described the principles demonstrated by the 1902 glider and included no references to powered aircraft.

During the winter of 1902-03, the Wright brothers designed the aircraft that they called the "Flyer"; they calculated that the airplane would weigh 625 pounds with a pilot, assuming that the engine and propellers weighed 200 pounds. No commercially available four-cycle engine met their specifications of eight or nine horsepower with a weight of under 180 pounds. Charlie Taylor designed a four-cylinder, twelve-horsepower engine with cast-iron cylinders in a cast-aluminum crankcase cooled by a water jacket; it had no radiator or water pump because the water did not circulate.

The Wrights chose two pusher propellers mounted behind the wings, and they connected the contra-rotating propellers with the engine using bicycle sprocket and chain technology. The efficiency of existing propellers disappointed them; they realized they would have to design their own. Wilbur and Orville considered propellers to be wings that moved in a rotary motion. The propellers were 8 1/2 feet in diameter and were made from three laminations of 1 1/8-inch spruce. The 1903 craft had a wingspan of forty-four feet and four inches, a 6 1/2-foot chord, and a wing area of 510 square feet.

In September 1903, the Wrights left for Kitty Hawk. Over the next three months, they experienced bad weather, many technical problems, and some disappointing flights with the 1902 glider. The loaded weight of the 1903 aircraft had increased from 625 to 700 pounds. The engine misfired frequently, placing severe strain on the propeller shafts. The damaged shafts had to be returned to Dayton for repair. The reinstalled shafts shook loose the nuts holding the sprockets in position. Bicycle cement on the nuts solved that problem.

The steel-tube propeller shafts broke again, and Orville returned to Dayton to make new shafts out of solid spring steel. He returned on December 11, and, three days later, Wilbur won the coin toss to fly the plane on its first lift-off from the sixty-foot-long launching rail.

The "Flyer" lifted off the rail (used to guide the craft during take-off) at the forty-foot point, reached an altitude of fifteen feet, stalled, and dropped onto the sand, damaging the forward elevator and one of the skids. This 3 1/2 second flight over 100 feet was not considered a real flight. Wilbur had not anticipated the sensitivity of the elevator, and he had overcontrolled the craft.

On December 17, the temperature was freezing and the wind was blowing at twenty-seven miles per hour. It was Orville's turn to pilot the airplane; the brothers shook hands as though they were not going to see each other again. At 10:35 a.m., the "Flyer" lifted off after traveling about forty feet and flew 120 feet in twelve seconds.

This flight was considered the first true flight. Orville commented: "This flight lasted only twelve seconds, but it was nevertheless the first in the history of the world in which a machine carrying a man had raised itself by its own power into the air in full flight, had sailed forward without a reduction in speed, and had finally landed at a point as high as that from which it started."

Wilbur flew the second flight of the day over a distance of 175 feet, followed by Orville in a flight of over 200 feet that lasted fifteen seconds. Wilbur flew the "Flyer" on the last flight of the day—a flight of 852 feet with a duration of 59 seconds. While they were discussing the flights, a gust of wind overturned the "Flyer," breaking spars, struts, most of the wing ribs, and the engine crankcase. No more flights were conducted in 1903; however, the Wright brothers had accomplished their goal of pioneering powered flight.

In 1904 and 1905 the brothers built two more powered aircraft to continue with their experiments. However, they moved their test flights from Kitty Hawk to Huffman Prairie, eight miles from Dayton. The success of the last 1903 flight was not matched until the forty-ninth flight in 1904. On September 20, 1904, they made their first circular flight; it lasted ninety-six seconds and covered 4,080 feet. On October 5, 1905, Wilbur circled the field thirty times in thirty-nine minutes covering a distance of 24 1/2 miles. Incremental improvements were vital to the success of the Wright brothers.

In 1908 and 1909, the brothers successfully marketed their air-craft in the United States and Europe through sales and licensing agreements. In 1910, they established the Wright Company for manufacturing aircraft, conducting exhibitions, and training pilots. Orville ran the company while Wilbur fought patent infringement suits. Weakened by the strain of the legal process, Wilbur died on May 30, 1912, four weeks after contracting typhoid fever.

In 1914, Orville brought the suits to successful conclusion. The following year, he sold his interest in the Wright Company and retired a wealthy man. Orville lived a long, quiet life in retirement. He suffered a heart attack and died on January 27, 1948.

JOHN ATANASOFF (1903-1995) Inventor of the Computer

"One night in the late 1930s, in a bar on the border of Illinois and Iowa, a professor of physics at Iowa State College had an idea. After a frustrating day performing tedious mathematical computations in his lab, John Vincent Atanasoff realized that a combination of the binary number system and electronic switches, together with an array of capacitors on a moving drum to serve as memory, could yield a computing machine that would make his life—and the lives of similarly burdened scientists—easier. Then he went back and built the machine in the basement of the physics building. It worked. The whole world changed."

Jane Smiley, *The Man Who Invented the Computer*

John Vincent Atanasoff was born on October 4, 1903, the son of Bulgarian immigrants. Atanasoff's father, a graduate of Colgate University, worked as an industrial engineer in New York and New Jersey before moving the family to Brewster, Florida. Young John was a precocious student, with practical interests as well, such as repairing his father's Model T Ford. After graduating from high school, he worked for a year and taught math classes to earn money for college.

Atanasoff was creative from his youngest days. In *Explaining Creativity,* R. Keith Sawyer cites the traits of creativity: self-confidence, independence, high energy, willingness to take risks, above-average intelligence, openness to experience, and preference for complexity. Atanasoff displayed all of these qualities in addition to what Sawyer describes as "problem finding"—the ability to productively formulate a problem so that the terms of the problem lead to the solution.

Atanasoff majored in electrical engineering at the University of Florida. When he graduated in 1925, he had the highest grade point average up until that time at the University. He applied for master's programs in physics, his first love. Iowa State was the first to reply with an offer of admission and aid. Later, he was accepted for graduate study at Harvard, but he had already been accepted by Iowa State. In addition to taking graduate courses, Atanasoff also taught undergraduate math courses.

Atanasoff met Lura Meeks, an undergraduate student at Iowa State. She had grown up on a farm in Oklahoma. She was intelligent, energetic, and enterprising. They were married when he received his master's degree in physics in June 1926.

Atanasoff accepted a position teaching mathematics and physics at Iowa State while taking additional graduate physics courses to prepare himself for doctoral studies at the University of Wisconsin, which he began in the winter of 1927. He specialized in quantum mechanics, the science that predicts what happens in systems. His professor of quantum mechanics was John Hasbrouck Van Vleck, who was to win the Nobel Prize in 1977.

Atanasoff's theoretical physics dissertation was "The Dielectric Constant of Helium." Dielectric constant is a practical measurement, the ratio of the electric field in a vacuum to the electric field in a medium. Obtaining solutions to the linear equations that his work required was laborious and time consuming.

Atanasoff got his Ph.D at the University of Wisconsin in July 1930. He accepted a position as assistant professor of mathematics and physics at Iowa State. After committing to the position, he was offered a job at Harvard, which he again turned down. He was a gifted teacher who engaged his students in discussions and questioned them to determine their areas of knowledge and ignorance.

Most calculators in 1920 were analog, not digital. Atanasoff read about the Differential Analyzer, developed at MIT in 1927-31 by Vannevar Bush. At Harvard, Howard Aiken was looking for a way to improve the 1822 Difference Engine of Charles Babbage, which had never really worked. Babbage later designed an Analytical Engine using gears and shafts, with which he tried to accomplish too much by building a universal machine.

Aiken attempted to update Babbage's ideas with modern techniques. This included using a power supply and electric motor for driving the machine, and master control panels controlled by instructions on punched rolls of paper tape synchronized with the machine along with manual adjustments for controlling the calculation of functions. It used a decimal (base ten) numbering system.

Aiken was driven to develop a calculating machine that could solve differential equations. His doctoral dissertation at Harvard was "Theory of Space Charge Conductions." It was similar to Atanasoff's dissertation in that it considered the properties of vacuum tubes—

devices in which electric currents pass through a vacuum between two metal electrodes. The simplest vacuum tube was a diode in which a cathode is heated, releasing negatively charged electrons that flow to a positively charged anode.

Atanasoff wrestled with a number of approaches to building a calculating machine. By the winter of 1937, he knew that whatever design he chose, it had to separate memory from computation. All of his design ideas were unsuccessful, and "I was in such a mental state that no resolution was possible. I was just unhappy to an extreme degree." He knew that he had to get away, at least briefly. He got in his new Ford V8 and drove east, with no destination in mind, until he was across the Mississippi River in Rock Island, Illinois, 189 miles from home.

Atanasoff noticed a tavern sign and went in and ordered a drink. As he waited for his drink, the general design of his computing machine came to him as a logical whole. He began to visualize how the component pieces would come together. For several hours he thought about his design, particularly how the memory would work and how an electronically based on-off (binary) system would calculate. Specifically, he pondered the working of the calculator's "regenerative memory"—the mechanism by which capacitors and vacuum tubes would charge one another in a feedback loop.

In 1938, Atanasoff worked on theoretical and practical aspects of four related ideas that he had thought of in the tavern in Illinois:

1. Electronic logic circuits that performed a calculation by turning on and off
2. A binary numbering system, using only 0 and 1 to indicate off and on
3. Capacitors for regenerative memory, which can store electrical charge while not connected to a source
4. Computing by direct logical action, not by enumeration, that is, by counting rather than measuring; the numbers represented by 1s and 0s, the on-off states of the vacuum tubes, which would directly be added and subtracted

In March 1939, Atanasoff submitted an application for a grant of $650 to attempt to build a calculator. In May, his request was granted: $200 for materials and $450 to pay for a student assistant.

Atanasoff was fortunate in obtaining the services of Clifford Berry as his assistant. Berry was knowledgeable, enthusiastic, and enterprising. He combined an exceptional intelligence and mechanical ability with a strong work ethic. Atanasoff and Berry had a "breadboard" prototype ready to test in October 1939. It incorporated seven innovations:

1. Electronic computing
2. Vacuum tubes as the computing mechanism and operating memory
3. Binary calculation
4. Logical calculation
5. Serial computation
6. Capacitors as storage memory
7. Capacitors attached to a rotating drum that refreshed the power supply of the vacuum tubes to regenerate the operating memory

In January 1940, the construction of the new prototype began. The goal was to focus the design of the machine on the solution of differential equations. The calculator would be able to solve equations containing up to twenty-nine unknowns, three times the number then considered possible with current methods.

Atanasoff and Berry constructed what they called the ABC, the Atanasoff-Berry Computer, in the basement of the physics building. The frame of ABC was seventy-four inches long, thirty-six inches deep, and forty inches tall, including casters. Solving twenty-nine linear equations with twenty-nine unknowns took thirty hours with periodic inputs from the operator, but it could be done and done accurately by the ABC.

In August 1940, Atanasoff completed a thirty-five page manuscript, in which he described the ABC in detail, including a list of nine types of linear algebraic equations a larger machine would be able to solve. He described practical applications in physics, statistics, and technology, ranging from problems of elasticity to quantum physics.

Atanasoff planned to use the manuscript to obtain additional development money—$5,000 was needed for the next phase. Atanasoff made three carbon copies of the original manuscript: one for the research corporation, one for Berry, and one for the patent process that Atanasoff thought the machine was ready for.

In December 1940, Atanasoff attended the annual meeting of the American Association for the Advancement of Science in Philadelphia. He also planned to do some patent research in New York and Washington, D.C. One of the reasons Atanasoff attended this annual meeting was to find out what other inventors were doing.

John Mauchly, a physics professor from Ursinis College in Collegeville, Pennsylvania, gave a talk about correlating weather patterns with solar phenomena. He mentioned that he had developed a calculator, the "Harmonic Analyzer," to do the correlations. He discussed his design and talked about his plans for the future. Although the "Harmonic Analyzer" was an analog machine, he thought the future of computing was electronic (digital).

After Mauchly's talk, he and Atanasoff compared notes on their development efforts. Atanasoff invited Mauchly to Ames to see the ABC. When Atanasoff returned home, he met with college officials to persuade them to hire Richard Trexler, an eminent patent attorney from Chicago to process the patent. Atanasoff sent Trexler a copy of the thirty-five page manuscript describing the ABC.

College president Charles E. Friley and college officials still did not appreciate the value of obtaining a patent, but Atanasoff prevailed. Friley wanted the college to get 90% of the potential profits with nothing for Berry. After six months of negotiations, In July 1941, Friley agreed to giving Atanasoff 50% of the profits, less expenses. Berry would receive 10% of Atanasoff's portion.

Mauchly visited Iowa State for four days in July 1941. Atanasoff was very open with him in discussing the ABC. He was pleased to find someone who was interested in his project. The staff at Iowa State wasn't all that interested. Atanasoff loaned Mauchly a copy of his manuscript on the ABC but would not let Mauchly take a copy back to Philadelphia with him.

Mauchly spent considerable time in the basement of the physics building with the ABC, talking with Berry and others. Mauchly had hands-on access to the ABC and actually helped Berry do a few repairs. He and Atanasoff spent every evening talking about the principles of the ABC. One evening, Mauchly asked Lura for some bond paper and she noticed that Mauchly stayed up late at night with his light on. She suspected that he was copying the thirty-five page manuscript. She was concerned he might be stealing her husband's ideas.

Later, Mauchly claimed that the ABC he viewed in Ames was not a working model. Professor George Snedecor of the Iowa State statistics department noted that he "would send problems over to Atanasoff and the ABC would solve them. Then the secretary would check the results on a desktop calculator. And they would be correct." The ABC was in working order.

In the summer of 1941, Mauchly took a course at the Moore School of Electrical Engineering at the University of Pennsylvania. It was a cram course in electronics sponsored by the War Department for scientists in other fields. There he met his future partner, J. Presper Eckert, who had just graduated from the Moore School. Upon completion of the course, Mauchly was invited to join the staff of the Moore School.

Mauchly wrote to Atanasoff to ask, "Is there any objection from your point of view to my building some sort of computer which incorporates some of the features of your machine? In the event that your present design were to hold the field against all challengers, and I got the Moore School interested in having something of the sort, would the way be open to build an 'Atanasoff Calculator' here?"

In September 1942, Atanasoff left Ames for a war-related position at the Naval Ordnance Laboratory in Washington, D.C. Iowa State told Atanasoff that the patent process was well in hand. He left the ABC in the basement of the physics building. Atanasoff worked for the Naval Ordnance Laboratory for the next seven years, during which time he was out of touch with the patent submission at Iowa State. When he inquired about the patent process, he was not given clear answers.

In the spring of 1943, Mauchly visited Atanasoff at the Naval Ordnance Laboratory. He told Atanasoff about a project at the Moore School calculating trajectories of large artillery pieces. Mauchly described how he and Eckert were devising a machine the army could use to make firing-range calculations. In his paper, "The Use of High-Speed Vacuum Tubes for Calculation," Mauchly described "an electronic device operating solely on the principle of counting." It would do the same tasks as an analog device but would do them faster.

The Moore School began to develop the ENIAC (Electronic Numeric Integrator and Computer). When it was finished, it weighed twenty-seven tons and was eight feet long, eight feet high, and three feet deep. It had 18,000 vacuum tubes, 7,200 diodes, 1,500 relays, and 10,000 capacitors for memory storage. It was not programmable.

Atanasoff met mathematician John von Neumann when he visited the Naval Ordnance Laboratory. Von Neumann wrote a paper describing a second version of ENIAC, "First Draft of a Report of the EDVAC." EDVAC stood for "Electronic Discrete Variable Automatic Computer." The paper described "Von Neumann architecture," in which the computer would contain a set of instructions in its memory, that is, it would be programmable.

In February 1946, Atanasoff attended the unveiling of ENIAC at the University of Pennsylvania. Neither Mauchly nor Eckert were present. He didn't learn much about the principles of the machine. He called Richard Trexler, the Chicago patent attorney, and was told that his patent was never filed because Iowa State had never paid the filing fee.

Another ongoing computer development project at the time was Howard Aiken's Mark I at Harvard, which was built by IBM, the supplier of the punched-card system for ENIAC. In the spring of 1946, Mauchly and Eckert formed their own company. Mauchly's responsibility was to manage the company and to obtain financing and contracts. Eckert was in charge of building the first UNIVAC (Universal Automatic Computer), which became available in March 1951.

The IBM 701 was announced in April 1952, followed by the 702, the 650, and the 705. The 701 and the 650 were designed for business use. Two of IBM's advantages were the punched-card systems in widespread use and the fact that IBM rented their machines.

Filmmaker Kirwin Cox noted that the EDVAC design was closer to the ABC design than the ENIAC configuration and that ENIAC was a hybrid machine—partially ABC, partially Bush Analyzer, and partially ganged calculators. Cox also observed: "John Vincent Atanasoff was a lucky man in many ways. He lived to see his hard work and enterprising intelligence vindicated. He spent a long life trying many things and, because of his energy, organizational skills, and and persistence, mastering everything he tried." Cox called him the "lone inventor" type, who explores and invents and then exhausts his interests in a given idea.

ALAN TURING (1912-1954) Father of Artificial Intelligence.

"Alan Turing was by any reckoning one of the most remarkable Englishmen of the century. A brilliant mathematician at Cambridge in the 30s, Turing discovered that his was precisely the kind of intelligence required by Britain during the war and became the presiding genius at Bletchley Park, the boffin centre which cracked the German Enigma code. There he became obsessed by the notion of machine intelligence and was, in effect, the father of the modern computer. Mistrust and bureaucracy, however, frustrated many of his plans after the war, when Turing was to discover that although he was master of his own sphere, politically he remained as he was in 1941 — a servant."

Richard Rayner, *Time Out*

Alan Turing was a pioneer computer scientist, mathematician, logician, and cryptanalyst. The general purpose computer, the Turing machine, that he developed provided a tool for him to use in developing the concepts of "algorithm" and "computation."

During World War II, Turing worked for the British Government Code and Cypher School at Bletchley Park, the code-breaking center. He devised techniques for breaking German ciphers, including development of an electromechanical device used in breaking the German Enigma code. His role in breaking intercepted coded messages allowed the Allies to defeat the Nazis in several important battles. Winston Churchill noted that Turing made the single largest contribution to Allied victory in World War II. It is estimated that the efforts at Bletchley Park shortened the war in Europe by two to four years.

Turing was born in Maida Vale, London, on June 23, 1912, to Julius Turing and Ethel Stoney Turing. Julius Turing, the son of a Scottish clergyman, served with Indian Civil Service in British India. Ethel Turing's father, chief engineer of Madras Railways, was from Protestant Anglo-Irish gentry.

Turing's parents enrolled him at the age of six, at St. Michael's, a primary school in St. Leonardo-on-Sea. The headmistress recognized his talent very early, as did all of his subsequent teachers. In 1926, at the age of thirteen, he enrolled at the Sherbourne School in

Dorset. In 1927, he solved complex mathematical problems without having studied calculus. From 1931 to 1934, Turing studied as an undergraduate at King's College, Cambridge, where he earned first-class honors in mathematics. In 1935, at the age of 22, he was elected a Fellow at King's College.

Turing wrote a paper that described a "Universal Machine," now called the Universal Turing machine, that could perform the task of any computation machine that is capable of computing anything that is computable. John Von Neumann acknowledged that the central concept of the modern computer was based on this paper.

From September 1936 to July 1938, Turing studied with Alonzo Church at Princeton University, where he studied cryptology in addition to mathematics. In June 1936, he completed his dissertation, *Systems of Logic Based on Ordinals,* for his Ph.D.

Turing returned to Cambridge in 1939 and attended lectures by Ludwig Wittgenstein on the foundations of mathematics. He began to work part-time with the Government Code and Cypher School at Bletchley Park. He joined Bletchley Park full-time on September 4, 1939, the day after Britain declared war on Germany. In addition to working on the cryptanalytic machine, he uncovered the indicator procedure used by the German Navy and developed a statistical procedure for making considerably more efficient use of the cryptanalytic machines.

In the opinion of Hugh Alexander, Head of Hut 8 (code breakers), Bletchley Park During World War II:

> There should be no question in anyone's mind that Turing's work was the biggest factor in Hut 8's success. In the early days he was the only cryptographer who thought the problem worth tackling and not only was he primarily responsible for the main theoretical work within the Hut but he also shared with Welchman and Keen the chief credit for the invention of the bombe (cryptanalytic machine). It is always difficult that anyone is absolutely indispensible but if anyone was indispensable to Hut 8 it was Turing. The pioneer's work always tends to be forgotten when experience and routine later make everything seem easy

and many of us in Hut 8 felt that the magnitude of Turing's contribution was never fully realized by the outside world.

Turing was a talented long-distance runner. Occasionally, he would run the forty miles to London to attend a meeting. He tried out for the 1948 British Olympic team even though he was hampered by an injury. His tryout time was only eleven minutes slower than British silver medalist Thomas Richards's Olympic race time

In 1945, Turing was awarded the Order of the British Empire (OBE) by King George VI for his wartime service. Nevertheless, his work remained secret for many years.

From 1945 to 1947 Turing lived in Hampton, London, and worked on the design of the ACE (Automatic Computing Engine) at the National Physical Laboratory. He wrote a paper in February 1946 that was the first detailed design of a stored-program computer. In late 1947, Turing left the ACE project and spent a sabbatical year at Cambridge.

In 1948, Turing was a Reader in the Mathematics Department at the University of Manchester. In 1949, he was appointed Deputy Director of the Computing Laboratory at the University, where he worked on software for one of the first stored-program computers, the Manchester Mark I.

Turing addressed the subject of artificial intelligence. He proposed a test known as the Turing Test, which attempted to define a standard for a machine to be called "intelligent." The concept was that a computer could be said to "think" if a human interrogator could not tell it apart from a human being.

On June 8, 1954, Turing's housekeeper found him dead. A postmortem examination determined that the cause of death was cyanide poisoning. An inquest established that his death was suicide. Philosophy professor Jack Copeland and Turing's mother refused to believe that he had committed suicide. They believed that his death was caused by his careless storage of laboratory chemicals. Although he had had problems, including criticism of his homosexuality and financial problems, he was not depressed or despondent. In fact, he had made a list of tasks he intended to accomplish when he returned to the laboratory after the weekend.

STEPHEN HAWKING (1942-   ) Cosmologist and Researcher

"It is the most persistent and greatest adventure in human history, this search to understand the universe, how it works and where it came from. It is difficult to imagine that a handful of residents of a small planet circling an insignificant star in a small galaxy have as their aim a complete understanding of the entire universe, a small speck of creation truly believing it is capable of understanding the whole."

Murray Gell-Mann

As an undergraduate, Stephen Hawking was an undistinguished student. He was not highly motivated; he studied an average of one hour a day. In 1963, at the age of twenty-one, Hawking was told that he had amyotrophic lateral sclerosis (ALS), which is known as motor neuron disease in Britain and Lou Gehrig's Disease in the United States. ALS attacks the nerves of the spinal cord and the portion of the brain that controls voluntary motor functions of the muscles. The nerve cells degenerate, causing muscles to atrophy throughout the body, resulting in paralysis. Memory and the ability to think are not affected.

ALS, which worsens in stages, forces the patient to deal with a series of progressively limiting plateaus. Hawking has made incredible contributions to science by ignoring his ailment, to the extent of his ability. He has probably done more than any scientist to expand our understanding of the origin and nature of the universe, and his theoretical work on "black holes" was innovative. He is especially well known for his book, *A Brief History of Time*, a best seller.

Stephen Hawking was born in Oxford, England, on January 8, 1942, the three-hundredth anniversary of the death of the Italian scientist Galileo. Both of Hawking's parents, Frank and Isobel Hawking, had attended Oxford University. Stephen Hawking wanted to major in either physics or mathematics in college, but his father insisted that his son take chemistry so that he could follow him in a medical career.

Hawking won a scholarship to University College, Oxford University. When he completed his undergraduate studies at

Oxford, he took the final examinations upon which admission to graduate school were based. Hawking achieved the first-class honors degree that he needed to be admitted to graduate school at Cambridge University to study cosmology with Dr. Fred Hoyle, the foremost British astronomer of his time. In October 1962, when Hawking began his graduate studies at Cambridge, he could choose between two areas of research, elementary particles—the study of small particles, or cosmology—the study of large objects. Cosmology is the study of the origin, evolution, and destiny of the universe.

In Hawking's words, "I thought that elementary particles were less attractive, because, although they were finding lots of new particles, there was no proper theory of elementary particles. All they could do was arrange the particles in families, like in botany. In cosmology, on the other hand, there was a well-defined theory—Einstein's general theory of relativity."

Instead of studying with Fred Hoyle, Hawking was assigned to Dennis Sciama, an unknown to him. He was discouraged by this until he realized that Hoyle, who traveled abroad frequently, would not have been as good a mentor as Sciama, a respected scientist who conscientiously guided him in his research.

Hawking also had a personal problem with which to contend. He began to have difficulty tying his shoelaces, he bumped into walls and furniture, and, on a few occasions, he fell. Also, he experienced slurred speech without having a drink to blame it on. When he arrived home for Christmas vacation in 1962, his parents, who hadn't seen him for several months, knew immediately that something was wrong. His father thought that he might have contracted a disease in the Middle East during a trip with him over the summer. His parents referred him to a specialist.

At several parties over the holidays, Hawking met and talked with Jane Wilde, the friend of a friend, who attended the local high school. Jane planned to read modern languages at Westfield College in London in the fall. She was attracted to this intellectual and somewhat eccentric character. Their relationship blossomed from their first meeting.

In January, Hawking underwent a battery of tests; the diagnosis was ALS. He faced decreasing mobility, gradual paralysis, and ultimately death as respiratory muscles lost their functionality or he contracted pneumonia. Many ALS patients do not live two years beyond the diagnosis. He went into a deep depression, locked himself in his room, and listened to classical music, particularly Wagner. If Hawking had decided to study experimental physics instead of theoretical physics, his career would have been over.

Hawking questioned continuing with his research, because he might not be around long enough to get his Ph.D. Literally, he felt that he had nothing to live for. He was not a deeply religious person; nevertheless, he had an experience that helped to put things into perspective: "While I was in hospital, I had seen a boy I vaguely knew die of leukemia in the bed opposite me. It had not been a pretty sight. Clearly there were people who were worse off than me. At least my condition didn't make me feel sick. Whenever I feel inclined to feel sorry for myself, I remember that boy."

Jane visited Stephen early in his stay in the hospital and was surprised to find that he had lost the will to live. Their relationship strengthened; she was a major factor in Hawking's turning his life around. His interest in his research was revived.

During his first two years at Cambridge, Hawking's physical condition worsened. He had to use a cane, and, occasionally, he fell. He rejected offers of help in getting around. His speech grew increasingly difficult to understand. He and Jane became engaged. She said, "I wanted to find some purpose to my existence, and I suppose I found it in the idea of looking after him. But we were in love." For Hawking, their engagement gave new direction to his life and something to live for.

Hawking met applied mathematician Roger Penrose at a scientific meeting at Kings College in London. Penrose explained his concept of a singularity—a mass with zero size and infinite density—occurring at the center of a black hole, a region in space where gravity is so strong that not even light can escape. He showed that the collapse of a star could lead to the formation of a singularity. One night on the train back to Cambridge from London, Hawking turned to Dennis Sciama and speculated what would happen if Penrose's singularity theory were applied to the entire universe.

Penrose had showed that the collapse of a star could cause the formation of a singularity. Hawking conjectured that an important event had begun with the singularity. The event was the reverse of Penrose's collapse, an outward explosion named by Fred Hoyle the "big bang," the origin of the universe. The "big bang" refers to the tremendous explosion believed to have begun the expansion of the universe fifteen billion years ago.

When Hawking applied Penrose's ideas to the entire universe, he really began to devote himself to his work: "I started working hard for the first time in my life. To my surprise, I found I liked it. Maybe it is not really fair to call it work. Someone once said, 'Scientists get paid for doing what they enjoy.'" This effort became the final chapter of Hawking's dissertation, "Properties of the Expanding Universe," the work for which he was awarded a Ph.D by Cambridge University. Hawking looked for a post with a salary so he and Jane could get married. He applied for a theoretical physics fellowship at Caius College, Cambridge University. He was awarded the fellowship, and he and Jane were married in July 1965.

Hawking's condition continued to decline. He now needed crutches to walk, and his ability to speak worsened. He had a difficult time getting around their house, but he refused offers of help. His strong-willed nature presented a challenge for Jane. She said, "Some would call his attitude determination, some obstinacy. I've called it both at one time or another. I suppose that's what keeps him going." When asked whether he ever became depressed over his condition, Hawking replied, "Not normally. I have managed to do what I wanted to do despite it, and that gives a feeling of achievement." He maintained a positive outlook, and he was generally cheerful. He didn't waste time worrying about his health.

In the late 1960s, Jane and their friends convinced Hawking that he should be in a wheelchair. He didn't let this change bother him; in fact, he admitted that it enabled him to get around better. His approach to life didn't change. Jane said, "Stephen doesn't make any concessions to his illness, and I don't make any concessions to him."

Hawking recalls when his first black hole breakthrough occurred. In November 1970, he was thinking about black holes while getting ready for bed. As he remembers it: "My disability makes this a rather slow process, so I had plenty of time. Suddenly, I realized that many of the techniques that Penrose and I had developed to prove singularities could be applied to black holes."

Over a six-year period, Hawking co-authored *The Large Scale*

Structure of Space Time with George Ellis. In March 1974, Hawking became a Fellow of the Royal Society at the age of thirty-two. He continued to collect prizes, six major awards in two years: the Eddington Medal from the Royal Astronomical Society, the Pius XI Medal awarded by the Pontifical Academy of Science in the Vatican, the Hopkins Prize, the Dannie Heineman Prize, the Maxwell Prize, and the Hughes Medal of the Royal Society, which cited "his remarkable results in his work on black holes."

In 1978, Hawking was awarded the Albert Einstein Award by the Lewis and Rose Strauss Memorial Fund. During the following year, Hawking co-authored *General Relativity: An Einstein Centenary Survey* with Werner Israel. Hawking was appointed Lucasian Professor at Cambridge University in 1979, 310 years after Isaac Newton was given the same honor. At about this time, an interviewer asked Hawking again about his disability. He responded: "I think I'm happier now than I was before I started. Before the illness set in, I was very bored with life. It really was a rather pointless existence."

Cambridge University Press hoped that Hawking's latest book, *The Very Early Universe,* would sell better than his previous one, *Superspace and Supergravity*, which even scientists had difficulty understanding. The University Press suggested to Hawking that he write a popular book about cosmology. The Press had success previously publishing popular science books by Arthur Eddington and Fred Hoyle. Hawking was a tough negotiator, and the University Press didn't think that they could afford the generous advance that he demanded. The initial sample of a section of the book that Hawking provided was much too technical. In particular, it contained too many equations. The Press told him that every equation would reduce sales significantly.

Prior to signing with Cambridge University Press, Hawking heard that Bantam Books was interested in his popular book about cosmology. Bantam offered an advance for the United States and Canada. He accepted their offer. Bantam's editors also suggested that the technical content of the manuscript should be reduced.

By Christmas 1984, the first draft of the manuscript was finished. Bantam began to promote the book: "Hawking is on the cutting edge of what we know about the cosmos. This whole business of the unified field theory, the conjunction of relativity with quantum mechanics, is comparable to the search for the Holy Grail."

In 1985, Hawking spent the summer in Geneva, Switzerland, at CERN, the European Center for Nuclear Research, where he continued his research and made corrections to the manuscript of his book. One night in early August, Hawking suffered a blockage in his windpipe and later contracted pneumonia. He was placed on a life-support machine but was not in critical condition. Because he was unable to breathe through his mouth or nose, doctors recommended a tracheostomy. A cut would be made in his windpipe and a breathing device would be implanted. However, Hawking would never be able to speak again.

A California computer technologist, Walt Woltosz, gave Hawking a program called Equalizer that provided a menu of 3,000 words from which to construct sentences. The sentences were sent to a voice-synthesizer that spoke for him with an American accent. Hawking's life was transformed by this technology.

In early spring of 1988, Hawking's popular book about cosmology, *A Brief History of Time: From the Big Bang to Black Holes,* was released. Within a few weeks, this book about equating relativity theory with quantum mechanics was at the top of the best-seller list, where it stayed for many months. Stephen Hawking fan clubs were formed. Sales of the book exceeded everyone's estimates, particularly Bantam's.

More than any previous accomplishment, *A Brief History of Time* made Stephen Hawking a household name. A documentary, "Master of the Universe" won a Royal Television Society award, and ABC presented a profile of Hawking on its *20 / 20* program. Earlier, Commander of the British Empire (CBE) honors had been conferred upon Hawking, and, in 1989, he was made a Companion of Honor by Queen Elizabeth.

Hawking's list of achievements is impressive, particularly when his handicap is considered. However, he has suggested that his accomplishments might not have been as great if he hadn't been diagnosed with ALS at the age of twenty-one. Hawking, a strong-willed, creative individual who was highly motivated, always maintained his sense of humor; his upbeat outlook on life contributed significantly to his success. He observed, "One has to be grown up enough to realize that life is not fair. You have to do the best you can in the situation you are in."

CHAPTER 5

ARCHITECTS / ENTREPRENEURS

"The creative person is both more primitive and more cultivated, more destructive, a lot madder and a lot saner than the average person."

Frank Barron, *Think*

SIR CHRISTOPHER WREN (1632-1723) Architect of St. Paul's Cathedral

"A man in earnest finds means, or if he cannot find them, creates them."

Channing

Christopher Wren was born on October 20, 1632, during the reign of Charles I. His father, Christopher Wren, Sr., was Rector of East Knoyle, Wiltshire. Soon after his son's birth, Christopher, Sr., succeeded his brother Matthew as Dean of Windsor and Registrar of the Order of the Garter. The brothers had ties to the court, and both suffered for being High Church and Royalists during the Civil War. Dean Christopher's house was sacked twice, causing him to move to West Country and then to seek refuge with his son-in-law, William Holder. Matthew was imprisoned for eighteen years in the Tower of London.

The Civil War broke out when young Christopher was ten years old. He studied at Westminster School with the highly regarded headmaster, Dr. Busby. Christopher, a serious student, wrote a letter to his father from Westminster School containing the message, "What in me lies I will perform, as much as I am able lest these gifts should have been bestowed on an ungrateful soul. May the good God Almighty be with me in my undertakings. "

Wren attended Wadham College, Oxford, in the late 1640s and was awarded a B.A. degree in 1651. In 1654, he was a Fellow at All Souls College when diarist John Evelyn referred to him as "that miracle of a youth, Mr. Christopher Wren." At that time, considerable overlap existed between the arts and sciences. Wren had a good classical education and was well versed in Latin; astronomy was his principal academic interest. In 1657, he was appointed Professor of Astronomy at Gresham College, London. His other interests included the study of the laws of motion, meteorology, optics, and physiology.

In 1657, Wren attended a series of scientific meetings at Gresham College. The attendees formed a society in 1660 that was granted a King's Charter as the Royal Society the following year and evolved into the most distinguished international scientific society. In 1661, Wren succeeded Dr. Seth Ward, his teacher at

Oxford, as the Savilian Professor of Astronomy. Later that year, Wren was honored with a Doctor of Laws degree by Oxford University.

King Charles II visited Oxford, and Wren organized a Philosophical Society program for him in which Wren made his first direct reference to the field of architecture. In 1663, the King appointed Wren assistant to Sir John Denham, the Surveyor-General of Works. Denham was a failure as an architect. John Evelyn observed of Denham, "I knew him to be a better poet than architect, although he had Mr. Webb to assist him." John Webb was noted architect Inigo Jones's assistant and married his daughter. Jones was the dominant English architect prior to Wren. Working under Denham, Wren became the Surveyor-General of Works in fact if not in name.

Wren's efforts shifted from other scientific pursuits to architecture. His first architectural endeavor was the chapel at Pembroke College, Cambridge, followed by his design for the Sheldonian Theatre at Oxford.

During the summer of 1665, Wren received an invitation to visit the Earl of St. Alban's, the English Ambassador to France, in Paris. Wren's first trip to the Continent gave him the opportunity to view its architecture. He made daily visits to the Louvre, which was under construction at the time, and was impressed by the College of the Four Nations (University of Paris and its four colleges: Arts, Law, Medicine, and Theology.)

Wren was introduced to François Mansart, who did the initial designs for the Sorbonne and the Church of Val-de-Grâce, and to Giovanni Bernini, who showed Wren his architectural design for the Louvre. Bernini, an extremely successful sculptor and architect, believed that "in order to excel in the arts, one must rise above all the rules and create a manner peculiar to oneself." Wren visited Fontainbleau and the Palace at Versailles as well as many villas, including Chantilly, Constances, Le Raincy, Liancourt, Maisons, Ruel, Vaux, and Verneuil.

When he returned from the continent, Wren, as Deputy Surveyor-General, was appointed to a commission overseeing the repair of St. Paul's Cathedral, which was the second church on that site. The first St. Paul's, which had been built in the mid-seventh century, burned down in 1087. Late in the thirteenth century, construction of its replacement still hadn't been completed. During the reign of King Stephen, the Cathedral was again destroyed by fire. Reconstruction began immediately. The medieval Cathedral was rebuilt with a Gothic choir and a Romanesque nave. In the 1630s, Inigo Jones had recased the nave using pilasters instead of buttresses and had constructed a Corinthian portico at the west end of the Cathedral.

The older members of the Commission, Sir John Denham, Sir Roger Pratt, and John Webb, recommended repairing the existing Cathedral, but Wren suggested sweeping changes. He suggested refacing the inside of the nave as well as the outside and replacing the nave vault with saucer domes. Wren's proposals for St. Paul's all contained two principal components—a great central area and a high dome. His proposals encountered considerable opposition but were finally agreed upon.

An even more drastic change faced St. Paul's. Beginning on September 2, 1665, the Great Fire raged for three days, leveling most of the Cathedral as well as destroying or virtually destroying eighty-seven other churches. John Evelyn noted that "the stones of St. Paul's flew like grenades, the melting lead running down the streets in a stream, the very pavements of them glowing with fiery redness."

Wren was one of three members of a Commission appointed by the King to make recommendations on rebuilding London; the City also appointed three members. By September 11, Wren had completed plans for London that would have replaced the old narrow, winding streets with an orderly layout of streets radiating from a civic center where the Royal Exchange is located today. The plan included a civic center surrounded by buildings for "Ensurances," the Excise Office, the Mint, and the Post Office.

Before the plan could be executed, however, citizens who had lost their homes and had no place to live began to rebuild on the old foundations. All that the Commission accomplished was to institute the Rebuilding Act of 1667, which prohibited building timber houses and houses with upper stories overhanging the street. This Act reduced the hazard of fire in the future, but did nothing to make London a well-laid-out city.

Wren's next designs were for the Chapel of Emmanuel College, Cambridge, in 1668 and, a year later, the Customs House, which had been destroyed by fire in the early 1700s. Sir John Denham died in 1669, and Wren was appointed Surveyor-General to succeed him. Also that year, Wren married Faith Coghill, the daughter of Sir Thomas Coghill of Bletchingdon, whom he had known as a youth. They had a son, Christopher, who was only seven months old when Faith died in 1675 of smallpox. In 1677, Wren married Jane Fitzwilliam, the sister of Lord Fitzwilliam of Lifford. They had two children, Jane and William.

Paying for the rebuilding of London and St. Paul's was a challenge. The country was bankrupt; nevertheless, it had to find a way to rebuild the city for the hundred thousand homeless. Money also had to be made available to support the Royal Navy, whose ships anchored in the Medway were being attacked by the Dutch. Economy was foremost, and Wren would have to find a way to finance the rebuilding of St. Paul's.

Most of the other members of the Commission wanted to patch and repair the Cathedral. Wren knew that structural problems in the Cathedral existed even before the Great Fire; he knew that rebuilding was the only way to proceed. He observed, "Since we cannot mend this great Ruine we will not disfigure it." From this point onward, he would struggle with his strong feelings for his art and doing what he knew was right despite the ongoing resistance of those who wanted to economize.

Wren oversaw the demolition of the remnants of the old St. Paul's, which began in 1667 and continued for two years. He supervised the first use of gunpowder in demolition. Unfortunately, in Wren's absence, his crew used twice the amount of gunpowder in the second demolition effort. No one was killed, but the residents of the area were terrified by the flying debris. Wren wasn't permitted to use gunpowder again. The last columns had to be knocked down with a battering ram.

In 1669, Wren was commissioned to rebuild the Temple Bar, the gateway from Westminster to the City of London. This right of way had been maintained by the Mayor of London and the Corporation for almost 400 years. Wren's design of the Temple Bar was constructed of stone with a large central arch and a guard room containing recesses with statues of Charles I and Charles II on one side and of James I and Queen Elizabeth on the other. In 1872, the Temple Bar was moved to Theobald's Park to alleviate traffic congestion.

The first two churches that Wren rebuilt after the Great Fire were St. Christopher-le-Stocks, which was later torn down when the Bank of England was built, and St. Mary-le-Bow, which was destroyed in the air raids of World War II. Then he returned his attention to St. Paul's. In addition to the design approved before the Great Fire, Wren had prepared several designs with a classic dome in the center of the old Gothic Cathedral. In *Wren: His Work and Times*, John Lindsey commented on the next design:

> Then followed Wren's own favorite design, one of incomparable beauty, in the form of a Greek Cross, with a vestibule and portico, surmounted by a lesser dome, the points of the Greek Cross being connected by concave facades. The King was so taken by this design that he ordered a huge model to be made of it (which still exists). But the Chapter and other Clergy thought the model not enough of a cathedral fashion, in that the choir was designed circular, and there were no regular aisles or nave.
>
> Over these points the architect and the Chapter fought bitterly, Wren being reminded that "his" cathedral must conform as nearly as possible to the designs of other cathedrals and that side aisles were an absolute necessity if the processions in the cathedral were to have that dignity to which they had been used. Wren, grumbling that "they are impertinent, our Religion not using Processions" reluctantly abandoned the design and produced another, irreverently known as the "Nightmare" design.

The King approved this plan, but fortunately he allowed Wren "liberty in the prosecution of his work, to make some variations, rather ornamental than essential, as from time to time he should see proper, and to leave the whole to his management."

Wren availed himself of this permission to an incredible extent and constructed a building almost as different from the approved plan as St. Paul's Cathedral is from that of Salisbury.

Financing the construction was an ongoing problem. Clearly, rebuilding St. Paul's was a national undertaking, not merely a diocesan effort. The King honored his 1664 commitment of £1,000 to restore the old cathedral; in fact, he doubled it. Archbishop Sheldon, Bishop Henchman, and the Bishops of Durham and Winchester made significant contributions, but the other bishops didn't contribute to the building fund. Wren personally contributed to the fund.

On May 14, 1675, the King authorized the commencement of work on the Cathedral. On June 21, the first stone was laid without any accompanying ceremony. Wren walked around the site and marked the key locations of the foundation. He asked one of the workmen to bring him a flat stone from the rubbish pile to use as the guide from which all other measurements would be made. The workman struggled bringing a stone to be used as a marker and was relieved to drop the heavy load at the location indicated by the Surveyor-General. Many of the workmen around Wren looked down and read the word "RESURGAM"—I shall rise again—carved on the old marker that their fellow worker had selected. Wren and the workmen considered this to be a good luck omen.

Many talented tradesmen contributed to the building of St. Paul's, including Assistant Surveyor John Oliver, who supervised the workmen, purchased materials, and audited the accounts; Laurence Spenser, Clerk of the Works, who acted as the timekeeper and kept the account books; Master-Mason Thomas Strong, who was succeeded by his brother, Edward Strong; ironworker Master-Carvers Tijou, from France, and Thomas Robinson; Stone carvers Francis Baird and Caius Gabriel Cibber; and Jonathan Maine, who did the wood carving in the library and in the chapels on the west side of the Cathedral. The two most well-known wood carvers were Grinling Gibbons and Philip Wood.

Wren's friend, John Evelyn, met Grinling Gibbons at Gibbons's run-down thatched cottage near Sage's Court at Deptford. Gibbons was carving a crucifix of Tintoret that impressed Evelyn. Evelyn introduced Gibbons to Wren, who employed him as a wood carver at St. Paul's for many productive years. Gibbons's wood carvings for the choir-stalls in the Cathedral provide an outstanding example of his craft.

The story of Philip Wood's hiring as a wood carver at St. Paul's is an unusual one. Wood, who was too poor to afford to buy the necessary wood carving tools, hung around the building site until he saw that wood carving was about to start. He approached one of the overseers to ask if he could get a job as a wood carver. The overseer thought that Wood looked like a farmer and told him that: "They had no use for barn and stable work here." Wood continued to hang around the site until "a gentleman approached with papers in his hand and talked to the work people. At last his eye falling on me, he asked a workman, 'What does that fellow do here? I will have no persons about unless they do business.'"

The workman addressed by Wren told him that the young man was looking for work as a wood carver but had been told that there was no job for him. When Wren asked him what experience he had, he replied that he had carved pig troughs. The workman laughed heartily at the young man from the country. Wren told him that he should go home and prepare wood carvings of a sow and her piglets, since that was something with which he was familiar. The workman got another laugh out of the young man's discomfiture.

Wood went home in near despair and told his landlady about his experience. She cheered him up and told him that they would buy a good piece of pearwood to use in carving the pig family. He completed his task and returned to the building site the following week. Again the overseer turned him away, but Wood waited until the Surveyor-General appeared. Wren was accompanied by a group of people, and the overseer attempted to prevent Wood from approaching him.

Wood presented his wonderful carvings of the pigs to Wren, who looked at them closely. Mr. Addison, one of Wren's companions, asked Wood if he would sell the carvings. Wood agreed to sell them and was given ten guineas. Wren apologized to Wood for his earlier treatment and told him that he would have work as a wood carver at the Cathedral as long as there was wood carving to be done.

Work proceeded on the Cathedral despite differences of opinion between the Commissioners that required adjudication by Wren. Wren persevered in keeping the work on the Cathedral moving and in ensuring that the design was implemented according to his plan. Lack of funds was a chronic problem, particularly since construction was proceeding simultaneously on housing and on the other churches that had been destroyed by the Great Fire.

Biographer John Lindsey described the Cathedral:

> Wren's intention all along had been that the dome
> should be the central figure of the church both
> within and without. The choir, the nave, and the
> transepts he planned of exactly the same design,
> proportion, and ornamentation: thus, the arcade of
> three arches in the choir is the same as the arcade
> of three arches in the nave and that of one each in
> the transepts.

> The arcade of the choir is completed by the apse,
> that of the nave by the magnificent vestibule
> flanked north-west and south-west by the chapels
> of St. Dunstan and of St. Michael and St. George
> while the the arcade of each transept ends in a flat
> ornamental wall with a semi-circular porch out-
> side. Each "arm" of the church is attached to the
> dome by walls and vast panels supporting a barrel
> arch of identical pattern while a similar arch joins
> the choir to the apse.

Wren was influenced by many sources in his design of St. Paul's. The dome displays the influence of Bramante's unexecuted design for St. Peter's Basilica in Rome, and the ribbed section of the dome reflects the work of Michelangelo. The Corinthian portico is simi- lar to earlier Inigo Jones designs, and the execution of the dome design over eight arches was probably influenced by an unused Mansart plan. The overall plan for a Greek cross building may have come from a drawing of Webb's "ideal" churches. These influences take nothing away from Wren's overall effort. St. Paul's is a mag- nificent design with great proportion that displays considerable originality on the part of the architect.

St. Paul's Cathedral was under construction for thirty-five years, and the chief architect lived to see it completed. Wren persevered in confronting many obstacles, including the initial controversy of whether the Cathedral should be in the shape of a Greek cross or a Latin cross, plan for the placement of the organ and its accompanying screen that would have limited the space for worship to 400 people, and conflict about having Sir James Thornhill paint images of the life of St. Paul on the inside of the dome instead of using bright mosaics.

Furthermore, the chief architect was nagged continually that the work on the Cathedral was proceeding too slowly. In his *Annals*, Dean Milman noted that:

> A clause had crept into an Act of Parliament that, until the work should be finished, half his salary should be withheld from the Surveyor. The Commissioners proceeded to carry this hard clause into effect. This was not only a hardship, but a tacit imputation that the Architect was delaying the completion of the work for his own emolument. It is indeed stated plainly in one of the Commissioner's papers that Sir Christopher, or someone employed by him, who, by many affidavits, have proved guilty of great corruption, may be supposed to have found their advantage to this delay.

> In the matter of corruption and embezzlement the Commissioners, apart from suggesting that Wren himself had been responsible for the delay, concentrated their attacks on the workmen, notably the Master Carpenter, Jennings. Him they accused of selling quantities of material which had been charged to Cathedral accounts and, by pocketing the proceeds, making an income of fifteen hundred a year out of his deals. It is noteworthy that they were unable to produce any witnesses to these alleged illegal transactions, nor were they ever able to produce evidence that Jennings's accounts showed that he received anything more than his official salary.

Wren's son Christopher in his book, *Parentalia*, claims that his father laid the last stone for the Cathedral in 1710. In late 1711,

Parliament declared that work had been completed and made the final payments on Wren's salary that had been held in arrears. Wren stayed on as Surveyor-General until he was eighty-four years old and had been employed on the old and the new St. Paul's for over fifty years. The final insult to him occurred in 1718, when his appointment was terminated, and he was replaced by a political appointee with no knowledge of architecture who lasted only a year as Surveyor-General.

Biographer John Lindsey puts Wren's achievement in designing and constructing St. Paul's into perspective:

> The quality of St. Paul's with its triumphs and its compromises, can be understood only if all the limiting conditions are remembered. Wren was building, in the age of late Baroque, for a Protestant community, and a conservative clergy, who wished to preserve the Latin cross plan which they had inherited from the Middle Ages. Money was short, materials came in slowly and, at the beginning at least, Wren lacked experience as an architect. He gained it by ceaselessly adapting himself to circumstances and using his mathematical genius to overcome difficulties . . . Wren's triumph lies in his conquest of circumstances; and surely by any standards the design for the dome is great architecture. His own generation had no doubt about his quality. To them, the man had matched the moment.

Wren died on February 25, 1723. He was buried in the crypt under the choir at St. Paul's "with Great Funeral State and Solemnity." Initially, his grave was marked by an unadorned black slab of marble with the inscription in Latin, "Under this stone lieth the Founder of this Church and City, Christopher Wren, who lived more than ninety years not for himself but for the public good." His son had a Latin inscription placed on the wall over his grave that ends with "Lector si monumentum requiris circumspice." (Reader, if you seek his monument, look around you). He couldn't have chosen a more suitable epitaph.

GEORGE EASTMAN (1854-1932) Creator of the Photographic Industry

"Eastman was a stupendous factor in the education of the modern world. Of what he got in return for his great gifts to the human race, he gave generously for their good; fostering music, endowing learning, supporting science in its researches and teaching, seeking to promote health and lessen human ills, helping the lowest in their struggle toward the light, making his own city a center for the arts, and glorifying his own country in the eyes of the world."

New York Times, 1932.

George Eastman, founder of the photographic industry, was born in Waterville, New York, on July 12, 1854. He was the third child and first son of George W. Eastman and Maria Kilbourn Eastman. In 1842, Eastman's father had established a business school, Eastman's Commercial College, in Rochester. The school prospered in the thriving Erie Canal community, but George W. Eastman did not move his family from Waterville to Rochester until 1860.

George W. Eastman died in 1862, leaving the family in reduced economic circumstances. Maria Eastman took in boarders to supplement her income. Young Eastman's first employment was a part-time job with an insurance agency. He began his first full-time position as junior bookkeeper for the Rochester Savings Bank in 1874.

The first reference to photography in Eastman's diary was in 1869. His interest became serious during the summer of 1877, when he purchased $100 worth of "sundries and lenses" and arranged for a local photographer to teach him "the art of photography." Taking photographs in 1877 was a complex process requiring bulky equipment. Glass plates had to be exposed in the camera while wet, and development had to be completed before the emulsion dried. Eastman was bothered by the cumbersomeness of the process. He commented: "The bulk of the paraphernalia worried me. It seemed that one ought to be able to carry less than a pack-horse load."

Eastman's thinking was given focus when he read an article in the *British Journal of Photography* containing a formula for a sen-

163

sitive gelatin emulsion for glass plates that could be used when dry. He spent long hours experimenting until he found a combination of gelatin and silver bromide that had the photographic qualities that he wanted. Initially, he experimented to support his hobby of photography; he soon realized the commercial potential of his effort and resigned his job at the bank to make and market dry photographic plates.

By June 1879, Eastman was manufacturing quality photographic plates and had designed and built equipment for coating them. He sailed to England, the center of the photographic industry, and obtained his first patent on July 22, 1879. On September 9, 1879, his patent attorney, George Selden, submitted an application for him to the U.S. Patent Office for "An Improved Process of Preparing Gelatin Dry Plates for Use in Photography and in Apparatus Therefor."

In April 1880, Eastman leased the third floor of a building on State Street in Rochester to produce dry plates in quantity. An early investor in the Eastman Dry Plate Company was Colonel Henry Alvah Strong, who, with his wife, boarded with Maria Eastman. Strong was a partner in Strong-Woodbury and Company, a thriving manufacturer of whips.

During the winter of 1879-80, Eastman formulated four business principles upon which to build his enterprise:

- Production in large quantities by machinery
- Low prices to increase the usefulness of the products
- Foreign as well as domestic distribution
- Extensive advertising as well as selling by demonstration

In 1881, a near-fatal catastrophe struck the business—photographers complained that Eastman dry plates were no longer sensitive and did not capture an image. Customers discovered something that had not been realized until then: passage of time lessened the sensitivity of the emulsion on the plate. The New York City distributor had placed the recently received plates on top of the older plates and had sold the new plates before using up the old. By the time the older plates were sold, they had lost their photographic sensitivity. At significant expense for a small company, Eastman recalled all of his plates and replaced them.

Then Eastman received a second staggering blow—he could no longer make a satisfactory emulsion. During many weeks of sleepless nights with his factory shut down, Eastman conducted 469 unsuccessful experiments to produce a usable emulsion. On March 11, 1882, Eastman and Strong sailed for England, where they discovered that the problem was due to a defective supply of gelatin received from a manufacturer. It was not a problem with the emulsion formula or Eastman's equipment. On April 16, they returned to Rochester, conducted sixteen more unsuccessful experiments, and were successful on the seventeenth. Eastman learned two lessons from this experience: to test samples of material received and to control the supply, whenever practicable.

On October 1, 1882, the Eastman Dry Plate and Film Company was incorporated with $200,000 capital stock. Henry A. Strong was president, and Eastman was treasurer of the company, which purchased the plant and stock of the Eastman Dry Plate Company.

Eastman searched for a material to replace the fragile, heavy glass as a support for the emulsion. He experimented with collodion, which was made from gun-cotton (nitro-cellulose) and nitric acid. On March 4, 1884, he filed his first patent application for photographic film. Then he designed a mechanism to hold film in the camera, a roll-holder in a wooden frame. On March 26, 1885, the first commercial film was manufactured by the new company.

An early setback to the company was a serious fire on February 10, 1888, that destroyed most of the interior of the State Street factory and shut it down for two months. Eastman was back in business by April, and by June he had his first camera on the market.

Eastman conceived of the name "Kodak" as a trademark for his products. He liked the letter K, the first letter of his mother's maiden name. On September 4, 1888, "Kodak" was registered as a trademark in the United States. The first camera was the "No. 1 Kodak." Eastman explained the origin of the word to the British Patent Office:

> This is not a foreign name or work; it was constructed by me to serve a definite purpose. It has the following merits as a trademark word:
> First: It is short.
> Second: It is not capable of mispronunciation.

Third: It does not resemble anything in the art
and cannot be associated with anything
in the art except the "Kodak."

The small, inexpensive cameras sold well, and the company expanded to meet market demand.

Eastman used Dr. Samuel Lattimore, head of the department of chemistry at the University of Rochester, as a consultant. The first chemist hired by Eastman was Henry Reichenbach, one of Dr. Lattimore's assistants. Eastman was too involved with the operation of the business to devote much time to experiments; however, he continued to work on mechanical developments, such as roller mechanisms. On December 10, 1889, a patent for manufacturing transparent nitro-cellulose photographic film was granted to Reichenbach. Joint patents were granted to Eastman and Reichenbach on March 22, 1892, and July 19, 1892.

The next challenge that Eastman faced was one that he least expected—employee disloyalty. Reichenbach and two other employees secretly formed a rival company using the filmmaking formulae and processes of Eastman's company. Eastman investigated the rumors and found them to be true. He also found that they had made 39,400 feet of unusable film and had let 1,417 gallons of emulsion spoil. He discharged them.

On November 28, 1889, the Eastman Photographic Materials Company, Ltd., was incorporated in London to represent the Company in all areas of the world except the western hemisphere. In December 1889, the Eastman Company was incorporated in Rochester with $1 million capital to represent the firm in the western hemisphere. In August 1890, the Company purchased several farms in the Town of Greece that were to become Kodak Park, the world's largest film manufacturing complex.

On May 23, 1892, the name of the Eastman Company was changed to the Eastman Kodak Company, and the capitalization was increased to $5 million. Camera and film development continued as Kodak designed and made uncomplicated products that lived up to the slogan "You press the button and we do the rest."

In 1912, Eastman established the Eastman Kodak Company Research Laboratories and brought Dr. Kenneth Mees from

England to serve as its head. Mees and his chief assistant, S. E. Shepard, who were both graduates of the University of London, made significant contributions to the growth of the company. Motion pictures were introduced in the early 1920s, and Kodacolor film was announced in the late 1920s. Many significant film improvements followed, including Technicolor film, Kodachrome film, and the replacement of nitrate-based film with an acetate-based product.

Eastman never married; he lived alone in his mansion on East Avenue. He was instrumental in founding the Eastman School of Music at the University of Rochester and building the Eastman Theatre. He gave over $60 million to educational institutions, including the University of Rochester, the Massachusetts Institute of Technology, Hampton Institute, and the Tuskegee Institute. He funded the Eastman Visiting Professorship at Oxford University and gave $5.5 million to establish dental clinics in Brussels, London, Paris, Rome, and Stockholm.

On March 14, 1932, George Eastman took his own life at his East Avenue home. He left a note that read: "To my friends. My work is done. Why wait? G. E." His death shocked the community. Karl K. Compton, president of the Massachusetts Institute of Technology, wrote in the April 15, 1932, issue of *Science* magazine:

> Consider for a moment the full significance of his last words. He had invented the modern photographic plate; he had invented the photographic film; he had made the Kodak a household object throughout the entire world; he had created a business; he had created a great research laboratory which had strikingly fulfilled his faith in it; he had selected certain fields of education, health, and art to which he had devoted his fortune for the benefit of the entire world; he had satisfied his distinctive desires for the excitement of exploration and big game hunting; he had no close relatives; the infirmities of old age had come upon him and were about to master him. He who had always been his own master remained so to the last.

THOMAS J. WATSON (1874-1956) Founder of IBM Corporation

"Within us all there are wells of thought and dynamics of energy which are not suspected until emergencies arise. Then oftentimes we find that it is comparatively simple to double or treble our former capacities and to amaze ourselves by the results achieved. Quotas, when set for us by others, are challenges which goad us on to surpass ourselves. The outstanding leaders of every age are those who set up their own quotas and constantly exceed them. The great accomplishments of man have resulted from the transmission of ideas and enthusiasm."

Thomas J. Watson

Thomas J. Watson, founder of IBM Corporation, was born on February 17, 1874, in Campbell, New York, the first of five children of Thomas Watson and Jane White Watson. Watson's father, who was in the lumber business, wanted his son to study law. Watson didn't want to pursue a legal career; he applied for a temporary teaching certificate for three years and enrolled at the Albany Teachers' College. However, one day of teaching changed his mind: "I can't go into a classroom with a bunch of children at nine o'clock in the morning and stay until four."

Watson enrolled at the Miller School of Commerce in Elmira, New York, and, in May 1892, completed the accounting and business program. He accepted a position as a bookkeeper in Painted Post, New York, but soon decided that "I couldn't sit on a high stool and keep books all my life." He formed opinions early about what he didn't want to do, but he wasn't yet sure what he wanted to do.

Willard Bronson, a neighbor of the Watsons, operated a hardware store and consignment business. Bronson acquired Estey organs, pianos, and sewing machines and sold them on consignment from a wagon. Watson went on the road selling for Bronson; it was the first of his many sales jobs.

Watson learned the importance of a neat appearance and of making a good first impression. He sold for Bronson for two years without a raise and without many kind words of encouragement from his boss. Bronson was astounded when Watson quit after two years. Only then did Bronson offer him a raise; he even offered to sell him the business. Watson's father advised his son to find a position outside the region. He suggested the Buffalo area.

Watson accepted a position selling sewing machines for the Wheeler and Wilson Company in Buffalo. After a short time, he lost his job, not because of any shortcoming on his part, but because they had too many salesmen. C. B. Barron, a coworker who lost his position at the same time, accepted a job selling shares in the Buffalo Building and Loan Association and invited Watson to join him. Watson sold shares in the Building and Loan Association until Barron ran off with all of the building and loan funds, including Watson's commissions.

Watson applied for a job with the National Cash Register Company (NCR) and met the manager of the Buffalo office, John J. Range. Range wasn't interested in hiring him, but Watson persisted until he did. Watson made no sales during the first two weeks, and Range made his disappointment clear. Watson absorbed Range's constructive criticism and, within a year, was one of the most successful NCR salesmen in the East. By the time he was twenty-five, Watson was the top salesman in the Buffalo office.

John Henry Patterson, chief executive officer of NCR, made the cash register virtually indispensible to businessmen and then monopolized its manufacture and distribution. Patterson was a successful manager because he combined paternalism with an emphasis on training. He realized that salesmen responded to the fear of punishment and the promise of reward. Patterson knew just how hard he could push Watson. He became the shaper of Watson's life over the next eleven years.

In the summer of 1899, Patterson promoted Watson to manager of the Rochester office. Watson moved the sales of the Rochester branch from near the bottom of all NCR's offices to sixth from the top within several months. He used ruthless techniques to beat his main competitor, the Hallwood Company, and his performance was followed closely by Hugh Chalmers, NCR's general manager, and by Patterson.

NCR had between eighty and ninety-five percent of the sales of new cash registers. Patterson decided to be aggressive in reducing the impact of sales of used cash registers. Patterson gave Watson $1 million to set up a company to front for NCR in driving out used cash register competition in the United States. When told by his son that he had been given $1 million to establish a business, Watson's father advised him: "Before you spend a dollar of your company's money, consider it as your own dollar. Do not spend any of your company's money when you would not spend your own money."

Watson established Watson's Cash Register and Second Hand Exchange in Manhattan, undercut the prices of his main competitor, and bought him out. He repeated this activity in Philadelphia and Chicago. He made the second-hand machine business a profitable unit of the company and was offered a position at NCR headquarters in Dayton.

Eventually, Chalmers could no longer tolerate Patterson's dictatorial style and, as the number two man in the company, disagreed with some of Patterson's non-business decisions. Chalmers was fired; Watson was promoted to general manager in his place.

Patterson went to Europe for two years, and, by the time he returned, Watson had doubled the sales volume (to 100,000 cash registers in 1910). The increase in sales was due partly to the redesign of the cash register by Charles (Boss) Kettering, who replaced the manual operation of the machine with an electric motor. Kettering moved on to General Motors where he designed the self-starter for automobiles.

NCR management's monopolistic practices in the second-hand cash register business caught up with them. On February 22, 1913, Patterson, Watson, and twenty-eight other company managers were indicted on three counts of criminal conspiracy and were placed on trial in Cincinnati for restraining trade and maintaining a monopoly.

While awaiting trial, Watson met Jeanette Kittridge, whose father was president of a railroad car manufacturing company. The Kittridges were friends and neighbors of Patterson; Jeanette was Patterson's choice of a wife for Watson. The couple fell in love.

Patterson, Watson, and all but one of the other senior NCR managers were found guilty as charged. Patterson was released on $10,000 bail, and Watson was released on $5,000 bail. Watson suggested postponing the wedding until the results of the appeal were known. Jeanette disagreed. She was as strong-willed as he was; together they made a powerful team. Shortly after their marriage, Watson was fired, just as Chalmers had been abruptly dismissed earlier. Upon leaving his office for the last time, he observed to friends: "I've helped build all but one of those buildings. Now I'm going out to build a business bigger than John H. Patterson has."

Watson received a job offer from Charles Flint, who had assembled a company called the Computer-Tabulating-Recording Company (CTR) by combining a computing scales company, a time recorder company, and the Tabulating Machine Company. CTR was unprofitable, and Flint wanted a new manager. Watson accepted Flint's offer; however, he wasn't elected to the board of directors because of the pending NCR lawsuit. On March 13, 1915, the District Court verdict was set aside and a new trial granted. No new trial was conducted, and Watson was cleared of any wrongdoing. CTR promptly elected Watson president and general manager.

Watson authorized the redesign of the Hollerith (punched card) tabulator, and the Tabulating Machine Company became the premier unit of CTR. From 1914 until 1920, CTR's gross income increased from $4 million to $14 million. The recession of 1921 curtailed CTR's expansion plans, and sales that year were $3.5 million instead of the projected $15 million. All salaries, including Watson's, were cut by ten percent. Watson had difficulty meeting payments on CTR's loans. The president of the Guaranty Trust Company, holder of CTR's debt, told him, "I believe so much in the future of your business and in you as the head of it that Guaranty Trust will go along with you, and don't worry about it."

In 1924, Watson renamed the company International Business Machines (IBM). He was appointed chief executive officer and, for the first time, was really in charge of the company. IBM's revenues increased from $19.7 million to $39.5 million from 1928 to 1939. IBM was a tough competitor; by 1935, IBM had 85.7 percent of all leased tabulating machines.

An important source of IBM's profits was from sales of punched cards used in tabulating machines. Passage of the Social Security Act in 1935 and the Wages-Hours Act in 1937 contributed heavily to IBM's growth. Businesses were now required to record wages paid, hours worked, and overtime earned. The company's revenues grew from $39.5 million in 1939 to $141.7 million in 1945.

IBM's competitors in business machines were Burroughs, NCR, Remington Rand, and Underwood-Elliott-Fisher. IBM's principal competitor was Remington Rand. James Henry Rand had formed Remington Rand by merging companies that manufactured adding machines and typewriters to his original company that produced

Kardex systems. In 1927, Rand acquired the Powers Accounting Machine Corporation, a respected manufacturer of tabulating equipment.

Remington Rand's revenue decreased from $59.6 million in 1928 to $43.5 million in 1939 mainly because of the stiff competition from IBM in tabulating machines. However, from 1939 to 1945, Remington Rand's net sales increased from $43.2 million to $108 million, principally due to sales of material to support the war effort.

In the 1930s, IBM funded university research in computing, including development of a mechanical calculator for astronomers by Wallace Eckert at Columbia University. The calculator had no commercial value, but IBM's support was widely recognized. In 1939, Howard Aiken of Harvard University entered a joint agreement with IBM to build an automatic computer, the Automatic Sequence Controlled Calculator (Mark I), at the IBM plant at Endicott, New York. Four IBM engineers participated in the development of the machine, an electromechanical device with 760,000 components.

In 1944, the Mark I was completed and shipped to Harvard University, where it was demonstrated by Aiken, who took all of the credit for its development. IBM and Watson weren't mentioned, even though they had participated heavily and contributed $500,000 to its development. Watson had involved IBM more from a public relations than from an earnings point of view; he was furious with Aiken. Aiken's betrayal motivated Watson to develop a machine that could outperform the Mark I. In 1948, the first step was taken with the introduction of the Selective Sequence Electronic Calculator (SSEC), IBM's first commercial electronic computer. The SSEC contained 12,500 vacuum tubes and 21,400 relays.

In June 1950, Communist forces crossed the thirty-eighth parallel into South Korea. Watson immediately sent a telegram to President Truman offering the services of the IBM Corporation. A team was formed to plan IBM's contribution during the Korean conflict. The team foresaw a need for "more computational power," so the Corporation developed the "IBM Defense Calculator," later renamed the IBM 701. In March 1953, the first IBM 701, which leased for $24,000 per month, was installed at the Atomic Weapons

Development Center at Los Alamos, New Mexico.

In 1952, Thomas Watson, Jr., became president of IBM; his brother Arthur was appointed general manager of the IBM World Trade Corporation. From 1914 through 1953, assets had grown by twenty-four times, employees by thirty-four times, the data processing business by 316 times, and development expenditures by 500 times. On May 8, 1956, Thomas Watson, Jr., became chief executive officer of the IBM Corporation. Just over a month later, on June 19, Thomas Watson, Sr., died of a heart attack.

IBM's founder definitely made his mark on U.S. industry. The *New York Herald Tribune* called Watson "a man who could well stand as a symbol of the free enterprise system." *Time* magazine called him "one of the first of a new breed of U.S. businessmen who realized that their social responsibilities ran far beyond their own companies." President Eisenhower considered his friend "an industrialist who was first of all a great citizen and a great humanitarian."

Thomas Watson, Jr., maintained the growth that was the legacy of his father. The IBM 701, a scientific computer, was followed by a commercial version, the IBM 702. In 1954, the IBM 704, the successor to the IBM 701, was placed on the market. The IBM 705, the successor to the IBM 702 and the first commercial computer with magnetic memory, was introduced in 1956.

In the early 1960s, IBM spent $5 billion developing the IBM 360 series of computers in the first development activity that used all international units of the company. It was considered a "you bet your company" effort; it resulted in a phenomenally successful family of computers.

CHESTER CARLSON (1906-1968) Inventor of the Dry Copying Process

"Now, through the use of the copying machine, the twenty-five page document can be reproduced in a manner of minutes, and one can have as many copies as one desires. This is true in every profession, in every business, in government agencies in colleges and hospitals and institutions of all sorts, whenever people communicate with written words or charts or pictures. That is why Chester F. Carlson's invention has so often been called one of the most significant of our age."

John Dessauer, *My Years With Xerox, The Billions Nobody Wanted*

Chester Carlson began experimenting with a dry copy process in 1935, and, on October 22, 1938, he produced the first crude copy using his electrophotography process. Carlson, whose job involved processing patents, filed a comprehensive patent in 1939. He spent five years looking for a sponsor to finance the further development and commercialization of his new technology. Over those years, he was turned down by the National Inventors' Council, the U.S. Army Signal Corps, and thirty-two companies, including A. B. Dick, Eastman Kodak, IBM (twice), General Electric, and Remington-Rand (UNIVAC). Carlson said that they all displayed "an enthusiastic lack of interest."

In 1944, Carlson found a sponsor, the Battelle Memorial Institute of Columbus, Ohio. Battelle was to receive sixty percent of future proceeds in return for helping to develop the technology. They suggested the use of selenium instead of sulphur in the process and the use of a specific black toner powder. They, too, were unsuccessful in promoting the product. An Ohio State University professor renamed the process "xerography," from the Greek words "xeros," meaning dry, and "graphos," meaning writing.

Finally, John Dessauer of the Haloid Corporation of Rochester, New York, saw an article about electrophotography in *Radio News*. Dessauer's boss, Joe Wilson, Jr., wanted to increase the $100,000 yearly earnings of the company and had asked him to read technical journals to look for new products or processes. Haloid

Corporation purchased the patent and rights to Carlson's technology from Battelle. They produced a flat plate copier in 1949 that required 3-5 minutes per copy, spent more on research and development than they earned each year, and, by 1956, received forty percent their sales from xerography. The name of the company was changed to Haloid-Xerox.

In 1959, IBM was asked to manufacture copiers for Haloid-Xerox. IBM commissioned Arthur D. Little, a consultant from Cambridge, Massachusetts, to do a study of the market potential. The study identified a total potential market of 5,000 units of sales for Haloid-Xerox's new 914 copier. IBM declined the offer to participate in Xerography a second time, and Haloid-Xerox began to manufacture the model 914 copier itself. By 1968, they had produced 200,000 of them. The fallacy in the Arthur D. Little study was in basing their recommendations on the estimate of the number of copies made at the point of origin, using the original. Most copies are made at the point of receipt from copies made elsewhere.

Haloid-Xerox changed its name to the Xerox Corporation in 1961. By 1988, three billion copies were being made each day worldwide, and the business of making copies had become a $22 billion a year business. The technology that nobody wanted made millionaires out of many people and revolutionized the way in which we communicate with one another.

BILL GATES (1955-   ) Co-founder of Microsoft Corporation

"Genius is only the power of making continuous efforts. The line between failure and success is so fine that we scarcely know when we pass it; so fine that we are often on the line but don't know it. How many a man has thrown up his hands at a time when a little more effort, a little more patience, would have achieved success. As the tide goes out, so it comes in. In business sometimes, prospects may seem darkest when they are really on the turn. A little more persistence, a little more effort, and what seemed hopeless failure may turn into glorious success. There is no failure except in no longer trying. There is no defeat except from within, no really insurmountable barrier save our own inherent weakness of purpose."

                                                      Elbert Hubbard

William Henry Gates III, the second child of William Henry Gates, Jr., and Mary Maxwell Gates, was born on October 28, 1955, in Seattle. Bill Gates, Jr., a graduate of the University of Washington Law School, was a partner in a Seattle law firm.

Young Bill was a competitive child and a good student. He wasn't disciplined heavily, and Mary Gates observed that, to a large extent, he did what he wanted to from the age of eight. By the time Gates was eleven, he was ahead of his fellow students in the public schools and needed additional academic challenges. Gates's parents enrolled him in the Lakeside School, an exclusive private prep school for boys in Seattle. Lakeside was known for its challenging academic atmosphere in which students were encouraged to develop their own interests.

In the spring of 1968, Lakeside introduced its students to the use of computers. Large mainframe computers were beyond the budget of even a well-endowed private school. Minicomputers developed by the Digital Equipment Corporation (DEC) were also too expensive for a prep school with under 400 students. The Lakeside School purchased a teletype machine and connected it via telephone line to a DEC PDP-10 minicomputer owned by General Electric in downtown Seattle.

Gates and his friend, Kent Evans, became frequent users of the

PDP-10. Paul Stocklin, Gates's math teacher, who introduced him to time sharing using the teletype, admitted that "I knew more than he did for the first day, but only for that first day." Gates spent most of his free time on the computer. Paul Allen, Gates's future partner, who was two years ahead of him at Lakeside, was also hooked on the new technology.

Gates's first programs were a tic-tac-toe game, a lunar lander game, and Monopoly™, all of which he wrote in BASIC (Beginners' All-Purpose Symbolic Instruction Code). Gates and Allen had common interests and became close friends. Allen would challenge Gates by saying "Hey, I'll bet you can't figure this out." Eventually, Gates, Allen, Kent Evans, and a fourth friend, Richard Weiland, formed the Lakeside Programmers' Group to earn money using the computer.

Computer Center Corporation (CCC), a Seattle time sharing company, convinced the Lakeside School to shift their time sharing account to their company from General Electric. CCC offered free computer time to Lakeside programmers in return for finding bugs in its software. The four friends from Lakeside took advantage of CCC's offer and spent many hours learning about application programs, operating systems, and hardware. In March 1970, CCC went out of business. Gates and Evans purchased the DEC computer tapes from CCC at a bargain price and later sold them at a profit.

In early 1971, the Lakeside Programmers' Group accepted a contract with Information Sciences, Inc., a Portland time sharing company, to write a payroll program. The four classmates, who formed a partnership and completed the project successfully, were paid royalties and received computer time worth $10,000. Allen graduated from Lakeside in 1971 and enrolled at Washington State University, where he majored in computer science.

Gates and Allen formed a company, Traf-O-Data, to translate vehicle flow information collected by traffic boxes into usable reports. The traffic boxes, which were connected to rubber hoses placed across the road, produced output on 16-channel tape that municipalities used to set traffic-light timing. With the assistance of a Boeing engineer, Gates and Allen developed a computer to analyze the tapes directly, without the intermediary of punched cards. The two partners earned about $20,000 from this venture; the partnership lasted until Gates went to college.

In May 1972, in their junior year at Lakeside, Gates and Evans were asked to develop a program for generating the school's class schedules. Tragically, Evans was killed in a mountain climbing accident on Memorial Day weekend. A saddened Gates asked Allen to work with him on the project that summer. They earned about $2,000 for the program, which they then offered for sale, with modifications, to other schools in the area.

During his senior year at Lakeside, Gates was offered a job with TRW Corporation in Oregon to troubleshoot application programs that ran on the PDP-10. TRW had a contract to develop a power monitoring system for the Bonneville Power Administration's electric power grid for the northwestern United States. Gates immediately called Allen, who had dropped out of Washington State, to work on the project. Gates was given permission to skip the middle trimester of his senior year at Lakeside.

TRW had learned of Gates and Allen from DEC, which was familiar with their preparation of the PDP-10 Problem Report Book for CCC in Seattle. Gates returned to TRW for the summer before entering Harvard University. He became a more professional programmer while at TRW. John Norton mentored Gates that summer in Oregon, helping him to write more efficient code.

Gates and Allen talked about founding their own company some day. Allen said, "We always had big dreams." Gates was a driven individual with no shortage of self-confidence. When asked by a classmate just prior to graduation what his plans were for the future, Gates replied, "I'm going to make my first million by the time I'm twenty-five." The business experience that he had in high school contributed heavily to the success he achieved while still in his twenties.

Gates didn't consider himself a serious student at Harvard. He was permitted to take graduate courses in parallel with his undergraduate courses; his class schedule included two-thirds undergraduate courses and one-third graduate courses. He spent many hours on the PDP-10 at the Aiken Computer Center. His schedule was erratic; it included little time for sleep. Gates accepted a job programming for Honeywell in Boston that summer. He was joined by Allen, who stayed on at Honeywell after Gates returned to Harvard for his sophomore year.

Gates's energy wasn't all expended on academic pursuits. He played poker frequently. His roommate, Andy Braiterman, later commented that Gate's approach to poker reflected his approach to life: "Bill had a monomaniacal quality. He would focus on something and really stick with it. He had a determination to master whatever it was he was doing. Perhaps it's silly to compare poker and Microsoft, but in each case, Bill was sort of deciding where he was going to put his energy and to hell with what anyone else thought."

One of Gates's residence hall friends was Steve Ballmer, who later played a significant role in the development of Microsoft Corporation. Gates and Ballmer, an applied mathematics major, had high energy levels, were very intense, and required little sleep. They could absorb large quantities of information, a trait that in Gatesspeak is called "high bandwidth communication."

In December 1974, Allen was walking across Harvard Square to visit Gates when he saw the January issue of *Popular Electronics* at a news kiosk. The cover had a picture of the Altair 8800 with the headline "World's First Microcomputer Kit to Rival Commercial Models." When Allen saw Gates, he told him, "Well here's our opportunity to do something with BASIC."

The Altair 8800 was developed by Ed Roberts of Micro Instrumentation and Telemetry Systems (MITS) in Albuquerque, New Mexico. Based on the Intel 8080 microprocessor chip, it had 256 bytes of memory (expandable to 4K). It had neither a keyboard nor a display. Since a high-level programming language hadn't yet been written for the Intel 8080 microchip, the Altair had to be programmed in machine language by flipping switches on the front panel. It responded by flashing red lights near the switches.

Programming languages available for mainframe and minicomputers at the time included FORTRAN (Formula Translation), which is a scientific language, and COBOL (Common Business-Oriented Language). No BASIC programming language had yet been developed for the Intel 8080 microprocessor. Gates called Roberts to tell him that he and Allen had developed BASIC for the Altair 8800 and would license MITS to sell their software for royalty payments. Roberts said, "We just told everyone, including those guys, that whoever showed up first with a working BASIC had the deal."

After telling Roberts that they had a working BASIC, Gates and Allen worked furiously to develop it. They didn't have an Altair 8800 to use in developing their software, but this didn't slow them down. They bought an Intel 8080 manual written by Adam Osborne, who was an Intel engineer at the time. Gates and Allen developed their programs by simulating the Altair 8800 on the PDP-10 in the Aiken Computer Center at Harvard. Allen observed, "We were in the right place at the right time. Because of our previous experience, Bill and I had the necessary tools to be able to take advantage of this new situation."

With only 4K memory for both his operating system and application program, Gates was faced with a difficult challenge. He said, "It wasn't a matter of whether I could write the program, but rather if I could squeeze it into 4K and make it super fast. It was the coolest program I ever wrote."

In late February, Allen delivered the BASIC software to MITS in Albuquerque. While on the plane to New Mexico, Allen realized that they hadn't written a "bootstrap" program to load the BASIC software into the Altair 8800. He wrote the program in assembler language and completed it before his flight touched down in Albuquerque. Roberts met Allen at the airport and drove him to MITS, which was located in a mall in the previous home of "The Enchanted Sandwich Shop," adjacent to a laundromat and a massage parlor.

Allen keyed in his bootstrap program on the teletype connected to the Altair 8800 and loaded the BASIC program on paper tape. It worked on the first try. Roberts said: "I was dazzled. It was certainly impressive. The Altair was a complex system, and they had never seen it before. What they had done went a lot further than you could have reasonably expected. I'd been involved with the development of programs for computers for a long time, and I was very impressed that we got anywhere near as far as we did that day."

When he returned to Boston, Allen celebrated with Gates, but their celebrating was short-lived. Harvard found out that they had used the Aiken Computer Center PDP-10 to develop a commercial product. The university administration was concerned, and Gates was admonished for allowing Allen, who had no association with Harvard, to use the PDP-10. Gates wasn't formally reprimanded because there were no guidelines for using university computers.

Harvard implemented guidelines the following year. Gates and Allen purchased computer time from a time sharing service to finish their development work.

Allen moved to Albuquerque to get BASIC ready for the Altair 8800 and to make enhancements. In effect, he was the entire software development department for MITS; all of the other MITS employees were working overtime to fill the high volume of orders for the Altair. MITS received 4,000 orders within the first several weeks of the *Popular Electronics* article and went from $300,000 in the red to $250,000 in the black. The Altair was unreliable and had extremely limited functionality. Nevertheless, customers willingly mailed $495 checks to MITS to buy them.

Gates worked in Albuquerque during the summer of his sophomore year at Harvard. Gates and Allen realized that they should establish a formal partnership. Microsoft, which was originally Micro-Soft (for microcomputer software), was founded in the summer of 1975. The original ownership was sixty percent for Gates and forty percent for Allen, because Gates had done more of the BASIC development work.

Gates and Allen developed an 8K version of BASIC as well as extended versions that used 12K and 16K of memory. They signed an agreement giving MITS "exclusive, worldwide rights to use and license BASIC to third parties." The agreement included the key phrase "The company (MITS) agrees to use its best efforts to license, promote, and commercialize the Program (BASIC)."

Gates and Allen received $3,000 for signing the agreement, which stipulated royalties of $30 for each copy of the 4K version of BASIC sold with hardware, $35 for the 8K version, and $60 for the extended versions. Microsoft received fifty percent of all sales of software sold without hardware. Gates's father and an Albuquerque lawyer helped him draft the agreement, which pioneered software licensing agreements. Although he was only nineteen, Gates was the principal architect of the groundbreaking agreement.

Gates returned to Harvard in the fall and spent his time attending classes, studying, writing software, and negotiating agreements for Microsoft. Allen stayed in Albuquerque to work with MITS, which wasn't an efficiently run company. Among other problems, their circuit boards were unreliable, which reflected negatively both on MITS and Microsoft. Between semesters, Gates flew to Albuquerque to write the Disk BASIC software to be used with the floppy disk-based version of BASIC for the Altair.

Gates had to contend with software pirates, including members of computer clubs with loose practices—such as the Homebrew Computer Club of Menlo Park, California. The Altair with BASIC was demonstrated to the club. A club member picked up a punched paper tape containing BASIC from the floor next to the Altair, made copies of the program, and distributed the copies without charge at the next Club meeting. Gates was irate when he heard about it. He wrote "An Open Letter to Hobbyists" in the Altair newsletter, *Computer Notes*, complaining about computer hobbyists stealing his software programs.

Gates's letter created a stir in computer club circles. Many members responded angrily, claiming that the software was in the public domain. Gates published "A Second and Final Letter" in the April issue of the Altair newsletter, in which he toned down his accusations. He said that it wasn't his intention to make a blanket indictment of all computer hobbyists.

Gates and Allen chose FORTRAN as their next product to run on microcomputers. In late 1976, Microsoft signed contracts to provide BASIC to General Electric and to develop Stand-alone Disk BASIC for the NCR Corporation. Gates and Allen added programmers, including Chris Larson, Mark McDonald, and Richard Weiland from Lakeside, to the Microsoft staff. In January 1977, Gates dropped out of Harvard. His parents weren't happy with his decision.

According to the agreement with MITS, Microsoft had to obtain permission from MITS to sell Intel 8080 BASIC to other companies. Roberts of MITS didn't block these sales unless they were to direct competitors, which initially wasn't a problem. However, as the personal computer industry grew, the agreement limited Microsoft's growth potential. Three early MITS Altair competitors were the Commodore PET computer, the Radio Shack TRS-80, and Apple Corporation's Apple II.

The Microsoft royalty agreement with MITS included a cap on royalties of $180,000. Furthermore, Roberts was contemplating selling MITS to Pertec, a manufacturer of peripherals, including disk drives and tape drives. Gates realized that Microsoft had to get out of the agreement with MITS. He sent Roberts a letter terminating the agreement for several reasons, including Roberts's lack of success in using his "best efforts to license, promote, and commercialize BASIC." The agreement had stipulated that any arguments would be addressed by an arbitrator. Roberts filed a restraining order that dried up Microsoft's revenue stream for several months.

On May 22, 1977, Pertec purchased MITS from Roberts for Pertec stock worth several million dollars. Pertec wrote a letter to Gates containing the statement that "it would no longer market BASIC or allow it to be licensed because it considered all other hardware companies competitors." This was counter to the "best efforts" provision of the agreement with Microsoft. The arbitrator sided with Microsoft in a hearing that lasted three weeks.

This decision played a significant role in the shaping of the software industry and of Microsoft's role in it. Both MITS and Pertec had underestimated their twenty-one-year-old adversary, Bill Gates. In *Hard Drive*, James Wallace and Jim Erickson observed, "Given his white-hot drive, and his determination to trounce the opposition, to do whatever had to be done to dominate the software market, this rare combination of technical genius and managerial acumen was an unbeatable combination."

Gates signed a contract to supply Radio Shack with BASIC for its TRS-80 computer. He negotiated the contract with John Roach, vice-president of marketing, who later became president of Tandy Corporation, Radio Shack's parent. Roach was an advisor and mentor to Gates, particularly in the area of marketing. Gates looked for ways of expanding Microsoft's business. In 1977, he expanded its market into Japan through Kuzuhiko Nishi, a native of Kobe with similar interests to Gates in computers.

Gates and Allen realized that New Mexico wasn't the optimal location for a fast-growing software company. They considered two other locations, the San Francisco Bay area and Seattle. San Francisco was the location of Silicon Valley and many computer-related companies; however, Seattle was home. Allen had a strong preference for Seattle, and Gates felt that it would be easy to attract programmers to the Northwest. In December 1978, Microsoft moved to Seattle. For the first time, the start-up had its own computer, a DEC PDP-20, instead of time sharing on a school computer as in Albuquerque.

Software has three levels: the operating system; language, e.g. BASIC, FORTRAN, and COBOL; and application software, such as word processing and spreadsheet applications. The operating system, usually written in a low-level language such as assembly language, performs tasks such as selecting the portion of the disk to be written upon. Microsoft licensed the CP/M (Control Program for Microcomputers) operating system from Digital Research to use with their programming language packages, such as FORTRAN and COBOL.

The CP/M operating system was developed in late 1973 by Gary Kildall, the founder of Digital Research. In 1978, Kildall refined CP/M by separating the basic input-output system (BIOS) from the rest of the software package that included device-driver software for peripheral devices, such as disk and tape drives, monitors, and printers. Only the BIOS had to be modified to adapt CP/M for use with a new computer. In the late 1970s, CP/M was becoming the de facto standard operating system, even though Apple, Commodore, and Tandy all used their own operating systems. The popularity of CP/M was due partly to the efforts of its New York distributor, Lifeboat Associates, which had started as a CP/M users' club.

In 1980, observing the success of Apple Computer and others in the personal computer market, IBM decided to enter the market. In July 1980, IBM contacted Gates to discuss Microsoft's possible participation in their personal computer development effort. Jack Sams and two other IBMers met in the Microsoft offices in Bellevue with Gates, Allen, and Steve Ballmer, Gates's friend from Harvard, who had just joined Microsoft as the assistant to the president. Sams asked them to sign a document stating that they would treat all of their discussions as confidential, and that they would never sue IBM. The trio from Microsoft signed without hesitation.

In August, at a second meeting with IBM, Gates was asked if he could develop a BASIC program by April 1981, based on specifications for an 8-bit computer provided by IBM. Gates said that Microsoft could do it, but he suggested that it should be for a 16-bit computer, which was the next generation of microcomputers. In September, Sams asked Microsoft to furnish FORTRAN, COBOL, and Pascal, in addition to BASIC. Gates pointed out to IBM that he would need an operating system to use with the the FORTRAN and COBOL software, which currently used CP/M.

Gates contacted Kildall at Digital Research in Pacific Grove, California, and asked him to meet with a "very important client" of Microsoft. When the IBMers arrived at Digital Research, they found that Kildall was away on a business trip. They spoke with Dorothy McEwen, Kildall's wife, who was asked to sign the same confidentiality agreement that Microsoft had signed with IBM. Digital Research's general counsel advised her not to sign, and the meeting was concluded. When Kildall returned, he didn't object to signing the document, but other priorities caused him to put off IBM. IBM lost interest and turned to Microsoft.

Gates realized that Microsoft would have difficulty adding the workload of development of an operating system to its current development efforts for BASIC, FORTRAN, COBOL, and Pascal. He contacted Tim Paterson of Seattle Computer Products, who had developed an operating system for use with their new 16-bit computer. Paterson had programmed QDOS (Quick and Dirty Operating System) to allow programs written for use with CP/M to be easily ported to QDOS. Microsoft licensed QDOS from Paterson.

In October 1980, Gates and Ballmer met with IBM in Boca Raton, Florida, to discuss a contract for developing software for the IBM personal computer. The Microsoft contingent was late for the meeting because Gates had forgotten to bring a necktie, and he had to stop at a store to buy one.

The Microsoft cause was aided by a conversation that Don Estridge, who was responsible for IBM's personal computer development, had with John Opel, IBM's chief executive officer, several days earlier at lunch. Estridge mentioned to Opel that he was negotiating with Microsoft to develop software for IBM. Opel said, "Oh, that's run by Bill Gates, Mary Gates's son." Opel knew Mary Gates from serving on the national board of the United Way. The contract between IBM and Microsoft was signed on November 6, 1980.

Microsoft knew that other companies were interested in using QDOS. Microsoft had a nonexclusive license with Seattle Computer to use QDOS; Seattle Computer could negotiate licenses with other companies. In 1981, Microsoft negotiated with Seattle Computer to obtain an exclusive agreement. Before the contract was signed, Gates personally changed the wording so that, for

$50,000, Microsoft would own QDOS and license it back to Seattle Computer.

Rod Brock, the owner of Seattle Computer, needed the $50,000 to pay for ongoing development and, since he had recently lost the services of QDOS developer Paterson, liked the idea of receiving updates to the operating system from Microsoft. He wasn't the only one who failed to perceive the potential market for personal computer software. By 1991, the operating system he sold for $50,000 had earned in excess of $200 million for Microsoft.

For two years after the IBM personal computer was introduced, MS-DOS (Microsoft Disk Operating System renamed from QDOS) and CP/M vied for leadership of the operating system market for personal computers. Eventually, the success of IBM's personal computer with its effective Charlie Chaplin-like "Little Tramp" advertising campaign assured that MS-DOS would win the race.

After 1983, Allen no longer played an active role in running Microsoft. He resigned from Microsoft's board of directors in 1985 to form his own software development company.

On October 28, 1985, the board of directors of Microsoft Corporation met to decide whether to proceed with an initial public offering of Microsoft stock. Frank Gaudette, Microsoft's chief financial officer, guided the effort of going public. Microsoft chose Goldman, Sachs as the lead underwriter and Alex Brown & Sons as the specialty investment banker.

On March 13, 1986, public trading of Microsoft's stock opened at $25.75. Two and a half million shares were traded on the first day of trading, and Microsoft's stock was worth $661 million. Gates owned forty-five percent of the total shares, which was worth $311 million after selling 80,000 shares. Allen owned 6,390,000 shares, twenty-eight percent of the total, before selling 200,000 shares. Ballmer owned stock worth $35 million after selling shares worth $630,000. By March 1987, Microsoft stock had climbed to $84.75, and Gates had become a billionaire at the age of thirty-one. Allen's twenty-two percent of the stock was worth $640 million.

Microsoft was phenomenally successful throughout the 1980s. In February 1986, Microsoft moved into new facilities on 400 forested acres in Evergreen Place, Redmond, Washington. The original four X-shaped buildings were designed to be egalitarian. Everyone had a private office of the same size; there were no private parking spaces. In 1987, Microsoft became the largest micro-computer software company.

Bill Gates has always been the fundamental ingredient of Microsoft's success. He stayed focused in addressing the problems and the future of Microsoft. Stewart Alsop, a highly regarded observer of the computer industry, commented:

> People are scared of Microsoft because they are so persistent. They have executed better than any other company. Others don't feel they are capable of competing with Microsoft. It's a lack of self-confidence. Every other company has screwed up. Does Microsoft have an unfair advantage that results in inferior products in the industry? That's the myth. That's what all the competitors want you to believe . . . Microsoft has made it harder to compete because it's constantly addressing problems. The reason that Microsoft has such a hold on the industry . . . is that they make better products.

By 1996, Gates was worth over $14.8 billion and over five to six times that by the end of the decade. However, net worth is not the only measure of success; it certainly isn't Bill Gates's principal measure. He has remained focused on the needs of the software industry and has persevered in creating the software products to meet those needs.

CHAPTER 6

ENGINEERS / SCIENTISTS

"Man unites himself with the world in the process of creation."

Eric Fromm, *The Art of Loving*

REGINALD J. MITCHELL (1895-1937) Designer of the Supermarine Spitfire

"When things go wrong, as they sometimes will,
When the road you're trudging seems all uphill,
... When care is pressing you down a bit,
Rest, if you must—but don't you quit.
... Often the goal is nearer than
It seems to a faint and faltering man,
Often the struggler has given up
When he might have captured the victor's cup."

Edgar A. Guest

Reginald Joseph Mitchell was born on May 20, 1895, in the English village of Talke, Staffordshire. His father was a teacher who later became a school headmaster. At the age of seventeen, Mitchell was apprenticed to Kerr, Stewart, and Company locomotive works at Stoke-on-Trent. He studied mechanics and mathematics as part of his engineering studies in addition to studying drafting in night school. In 1917, he accepted the position of assistant to the chief engineer and designer at the Supermarine Aviation works near Southampton. Mitchell was married in 1918 and settled in Southampton. In 1920, he was promoted to chief engineer and designer at Supermarine. At the time, most of his projects involved the design of large military flying boats such as the Martlesham Amphibian, for which he won a government prize.

"RJ" Mitchell established his reputation as an aircraft designer by creating aircraft to compete in the Schneider international seaplane races from 1922 to 1931. The Schneider Trophy race was the world's major aeronautical event. Lieutenant James Doolittle of the U.S. Army was the winner of the race in Baltimore in 1925; he flew a Curtiss biplane on twin floats at an average speed of 232.57 miles per hour. Britain won the Schneider race in 1929 and again in 1930. Britain would become the permanent holder of the Schneider cup with a win in 1931.

Due to the worldwide depression in the 1930s, government expenditures were significantly reduced. Prime Minister Ramsay MacDonald decided not to finance an entry in the 1931 Schneider cup race. The British public protested strongly. In January 1931, Lady Houston, the wealthy widow of a shipping magnate, contributed £100,000 to finance an entry in the 1931 race. The Supermarine S.6B, winner of the 1931 Schneider Trophy, was an early prototype of the Spitfire fighter aircraft. Thus a private citizen, Lady Houston, was a contributor to the development effort of one of the high-performance fighter aircraft of World War II.

All of the major design criteria for the evolving Spitfire had been defined by the summer of 1935. Changes to the design incorporated into the final prototype, which was built in the fall of 1935, included a thinner, elliptically-shaped wing, ducted radiator cooling, and eight machine guns instead of the four machine guns originally specified.

Mitchell was appointed chief designer but unfortunately was able to spend only limited time on the project. In 1933, "RJ" was diagnosed as having cancer and underwent surgery. If he had followed his doctor's advice and either taken an extended leave of absence or reduced his efforts, he might have been cured of cancer, or at least have extended his life. However, he continued to drive himself to develop the Spitfire prototype.

Mitchell was motivated by a visit to Germany in 1934, where he observed the production of military hardware by the Nazis. He was familiar with the Dornier, Heinkel, and Junkers airplanes, and he knew about the Bayerische Flugzeugwerke BF 109 fighter (the ME 109), which was designed by Willie Messerschmitt. Mitchell strongly believed that Britain must respond to the German threat and that Britain needed reliable, high-performance fighters that could be produced in quantity. He drove himself to ensure that his greatest design effort, the Spitfire, would be ready in time to defend England against a German attack.

On March 5, 1936, Spitfire prototype K5054 flew for the first time; it was piloted by chief test pilot J. "Mutt" Summers from the Eastleigh Airport in Hampshire. Mitchell watched his airplane perform. He knew that his perseverance had been rewarded, and that he had accomplished what he had set out to do—to create a revolutionary high-performance fighter for which a critical need existed. Having a high-performance aircraft was crucial for England in the late 1930s, when war was increasingly seen as unavoidable.

The two principal British fighter aircraft in World War II were the Spitfire and the Hawker Hurricane, which was designed by Sidney Camm. The Hurricane was actually a monoplane version of the Hawker Fury biplane that Camm had designed earlier. The Hurricane was more of a traditional aircraft in that it was built of wood and fabric and stiffened by tubular metal framework. Surprisingly, the fabric-covered fuselage survived cannon shells better than the metal-skinned Spitfire.

The Hurricane was a design halfway between the biplanes of the 1930s and the aircraft design of the 1940s, such as the Spitfire. In the Battle of Britain, the Hurricanes actually downed more German aircraft than the Spitfires, because of the way they were deployed. The faster Spitfires were assigned to engage the German fighters escorting their bombers. The Hurricanes, although slower than the Spitfires, provided an excellent gun platform for attacking the German bombers.

The ME 109 was the leading German fighter; it had similar flight characteristics to the Spitfire. The ME 109 had a tighter turning radius than the Spitfire, but the pilots rarely used this advantage because the ME 109's wings weren't strong enough to withstand the stress of tight turns. The visibility provided by the Spitfire's bubble canopy was superior to the ME 109, whose view to the rear was blocked by the fuselage. Also, the Spitfire pilot had the advantage of armor plate behind his seat. Mitchell never fully regained his strength after his operation in 1933. His condition worsened in early 1937, and his wife, Florence, accompanied him on a visit to a specialist in Austria; however, his cancer was too advanced to operate again. He returned to Southampton, where he died at his home in June 1937 at the age of forty-two.

The importance of Mitchell's design efforts should not be underestimated. A high-performance fighter, such as the Spitfire, was critically needed in the Battle of Britain to counter Germany's high-performance ME 109. By winning the Battle of Britain, England prevented Hitler's planned invasion across the English channel, and Hitler turned his attention to Russia.

Mitchell's drive in pushing the development of the Spitfire while in failing health resulted in an important contribution to Britain's war effort. It is virtually certain that Mitchell would have received a knighthood for his design efforts had he lived, as Sir Sidney Camm did for his design of the Hawker Hurricane.

ROBERT GODDARD (1882-1945) Rocketry Pioneer

"The secret of discipline is motivation. When a man [or a woman] is sufficiently motivated, discipline will take care of itself."

Sir Alexander Paterson

On October 19, 1899, at age seventeen, Robert Goddard climbed a large cherry tree in the backyard of his home to prune dead branches. He had recently read H. G. Well's *War of the Worlds*, which at least partially explains the significant emotional event that occurred.

He climbed down from the tree and made the following entry in his diary: "As I looked toward the fields at the east, I imagined how wonderful it would be to make some device which has even the possibility of ascending to Mars, and how it would look on a small scale, if sent up from the meadow at my feet . . . I was a different boy when I descended the tree from when I ascended, for existence at last seemed very purposive."

That phrase, "for existence at last seemed very purposive," was a great motivator for Goddard's subsequent endeavors. He felt that he now had a purpose in life and a goal to develop something that would go higher than anything had gone previously. Every year for the remainder of his life, he viewed October 19 as his "Anniversary Day."

Goddard began his research with rockets as an undergraduate at Worcester Polytechnic Institute and as a graduate student at Clark University. While recovering from an illness in 1913, he developed rocket designs. During this time, he applied to the U.S. Patent Office for the first two of approximately 200 patents he was granted in his lifetime. His first patent described the characteristics required by all modern rockets: a combustion chamber with a nozzle, a pump to force fuel into the combustion chamber, and the propellant, either solid or liquid, which burns in the combustion chamber.

Goddard's second patent outlined the concept of the multistage rocket that is the forerunner of all high-altitude rockets in use today. Earlier, Goddard investigated the efficiency of rocket fuel. A simple rocket using gunpowder placed in a cylinder closed at one end and ignited uses only about two or three percent of the energy of the fuel. His two principal goals were to improve the basic design of the rocket and to develop an improved propellant.

By the fall of 1914, Goddard was well enough to resume work on a part-time basis on the faculty of Clark University. Within a year, he had built some of the rockets that he had designed. He developed a nozzle design to improve propellant efficiency and to generate more thrust. By the summer of 1915, working with solid-fuel rockets, he had achieved a fuel efficiency of forty percent and was recording ejection velocities of 6,700 feet per second. After many partial successes, he launched a rocket that reached a height of 486 feet and had an ejection velocity of just under 8,000 feet per second.

Goddard realized that he could not afford to continue his research on his own. He wanted to begin his experiments with liquid fuels, and he knew that the effort would be costly. He wrote a paper to describe his rocket theory, the mathematics that supported it, and his expectations for further development. He forwarded his paper entitled "A Method of Reaching Extreme Altitudes" to several scientific institutions to promote interest in his endeavors.

The Smithsonian Institution, whose stated propose is the increase of knowledge, was one of the institutions to which he sent his paper. In his letter to the Smithsonian, he wrote, "For a number of years, I have been at work on a method of raising recording apparatus to altitudes exceeding the limit of sounding balloons . . . I have reached the limit of the work I can do singlehanded, both because of the expense and also because further work will require more than one man's time." Goddard and the Smithsonian scientists knew that it would be useful for meteorologists to have additional knowledge of the atmosphere hundreds of miles from the earth's surface.

The Smithsonian Institution decided to support Goddard's projects. Goddard provided the status of his development effort to the Smithsonian on a regular basis. In one of his communications, he mentioned the potential usefulness of rockets in wartime. When the United States declared war in 1917, Dr. Abbott of the Smithsonian passed on his suggestions to the U.S. Army Signal Corps.

Goddard left his teaching position at Clark University and began working on a rocket to be used by the U.S. Infantry against enemy tanks. A successful demonstration was conducted in the fall of 1918 at the Aberdeen Proving Grounds in Maryland. It appeared that this weapon, the forerunner of the World War II bazooka, would be put into immediate production. However, with the signing of the armistice on November 11, 1918, the U.S. Army suspended their interest in rockets for over twenty years.

Goddard returned to Clark University and evolved his designs for nose cones, combustion chambers, and nozzles; he also investigated liquid fuels. He realized early that liquid hydrogen and liquid oxygen would be an optimal fuel. However, liquid hydrogen was very difficult to manage, so he searched for a substitute. He chose gasoline since it was inexpensive and relatively dependable. Handling liquid oxygen was also problematical since its boiling point is 298 degrees below zero Fahrenheit, and it had to be kept under pressure.

Goddard conducted tests of his liquid fuel rockets at a farm owned by a family friend. He first launched a liquid-fuel rocket flight on March 16, 1926. The rocket reached a height four times its length and a speed of sixty miles an hour while traveling a distance of 220 feet. He had to redesign the original rocket because the combustion chamber burned through due to the intense heat. Use of sheet steel was a short-term solution to the problem. He experimented with increasingly large rockets, and he added a thermometer and a barometer as well as a small camera to record the instrument readings.

In July 1929, Goddard had his most successful flight so far. The rocket gained an altitude of ninety feet and traveled 171 feet in its eighteen and one-half seconds of flight. As Goddard and his associates picked up the reusable pieces of the rocket, the crash site was visited by an ambulance, several police cars, and cars with signs marked "Press." They had received a report of an airplane crash. This incident gave the rocket experiments bad publicity. The Smithsonian Institution supported Goddard by explaining that he was attempting to collect weather information at high altitudes. Commonwealth officials would not allow any more experimental rocket flights to be conducted in Massachusetts, however.

Goddard and his assistants looked for a more compatible location to resume rocket testing. They considered the amount of rainfall, topological factors, and general climate conditions and chose

Roswell, New Mexico, for future tests. In addition to the favorable climate, the area around Roswell was sparsely settled and met their criterion of having few neighbors to become alarmed by the noise of their experiments.

The first major test at the Roswell site was in December 1930. The purpose was to determine if compressed nitrogen gas from an outside tank could be used, when routed through tubes to the fuel and oxidizer tanks, to force gasoline and liquid oxygen into the combustion chambers. In this successful flight, the rocket reached a speed of 500 miles per hour and an altitude of two thousand feet and traveled 1,000 feet from the launch tower.

Goddard experienced continuing problems with the burning through of the narrow opening between the combustion chamber and the nozzle. He tried different metals but finally concluded that the walls of the combustion chamber needed cooling. He solved this problem by using curtain cooling. He evolved a design in which gasoline was sprayed on the inner wall of the combustion chamber prior to its ignition.

In effect, he placed a layer of burning gas around the inside of the combustion chamber that, because it was cooler than the burning gasoline and oxygen in the center of the chamber, resulted in the necessary cooling. In future tests, the problem of rocket engines burning through was reduced considerably. He also experimented with placing parachutes in the nose cone to lessen damage to the rockets as they returned to earth.

On April 19, 1932, Goddard conducted his first test of a rocket equipped with a gyroscope to control the guidance vanes of the rocket. These adjustable vanes were used to keep the rocket on a vertical course longer than had been possible previously. Also, the gyroscope was used to release the parachute as the rocket approached its maximum altitude.

The Guggenheim Foundation, which supported Goddard's research when the need for funds exceeded the amount provided by the Smithsonian Institution, was unable to provide support for the years 1933 and 1934. Goddard returned to Worcester and resumed teaching at Clark University. Resumption of the support from the Smithsonian Institution allowed Goddard to continue his design efforts.

The most significant development during Goddard's time back

in Worcester was a combustion chamber in which atmospheric air was used as the oxidizer. Obviously, this would not work for a high altitude rocket, but it worked for a rocket that traveled horizontally at low altitudes. This type of rocket could be much lighter than a high altitude rocket since it would not have to carry a tank of liquid oxygen.

Goddard used a funnel as the air intake at the front of the rocket motor. The air passed by a shutter-type intake valve on its way to the combustion chamber. The air came in while the shutters were open, the shutters closed, and combustion occurred, providing the thrust. Then the shutter opened and the process was repeated over again. This concept was used by the Germans on their V-1 rocket of World War II. The air resonance noise of the shutter opening and closing was the unusual sound that gave the "buzz-bomb" its name.

The Guggenheim Foundation resumed its support of Goddard's work in the fall of 1934. By this point, Goddard had concluded that the current design was too complex, and that it must be simplified to increase reliability. He wanted to eliminate the need for nitrogen gas and its associated tank and to use centrifugal pumps to force liquid oxygen and gasoline into the combustion chambers. The size of the tanks and their weight was the main difficulty. Goddard and his associates worked until 1940 to reduce the size and weight of the tanks and pumps.

By 1937, German scientists were performing rocket experiments at a large, liquid-propellant facility at Peenemunde. The Nazi government provided ample financial backing; they had an operational V-2 rocket by 1943.

In May 1940, Harry Guggenheim of the Guggenheim Foundation called a meeting of representatives of the armed forces that provided Goddard an opportunity to present his work and to promote the potential of liquid-propellant rockets in time of war. The Army representative stated that the next war, which had already started in Europe, "will be won by trench mortars." The only interest expressed by Army Air Corps and Navy authorities was for a rocket motor to assist short runway take-off of heavily loaded aircraft.

This joint Army Air Corps and Navy project was the first one assigned to Goddard to aid the war effort. Out of this work came the JATO unit, the jet-assisted take-off device that used solid fuel.

His next assignment was to develop a rocket motor with variable thrust that could be controlled by a pilot. This engine design was successful; a version of it was used later on the X-2 and the X-15 experimental aircraft. His last assignment was the development of a small liquid oxygen and gasoline-powered rocket for use in a guided missile.

Goddard laid out the principles underlying rocket flight, and all modern rockets evolved from concepts developed by him; unfortunately, the United States did not take advantage of his work. Documentation of many of Goddard's early rocket designs was provided upon request. Some of it was technical literature available from the Smithsonian Institution. German rocket scientists, including Werner Von Braun, acknowledged openly that their work was based on Goddard's earlier development.

Robert Goddard is example of an individual whose early academic work was not notable, but, once he had a firm goal in mind, he applied himself to achieve that goal. He was motivated to add to his chosen body of knowledge, even though he received little recognition for his efforts.

PALO ALTO RESEARCH CENTER Personal Computer Pioneers

"The scientists at PARC created more than a personal computer. They designed, built, and used a complete system of hardware and software that fundamentally altered the nature of computing itself. Along the way, an impressive list of digital 'firsts' came out of PARC. In addition to the Alto computer, PARC inventors made the first graphics-oriented monitor, the first hand-held 'mouse' inputting device simple enough for a child, the first word processing program for inexpert users, the first local area communications network, the first object-oriented programming language, and the first laser printer."

Douglas K. Smith and Robert C. Alexander, *Fumbling the Future*

In 1973, over three years before Steve Wozniak of Apple Computer designed and built the Apple I, Xerox's Palo Alto Research Center (PARC) created the first computer dedicated to the use of one person. PARC did more than design and build a computer. Its developers introduced a comprehensive system of hardware and software that changed the environment of computing. PARC called their computer Alto and its environment "personal distributed computing": "personal" because it was designed for use by an individual and "distributed" because it was connected via a network to shared resources, such as printers and other computers.

PARC was unable to convince anyone within Xerox to exploit the technology. PARC was a development and research center, not a manufacturing and marketing organization. The technology languished. Xerox failed to capitalize on their dramatic developments. Apple Corporation promoted the technology and became associated with the introduction of the personal computer. After Apple's initial success, Xerox introduced the Star computer, which was too late and too expensive. Xerox had missed the opportunity.

Xerox established PARC in 1970 as part of the company's plan to acquire or develop digital capability. IBM was entering the copier business, and Xerox knew that they had to expand into the computer business to remain competitive. However, Xerox didn't plan to take on IBM in large mainframe computers. Their goal was to fight it out with IBM in developing products for the "office of the future." In other words, they would develop and market equipment and systems to be used by managers and secretaries as well as by production and sales personnel.

Peter McColough, who had succeeded founder Joe Wilson as CEO of Xerox in 1968, decided to buy and expand an existing computer company rather than form a start-up. He approached Control Data Corporation, Digital Equipment Corporation, and the Burroughs Corporation, but no mutually beneficial agreements could be reached. In 1969, Xerox paid $900 million for Scientific Data Systems (SDS), a California-based company that had sales of $100 million in the previous year. Most of the SDS customers were in technical computing, but McColough planned to reorient his new acquisition to commercial computing markets.

SDS had no independent development laboratory. Jack Goldman, who succeeded John Dessauer as director of research at Xerox in 1968, recommended to McColough that Xerox establish a digital research and development center. McColough approved the request, and a talented team of scientists and engineers was assembled at Palo Alto to provide Xerox with future-oriented digital capability. Goldman chose George Pake, a well-regarded physicist with experience in both academia and industry, to establish and manage the new center.

Both Goldman and Pake believed in hiring highly capable people and then following a "bottom up" rather than a "top down" approach to research. Overall goals were conveyed to the researchers, but it was left up to them to tell their managers what they had to do to accomplish them. After all, development of the "architecture of information" involved in moving to the "office of the future" wasn't immediately obvious to high-level managers.

Pake divided the lab into three components:

- The General Science Laboratory (GSL)—conducted research in physics and other basic sciences
- The Systems Science Laboratory (SSL)—was responsible for broad "systems" research in engineering, information, mathematics, operations, and statistics
- The Computer Science Laboratory (CSL)—focused on com-

puter systems

Pake managed the GSL in addition to the laboratory as a whole. Bill Gunning, who had twenty years of computer science experience, was appointed to manage SSL. Jerry Elkind was selected to head CSL. Elkind had worked for NASA and for the computer consultant that designed ARPANet, the first nationwide computer communications network, for the Advanced Research Projects Administration (ARPA) of the Department of Defense. Bob Taylor, who had served as ARPA's chief administrator of computer funding, was named associate director of CSL.

With the high cost of mainframe computers and minicomputers that cost over $100,000, time-sharing was a popular tool. Many users at different terminals were connected to one central computer and shared its use.

Computers were considered fast and people were considered slow, so this was viewed as a good arrangement. However, it caused many computer scientists to work odd hours, such as the middle of the night, to gain access to the central computer. Developers' schedules were slaves to the computer's schedule. As the cost of computers came down due to the increased use of integrated circuits and microprocessors, an alternative to time-sharing was sought. Taylor recommended a "one computer, one person" solution to the problem.

CSL computer scientist Alan Kay had described a tool called FLEX in his 1969 doctoral dissertation that fit Taylor's concept. It was an interactive tool. "It must be simple enough so that one doesn't have to be a systems programmer to use it, and it must be cheap enough to be owned. It must do more than just be able to recognize computable functions." FLEX was an "idea debugger" and, as such, it was hoped that it was also an "idea media." Kay proposed that PARC develop a FLEX-like computer called "Dynabook," which he referred to as a "dynamic media for creative thought." When the Dynabook project was turned down by Xerox management, he countered with a project called "interim Dynabook."

Interest in the project began to build within the CSL, and Taylor obtained approval to develop a computer that met the "one person, one computer" criterion. It was called Alto. CSL scientist Butler Lampson described it as having an enhanced display monitor, being virtually as powerful as a minicomputer, operating in a network of distributed machines, and being affordable. He referred to the use of such a computer as "personal computing." Computer scientist Chuck Thacker had some ideas on putting it together. Their goals were to make it both better and cheaper than a minicomputer.

Lampson and Thacker used some of the tools developed by Douglas Englebart, an early advocate of interactive computing, including an input device called a "mouse" and displays that could be divided into multiple "windows." Englebart's mouse was a bulky analog device that was converted into a digital tool and made smaller and more reliable.

Lampson and Thacker planned to improve Englebart's displays. They favored a technique called bit-mapping, which associated each picture element (pixel) with a specific bit of computer memory. Specific binary bits are programmed to be "on "(one) while others are "off" (zero); in combination the bits create a character on the screen and retain it in memory for later use. Unfortunately, this one-to-one relationship of pixels on the screen with bits in the computer's memory required a large storage capacity and was expensive.

Another Alto innovation was multitasking, which allowed one processor to operate as many. A task was performed according to its priority. Multitasking slowed Alto down because the bit-mapped display used the processor two-thirds of the time, but provided more functionality for less cost. In April 1973, after four months of work, the first Alto was completed. Ten Altos were built by the end of the year, and forty were completed by the following summer.

However, hardware alone doesn't make a computer system. Still needed to obtain benefit from the machine were an operating system, programming languages, and application software. As the software became available, three applications were emphasized: communications, printing, and word processing.

The communications tool developed by Robert Metcalfe was called Ethernet, which didn't use telephone lines but relied on local cable runs within a building. Ethernet connected an Alto to shared equipment, such as printers and other Altos. PARC also developed the xerographic laser printer. Laser printers were expensive, but sharing them reduced the cost to individual computer users.

Lampson and CSL scientist Charles Simonyi developed a word processing application called "Bravo," which allowed the word image on the screen to be the same as that which was output by the printer. This feature, which was called "wysiwyg" for "what you see is what you get" wasn't available on earlier word processing packages. Subsequently, a more user-friendly version, called "Gypsy," was developed. Alto was used successfully in an experiment at Ginn & Company, a Xerox textbook publishing subsidiary, to streamline the publishing process.

The Alto effort seemed to be prepared for takeoff. Thacker observed, "It was certainly from my own experience the largest piece of creative effort I have seen anywhere. And it was like being there at the creation. A lot of people worked harder than I have ever seen, or have seen since, doing a thing they all felt was worthwhile, and really thought would change the world." However, no attempt was made to translate PARC's developments into products.

Xerox faced many challenges at the time. In 1972, the Federal Trade Commission (FTC) claimed that the company was monopolizing the plain paper copier market. The FTC accused Xerox of manipulating patent laws, setting prices that were discriminatory, insisting on leases over sales of equipment, and exploiting the market by using joint ownership arrangements with Rank in England and Fuji in Japan. In July 1975, the FTC discontinued the antitrust action. In order to comply with FTC demands, Xerox had to give up its patents, change its pricing policies, and allow supplies such as toner to be sold by other companies.

In late 1973, CEO McColough and president Archie McCardell, a Ford Motor Company financial executive who had joined Xerox in 1971 upon the death of Xerox founder Joseph Wilson, formed a team of four people to plan the future strategy of Xerox. The team was headed by Michael Hughes, who had a corporate planning background, and included George Pake, who had been assigned to corporate headquarters after directing PARC for three years.

The team evaluated four distinct strategies for Xerox and recommended the alternative that pursued the office of the future. They suggested combining computers, copiers, and word-processing typewriters with PARC's innovations in communications, microcircuitry, and software. No action was taken on their recommendation by Xerox management.

Xerox research director Goldman thought that PARC's inventions would be brought to market by SDS. When SDS hemorrhaged financially during the first half of the 1970s, he realized that another avenue would have to be used to capitalize on PARC's innovations. As the emphasis on financial analysis practiced by ex-Ford executives became prevalent at Xerox, Goldman's influence as the senior technical person waned.

In January 1973, Bob Potter became the General Manager of Xerox's Office Products Division, which was responsible for developing and manufacturing office products other than copiers. The division had few successes other than developing a popular facsimile machine. Potter wanted to move the division from Rochester, New York, to another location. Dallas and Silicon Valley were two of the favored locations. Goldman lobbied strongly for Silicon Valley because PARC was located there. However, Dallas was chosen for strictly financial reasons, such as lower costs for labor, taxes, and transportation. The financial types had won again; PARC was to remain isolated from the rest of the company. In Goldman's opinion, this decision had the greatest negative impact of any single decision on the future of digital technology at Xerox.

Potter visited PARC and observed the Alto technology, but decided to concentrate on word processing technology. Although his background was in both technology and operations, he thought that PARC's ideas were too futuristic. Also, he was influenced by the Xerox financial people, who emphasized short-term profits.

PARC was disappointed that the word "software" didn't enter into Potter's plans for Dallas. They thought that products that weren't programmable, such as Potter's electro-mechanical devices, would fail. Within a year and a half of entering the market, Potter's word-processing typewriter was out of date because of its display and communications shortcomings. Xerox's Display Word Processing Task Force recommended that the new word processor be Alto-based. However, a team from Dallas recalculated PARC's estimates for the new product and concluded that the Alto would take longer to build and cost more than the estimates. The task force's recommendation was ignored. Next, Goldman proposed that a small entrepreneurial team be formed to produce a general-purpose workstation using the Alto. That idea was also rejected.

The recession in 1974-75 impacted Xerox. The company found that customers made as many copies in bad times as in good times, but they made them with existing machines. They didn't buy or lease new copiers during a slowed economy. However, the greatest negative impact on Xerox was the staggering loss from the Scientific Data Systems acquisition. Taking on IBM head-to-head in the "office of the future" wasn't working.

Combining the copier and the computer businesses in a functional organization grouped by design and manufacturing, marketing and service, and planning had removed the focus of the computer business. In effect, SDS drifted without a general manager. In July 1975, CEO McColough admitted that the SDS acquisition had been a mistake. No buyer for SDS could be found. Xerox took a write-off of just under $1.3 billion and left the computer business.

In 1975-76, the Office Products Division began to manufacture the laser printer developed at PARC; a patent was received for Ethernet; and the Systems Development Division (SDD) was formed to translate PARC inventions into products. Some PARC-developed products were entering the marketplace. However, Xerox wasn't prepared to exploit the advances made on the Alto.

In 1976, PARC researcher John Ellenby was authorized to produce hundreds of Altos for use with laser printers within Xerox. He thought that at last technology transfer from the lab to the users was beginning to happen. In August 1976, Ellenby submitted a proposal on Alto to the Xerox task force determining new product strategies for the company. No action was taken on his proposal.

Ellenby was pleased when he was asked to organize the 1977 "Futures Day," at which Xerox showcased its new products within the company. His team worked hard and thought that they had made a strong case for proceeding with the Alto. By this time, McCardell had left Xerox to become CEO of International Harvester, and David Kearns from IBM had taken his place as president and chief operating officer. Ellenby was informed that Kearns had decided not to go into production with the Alto.

In 1979, a Xerox investment unit contacted Steve Jobs about investing in Apple. Jobs requested and received a tour of the PARC facility. Larry Tesler demonstrated Alto for Jobs, who saw its potential immediately. He asked, "Why isn't Xerox marketing this? You could blow everybody away." Once Jobs knew that it could be done, he set out to duplicate it at Apple. He hired Tesler immediately and later Alan Kay, who eventually became an Apple Fellow. Most of the "look and feel" of the Alto that provided its ease of use eventually was incorporated into the Apple Macintosh. Xerox was amazingly open with their technology.

In 1978, Xerox combined the Office Products Division in Dallas with other non-copier units. General Manager Potter left to join McCardell at International Harvester as chief technical officer. In 1979, the Office Products Division was again made independent, and Don Massaro hired from Shugart Associates to be Potter's replacement as General Manager. Massaro, who was known as an entrepreneurial type, announced a new word processor, readied two facsimile machines for the market, announced PARC's Ethernet as a product, and started an electronic typewriter project within the first year. Soon he became interested in Star, a product that had evolved from the Alto.

Massaro asked Xerox management for $15 million to make and sell the Star and was turned down. He scaled down his request and was turned down again. He proceeded on his own using his division's budget. The Star's strength, like Alto's, was its "user interface," including the contents of the screen and the tools provided to work with the display. The Star used icons, action choice menus, and multiple screen windows along with electronic file cabinets, in and out boxes, and wastebaskets. The Star was designed to be used by managers.

Much of the software had already been designed when a decision was made to replace the processor. Hardware is usually designed before software, and compromises had to be made that slowed the speed of the machine to incorporate the new processor. It was the first personal computer to offer the bit-map screen, a laser printer, the mouse, combined text and graphics in the same document, and "what you see is what you get" word processing.

However, it had limitations in addition to its slow speed:

- Because it was a distributed system, it was more expensive than a stand-alone computer. ($16,595 for the workstation, five times the cost of a stand-alone personal computer).
- It didn't offer a spreadsheet.
- Its design was based on a closed architecture, not an open architecture, and suppliers could not make and sell components to be used with it.
- Its programming language wasn't available to the public (only Xerox employees could write application software for it).

- It wasn't compatible with other computers.

In April 1981, the Star was introduced—eight years after the invention of the Alto. It wasn't a successful product; however, the Star (the Xerox 820) was the first personal computer introduced by a Fortune 500 Corporation.

Mishandling the introduction of the personal computer by Xerox was a classic case of missing an opportunity. Unfortunately for Xerox, the technology developed at PARC was exploited by others and Xerox didn't receive the benefit of its labors. An incredible body of talent had been assembled at PARC during the 1970s. Some of the key people seeded the laboratories of other companies: for example, Charles Simonyi, who was hired by the Microsoft Corporation. Butler Lampson, Bob Taylor, and Chuck Thacker joined the Systems Research Center of the Digital Equipment Corporation. In 1984, they received the System Software Award from the Association of Computing Machinery for the invention of personal distributed computing. In 1987, President Reagan awarded George Pake the National Medal of Science for the notable accomplishments of PARC.

STEVE JOBS (1955-2011) Founder of Apple Inc., Innovator

"His tenacity is what makes him great. Several years after leaving Steve's employ, Susan Barnes conducted a study about family run businesses. She found that the key to success was 'pure staying power, persistence, continually believing in something, doggedness to get things done, and continual optimism.' That was a good description of Steve Jobs. Steve was beaten down many times but 'he kept getting off the mat,' she says."

Alan Deutschman, *The Second Coming of Steve Jobs*

Steve Jobs was the first to envision that people would buy a computer for their home because they wanted to do some business tasks or to run educational applications for themselves or their children. Furthermore, he foresaw the need to link the home with a "nationwide communications network," now called the Internet. Jobs's role in the formation of the personal computer industry is described by Nathan Aaseng in *Business Builders in Computers:*

> Steve Jobs was the first person who saw the personal computer as a mass consumer product. He triggered the transformation of personal computers from hobby toys into useful products for the home and business. Jobs then went on to introduce a second revolution in personal computers—the user-friendly, point and click operating systems that are now standard. While Jobs did not originate the ideas that went into the Macintosh . . . his drive and energy helped bring the revolutionary computer into existence.

Steve Jobs was born on February 24, 1955, in San Francisco. Shortly after his birth, he was adopted by Paul and Clara Jobs. Paul Jobs worked for a finance company in Palo Alto; the family lived in nearby Mountain View. Young Steve was smart but was known as a loner. He was not subjected to much discipline as a child, and he was used to getting his way. He was not interested in team sports so he became a swimmer, where emphasis was on individual achievement.

Paul Jobs's hobby was buying and fixing up old cars. He took his son with him when he negotiated for cars and parts. This early experience helped Steve to develop his strengths as a negotiator.

Steve became interested in electronics at the age of ten. Many Hewlett-Packard engineers lived in his neighborhood, and he was intrigued with many electronics projects assembled in neighborhood garages. One neighbor instructed Jobs in electronics and enrolled him in the Hewlett-Packard Explorer Club, where he learned about calculators, diodes, holograms, and lasers.

Because Steve did not like the high school in Mountain View, his father secured a position as a machinist in Los Carlos and moved the family. Through a mutual friend, Jobs met Steve Wozniak. Jerry Wozniak, an electrical engineer at Lockheed, had instructed his son in electronics. Steve Wozniak was only eighteen when he met Jobs, but his knowledge of electronics was advanced for his age. He had won prizes in local electronics fairs against tough competition. He had already expanded his design for a one-bit adder-subtractor into a ten-bit parallel adder-subtractor, a precursor to a computer.

One of Jobs's first projects for the Explorer Club was building a frequency counter. He needed parts and obtained them with the boldness for which he later became known. He looked up Bill Hewlett in the Palo Alto phone book. Hewlett answered the phone and talked with Jobs for twenty minutes. He not only gave him the parts he needed but also gave him a summer job at Hewlett-Packard assembling frequency counters. Later, when Jobs needed another part, he called the Burroughs Corporation in Detroit collect, and asked them to donate it to him.

During high school, Jobs worked at a surplus electronics warehouse store in Sunnyvale, where he learned electronic part pricing. He purchased capacitors, resistors, and microchips at flea markets and resold them at a profit.

Wozniak enrolled at the University of Colorado but returned to San Francisco after one year. He took programming courses at the local community college and later enrolled at the University of California at Berkeley.

Despite his parents' objections, Jobs enrolled at Reed College in Portland, Oregon. Reed was a liberal school, and its students considered themselves anti-establishment. Jobs and a fellow student, Daniel Kottke, studied Zen Buddism and yoga. They became vegetarians and visited the Hare Krishna temple frequently. Jobs dropped out of school but stayed on the periphery of Reed. He lived in an unheated room and supported himself by maintaining electrical equipment. He usually went barefoot and only wore his sandals when it snowed.

In 1974, Jobs returned home and interviewed for a job at Atari as a technician. He insisted that they hire him, so they did. Nolan Bushnell had founded Atari in 1972 to develop video games. His first big success was the game "Pong." Jobs wanted to travel to India, as one of his Reed friends had done the previous summer. Jobs asked Atari's Chief Engineer to pay his way to India "to see his guru." The Chief Engineer laughed at him but thought of a way to give him time off. He asked Jobs to stop in Germany on his way to India.

Atari had a grounding problem with circuit boards in the games they sold in Germany, partly due to the difference between sixty-cycle and fifty-cycle power. The Chief Engineer gave Jobs a short course in ground loops. In Germany, Jobs solved the problem in two hours by ensuring that the chassis in which the board was inserted was properly grounded.

Jobs's friend Kottke joined him in India. They were moved by the poverty, which was greater than they had expected. Jobs's summer in India caused him to question many of his Eastern beliefs. His friends thought that his disillusionment with India made him seem detached. In the fall of 1974, Jobs returned home and contacted Wozniak.

Wozniak had dropped out of Berkeley during his junior year, married, and accepted a position as an engineer in Hewlett-Packard's calculator division. He became a regular attendee at meetings of the Homebrew Computer Club, a gathering place for computer hobbyists, engineers, programmers, and suppliers.

Attendance at Club meetings increased exponentially after the January 1975 issue of *Popular Electronics* was circulated. It included an article about the Altair 8800 computer kit produced by MITS in Albuquerque, New Mexico. The Altair central processing unit used an Intel 8080 microprocessor. The Altair was a collection of parts with meager documentation and little input / output capability. It required substantial knowledge of electronics to assemble, was usually missing parts, and cost $495. Orders from hobbyists for this first mail-order computer overwhelmed MITS. The Altair operating system was developed by Bill Gates and Paul Allen, who later founded Microsoft Corporation.

Wozniak designed his own computer. Initially, he based his design on the Motorola 6800 microprocessor, but later replaced it with the MOS Technology 6502. He drew on his previous experience in building a computer with limited capability in a neighbor's garage and in designing a "Computer Converser" for Call Computer. Wozniak was adept at designing efficient circuit boards with a minimum of components; the circuit board for this computer was no exception.

Wozniak took his computer to meetings of the Homebrew Computer Club, but they were not interested in it because it was not based on the Intel 8080 used in the Altair. He offered to give away circuit diagrams of his computer to club members, but Jobs suggested that they sell them. Better yet, Jobs suggested that they make the circuit-board computers and sell them. On April 1, 1976, Jobs and Wozniak formed a partnership called Apple Computer to make and sell computers. Jobs chose the name because it came before Atari in the phone book and because he liked the Beatles—Apple was the name of their record label.

Jobs invited Ron Wayne, Atari's Chief Field Service Engineer, to join the partnership to do artwork, advertising layout, and documentation. Wayne was given ten percent of Apple Computer, and Jobs and Wozniak each took forty-five percent. Wayne, a conservative engineer in his forties, favored low risk investments such as precious metals and stamps. He became nervous when Apple Computer committed substantial amounts of money for circuit-board parts. He withdrew from the partnership, a move that he regretted later.

Jobs found a source for economical circuit boards. He had gained experience in dealing with circuit-board houses when he negotiated circuit-board work for Wozniak's Computer Converser. Jobs developed a reputation as a tough negotiator. He was called "the rejector," because he usually turned down early designs and estimates.

Jobs met an electronics retailer at a Homebrew Club meeting

who offered to buy fifty circuit-board computers, now called Apple I, for $500 each. Apple Computer needed start-up capital, but no one was willing to lend it to them. Jobs had $1,000 from the sale of his van plus a small nest egg from selling Atari the video game "Breakout," which Wozniak had designed. Jobs's loan requests were turned down by banks and by his previous employer at the electronics warehouse store.

Finally, Jobs found a supplier of electronics parts in Palo Alto who would sell them $20,000 worth of parts on credit with no interest if they paid within thirty days. Jobs's sister had married and moved out of their parents' home, so they used her bedroom to assemble the circuit boards. The Jobs' garage is usually noted as the first location of Apple Computer. The garage was used when the work volume overflowed Jobs's sister's bedroom. Their customer was unhappy with the first delivery of the Apple I because it lacked a display, a keyboard, a power supply, and software. Nevertheless, he paid in cash.

Jobs hired his sister and his old friend Kottke to insert components into circuit boards. A classmate of Jobs at Reed kept the company's books. Wozniak obtained a $5,000 loan from friends to keep the enterprise going. In the fall of 1976, Jobs and Wozniak took Apple I to a computer fair in New York City. Commodore Business Machines offered to buy Apple Computer, but they thought that $100,000 and annual salaries of $36,000 a year for Jobs and Wozniak was too much to pay for a garage-based operation.

Jobs offered to sell Apple Computer to Nolan Bushnell of Atari and was turned down; Bushnell saw no future in microprocessors. Wozniak approached Hewlett-Packard about buying Apple, but they did not want to get into that "dubious" market. Finding no buyers for the company, Jobs and Wozniak addressed the shortcomings of the Apple I.

Wozniak had already started to design the next generation computer, so Jobs farmed out the design of the power supply. Jobs insisted upon a power supply that required no cooling fan. After another designer failed with a cassette interface, Wozniak designed a straightforward interface for use in loading BASIC programming language into the computer. Jobs devised a wooden case for the Apple I made by a local cabinet maker. It was heavy and did not dissipate heat well; unfortunately, it cost almost as much as the circuit board.

When Apple Computer outgrew their bedroom / garage operation, Jobs contracted out the insertion of components into circuit boards. The company he chose did not want the work, but Jobs succeeded with his "I'm not going to leave here until you agree" approach. Wozniak's next-generation computer incorporated a case, a keyboard, and a power supply. It was designed to be used with a standard television set as the display, both to hold down the cost and because it was less intimidating to the user.

Wozniak added expansion slots to the Apple II to be used by suppliers of add-on circuit boards. This important feature started a new industry when other vendors realized how easy it was to design and build products for the Apple II. Wozniak also designed a read-only memory chip to hold the BASIC programming language, thus eliminating the cassette interface. Jobs found a designer for Apple II's plastic case through contacts at Hewlett-Packard.

Jobs had been an individual in search of a cause. In promoting the personal computer, he had found his cause. He had a knack for convincing talented people to undertake projects for Apple.

One of Jobs's important early decisions was his choice of an advertising / public relations firm. He asked Intel who had handled their recent advertising campaign and was told it was the Regis McKenna Agency. McKenna turned him down. Jobs persisted; he called McKenna three or four times a day until he agreed to take on Apple as a client. McKenna's first action was to change the logo. Wayne had designed the original black and white logo with Isaac Newton sitting under a tree with one apple on a limb. McKenna redesigned the logo using an apple with multicolored bands and a bite, or byte, taken out. Apple used that logo until it was replaced in 1998.

The fledgling enterprise needed capital to expand. Jobs asked Nolan Bushnell of Atari to recommend a venture capitalist. Bushnell suggested Don Valentine of Sequoia Ventures, but Valentine was not interested. Valentine told Jobs and Wozniak they were not thinking big enough; he suggested that they talk with Mike Markkula, who had made his first million when Intel went public. Markkula, who had retired at the age of thirty-three, offered to devote four years to Apple and provide $250,000 to develop and manufacture the Apple II in return for a one-third ownership in the company.

Markkula's offer was dependent upon Wozniak leaving Hewlett-Packard and working for Apple full time. Wozniak refused even though his division of Hewlett-Packard was moving to Oregon, and he did not want to move. He changed his mind when his friend told him that he did not have to become a manager; he could continue as an engineer.

Markkula helped Jobs and Wozniak prepare a business plan. On January 3, 1977, Apple Computer Company was incorporated and, within three months, bought out the partnership for $5,308.96. Jobs, Wozniak, and Markkula each owned thirty percent and Rod Holt, designer of the power supply and finisher of Wozniak's projects, owned ten percent.

Markkula's strengths were business planning and marketing strategy. He had no desire to be president of Apple; he recommended his friend, Michael Scott, who was responsible for producing $30 million worth of components a year at National Semiconductor. Scott was an aggressive manager who could make tough decisions, in contrast to the diplomatic, mild-mannered Markkula.

As he had on Apple I, Jobs worked closely with the circuit-board contractor. The board, due to Wozniak's original design of sixty-two chips and integrated circuits and to Jobs's efforts as "rejector," was a work of art. It was easy to produce and it looked good when the cover was raised. Jobs persisted in negotiating bargain-basement prices for Apple's components.

Neither Markkula nor Scott could get along with Jobs; daily confrontations occurred between Scott and Jobs, partly because Markkula pushed off all of his dealings with Jobs onto Scott. Jobs was openly critical of the work of the young employees. As the business increased and company operations became more formal, Jobs went in several directions at once.

Wozniak fitted in less well with the expanding organization and was not consulted as often as he had been. The close working relationship between him and Jobs began to change. Wozniak spent so much time at Apple that his marriage broke up. He gave his wife fifteen percent of his Apple stock in the divorce settlement.

In early 1977, Apple II was demonstrated in an attention-gathering booth at a computer fair in San Francisco. Jobs bought the first suit he ever owned to wear at the fair. 13,000 attendees were captivated by Apple II, and 300 orders were placed.

During 1977, Markkula worked hard to obtain additional capital to fuel Apple's growth. He was amazingly successful. In January 1978, financing arrangements were completed, and Apple was valued at $3 million. Venrock, a venture firm that invested Rockefeller money, invested $288,000; Don Valentine, who earlier had declined investing in Apple, invested $150,000; Arthur Rock, who had made millions on Intel and Scientific Data Systems stock, invested $57,600. Rock also became an important advisor to the fledgling enterprise. Henry Singleton of Teledyne invested $108,000 and agreed to serve on the Board.

In early 1978, Wozniak completed his design for a floppy disk drive, and it went into production. Wozniak considered it his best design; it added important functionality to the Apple II by allowing programmers to produce software that could be transferred from computer to computer reliably.

Later in 1978, Markkula suggested that Apple enter the education market. His daughter was learning grade school math, and he could see the enormous potential of the market. His efforts ultimately led to the establishment of the Apple Education Foundation. The education market became a lucrative one for Apple.

The next product was an enhanced Apple II, Apple Plus, that had an improved start-up routine and an updated version of BASIC. Memory was doubled to 48 kilobytes. However, enhancement was not enough; the company provided additional improvements that customers and dealers had requested by:

- Increasing the width of the display from forty to eighty characters
- Providing lower-case as well as upper-case letters
- Providing additional memory to accommodate more sophisticated programs
- Ensuring compatibility between the Apple II and new machines
- Bundling the software and providing it with the purchase of the hardware

Wozniak was not directly involved with the new machine, the

Apple III, as he had been on earlier products. Jobs designed the case first and then made the designers fit within it as best they could. The designers did not have enough space, but Jobs would not enlarge the case. As a result, they designed a circuit board to piggyback onto the motherboard. To save money, they did not use gold contacts (which do not corrode) to connect the boards. The connectors corroded, and Apple III was not reliable. Fortunately, sales of Apple II, which had little competition in 1979, were strong.

Apple sold an additional $7,273,801 worth of stock that year. Also in 1979, the spreadsheet application entered the marketplace. Dan Fylstra, a Boston software entrepreneur, developed VisiCalc on an Apple II and offered it to Apple for $1 million. Apple declined; nevertheless, when VisiCalc was shipped in the fall of 1979, it only ran on the Apple II. The availability of a spreadsheet application and of Wozniak's floppy disk drive spurred Apple II sales.

Following Apple III's limited success, Jobs needed a new goal. He hired two Hewlett-Packard managers, one to manage software development and the other to manage engineering. Jobs's goal was a machine based on 16-bit architecture, rather than the Apple II 8-bit architecture, to sell for $2,000. The new machine, Lisa, was large, awkward-looking, and based on the 68000, the new microprocessor from Motorola.

Lisa was slow in both processing and in screen refreshment speed, but the software group had been innovative in using bit-mapping that provided a one-to-one correspondence between the bits in the computer memory and the picture elements (pixels) on the screen. Screen resolution was considerably higher than that of the Apple II and III. Jobs did not think that Lisa was "sexy" enough, and he did not think it was the right product for the office environment. He sought a partner; he considered IBM and Xerox despite the fact that Apple considered IBM the enemy.

Xerox had invested in Apple's second private investment placement. Jobs contacted the Xerox Development Corporation, the company's venture capital unit, and offered to let them invest $1 million in Apple if they would give him a tour of their Palo Alto Research Center (PARC). PARC had a talented staff of computer scientists who had made many breakthroughs that Xerox had failed to exploit. Xerox purchased 100,000 shares of Apple at $10.00 and

215

opened their doors to Jobs. The twenty-five-year-old entrepreneur had gotten his way again.

Larry Tesler of PARC demonstrated their Alto personal computer to Jobs and seven Apple developers, who were enthusiastic when they saw Alto's potential. User interaction with the Alto was revolutionary through the use of icons, menus (action lists), partitions of the screen (windows), and a "mouse." Jobs was moved by what he saw. He shouted: "Why aren't you doing anything with this? This is the greatest thing! This is revolutionary!" After the demonstration, Jobs hired Tesler to work for Apple. Later, Alan Kay, one of PARC's principal computer science visionaries, joined Apple and eventually became an Apple Fellow.

In August 1980, Markkula reorganized Apple into three divisions:

- Personal Computer Systems (Apple II and III)
- Professional Office Systems (Lisa)
- Accessories (add-on circuit boards, disk drives, printers, etc.)

Jobs had hoped to be given line authority of a division; instead, he was named Chairman of the Board.

On December 12, 1980, Apple Computer Corporation went public. Apple's 4,600,000 shares sold out within the first hour in the most oversubscribed initial public offering since Ford Motor Company had gone public in 1956. Apple was worth $1.778 billion on the stock market. The company had reached the Fortune 500 faster than any company in history. Forty new millionaires were made that day, including:

- Jobs, whose outstanding shares were worth $256 million.
- Markkula, who owned $239 million of Apple stock.
- Wozniak, who was worth $135.6 million.
- Scott, the President, who owned Apple stock worth $95.5 million.
- Holt, a key designer, who was worth $67 million.
- Wozniak's ex-wife, whose divorce settlement stock was worth $42 million

Without line responsibility, Jobs was again without a project.

He needed a subject for his evangelism. The Macintosh personal computer was the next project to provide an outlet for his zeal. Macintosh was in the R & D phase and had already survived one attempt by Jobs to kill it. Scott had rescued the project. Jef Raskin and his team of two developers planned a "luggable" machine that would be easy to use and would sell for about $1,000. Hardware and software designers would work together from the beginning, and software would be offered as part of the purchase price of the machine. Jobs promoted the Macintosh within Apple, and three developers were immediately added to the team. Jef Raskin had based the design on the Motorola 6809 microprocessor. Jobs insisted that the 6809 processor be replaced with the faster Motorola 68000; Raskin was overruled.

Jobs challenged Burrell Smith to redesign the Macintosh based on the 68000 by the end of 1980. Smith was a Wozniak-type designer who liked simple designs and worked on a project night and day until it was done. He also had Wozniak's ability to evaluate the elements of a complex design in his head. The Macintosh design had one circuit board that used off-the-shelf parts, compared to Lisa's five circuit boards with some custom components. Furthermore, it was twice as fast as Lisa and could be produced at one-third the price. Jobs took over the project and brought in developers from the successful Apple II, including Wozniak and Holt. Jobs managed the Macintosh Division when it was formed.

As the Macintosh development effort expanded, Jobs pulled talent from the rest of the company. In fact, he frequently and loudly announced that the future of the company was with the Macintosh "pirates." Ultimately, however, this split between Macintosh developers and other Apple developers divided the company. The development deadlines for the Macintosh were so tight that it forced them to contract writing some of the programs outside of Apple.

The first software developer Jobs sought out was Bill Gates of Microsoft, who wrote the first BASIC programs for personal computers. Gates and his partner, Paul Allen, provided the operating system software (eventually called MS / DOS) for IBM's personal computers. Gates had negotiated a non-exclusive agreement with IBM that allowed Microsoft to license IBM's operating environment to other customers.

Jobs and Scott, Apple's President, had a tempestuous working relationship. Scott was one of the few people that Jobs could not intimidate. Unfortunately, Scott's abrasive personality intimidated younger employees. Scott fired the Vice President of Engineering and was attempting to do that job in addition to his own. Finally, he was edged out by Markkula, who had brought him into the company.

Markkula was in a difficult position because his four-year arrangement with Apple was almost over. He looked outside Apple for a new president. He wanted John Sculley, President of Pepsi-Cola USA, who had taken market share from Coca-Cola. Initially, Sculley was not interested in joining Apple. Jobs flew to New York City and courted Sculley. After many long conversations about the future of Apple, Jobs asked Sculley if he intended to sell sugar water to children for the rest of his life when he could be doing something important with personal computers. The financial package Apple offered to Sculley was difficult to turn down.

Sculley spent many hours learning the technology. Within his first year on the job, he realized that cuts would have to be made. Apple II was carrying the company, and Lisa was a distinct disappointment. He streamlined the organizational structure and eliminated 1,200 jobs to keep the company profitable. Jobs retained his position as manager of the Macintosh Division in addition to serving as Chairman of the Board. Sculley redirected the company from producing most of its own software to increased reliance on outside software developers, an approach similar to IBM's.

The first disagreements between Jobs and Sculley occurred in 1983. By 1984, when Macintosh sales were considerably below Jobs's estimates, the rift was obvious to everyone. Apple lowered the price of Macintosh from $2,495 to $1,995, but sales continued to be disappointing. The initial demand for Apple IIc had declined; eventually 200,000 had to be sold through a liquidator. An attempt to market Lisa as Macintosh XL wasn't successful. In 1985, President Reagan awarded National Technology Medals to Jobs and Wozniak at the White House. Also that year, Wozniak left the company. He was unhappy with Apple's direction, particularly the lack of recognition of Apple II's contribution to the company's bottom line and the dearth of Apple II development funds.

At the Board of Directors meeting on April 11, 1985, Sculley removed Jobs as manager of the Macintosh Division and replaced him with Jean-Louis Gassee, the successful head of Apple France. Jobs then attempted to have Sculley removed as President and CEO. However, he misjudged Sculley's support from the Board.. Finally, their disagreements became so disruptive that the Board suggested that Sculley force Jobs out of the company.

When Jobs left Apple, he formed a new computer company called NeXT. He attracted many key Apple developers to his start-up. Apple was alarmed by the loss of critical personnel and concerned about a potential loss of technology. Jobs sought start-up capital for NeXT; Ross Perot invested $20 million for sixteen percent of the company. Jobs was only moderately successful with NeXT, which generated some income by selling software to Apple. In 1997, Apple's sales and earnings plummeted, and Jobs returned to Apple Computer as interim CEO and led Apple's rebound. He became CEO in 2000.

In 2001, Apple introduced the iPod and became a consumer electronics company and the major company in the media-player market. In 2007, Jobs announced the iPhone, a powerful pocket-sized personal computer, which incorporated a new touch screen and interface and dominated the smart phone market. In 2010, the iPad, a highly successful tablet computer, was introduced by Apple.

In his personal life, Jobs was diagnosed in 2004 with a rare form of pancreatic cancer that could be controlled. He underwent surgery and returned to work.

In 2005, Jobs gave the commencement address at Stanford University. He said, "Your time is limited, so don't waste it living someone else's life. Don't be trapped by dogma, which is living with the results of someone else's thinking. Don't let the noise of others' opinions drown out your own inner voice. And most important, have the courage to follow your heart and intuition. They somehow already know what you truly want to become. Everything else is secondary."

In 2009, Jobs received a liver transplant. He again returned to work. On August 24, 2011, Jobs turned over his CEO responsibilities to Tim Cook, the Chief Operating Officer. Jobs died from complications of pancreatic cancer on October 5, 2011.

In 2011, Apple's market capitalization exceeded that of ExxonMobil, making it the world's most valuable company. Jobs revitalized six industries: personal computers, animated movies, music, telephones, tablet computing, and digital publishing. He also had a significant impact on retailing with the establishment of the Apple retail stores.

Jobs, who considered himself an artist, had a passion for design. He combined art, technology, and ease of use in his products. Jobs did no market research. He did not ask customers what they wanted; rather, he gave them what he thought they should have.

Steve Jobs and Steve Wozniak made significant contributions to the computer industry. Working out of a garage, they succeeded where large corporations had failed; they pioneered the personal computer revolution. Together, they provided the expertise, determination, and vision to create an industry within an industry. In doing so, they changed the home and workplace environment forever.

SIR JONATHAN IVE (1967-   ) Chief Designer for Apple Inc.

"[Jony Ive] has more operational power than anyone else at Apple, except me. There's no one who can tell him what to do, or to butt out. That's the way I set it up."

Steve Jobs

Sir Jonathan Ive, a native of Great Britain, is the Chief Designer at Apple Inc. He has been responsible for the Industrial Design Group and provided direction for the Human Interface software teams. He has designed many Apple products, including the MacBook Pro, iMac, MacBook Air, Mac mini, iPod, iPod Touch, iPhone, iPad, iPad Mini, Apple Watch, and the iOS operating system. Steve Jobs considered him his "spiritual partner" at Apple.

Ive was born in Chingford, London, on February 27, 1967. His father was a silversmith lecturer at Middlesex Polytechnic Institute. Ive attended the Chingford Foundation School and then Walton High School in Stafford. He was very interested in cars in school and considered going into automobile design.

Ive studied industrial design at Newcastle Polytechnic Institute (now Northumbria University}. He decided on a career in product design. He worked at the London design agency Roberts Weaver Group, which was his college sponsor. After graduating with a first class Bachelor of Arts degree in 1989, Ive became familiar with Apple products as an undergraduate and was impressed with the mouse-driven system.

In 1988, while an undergraduate, Ive married British writer and historian Heather Pegg. They have twin sons and live in the Pacific Heights district of San Francisco.

After a year with Roberts Weaver, Ive joined a new design agency called Tangerine, where he designed products such as microwave ovens. Tangerine wasn't particularly impressed with his work and he wasn't impressed by their supervision. While at Tangerine, he consulted with Apple Inc., and created the initial PowerBook designs. Apple not only appreciated his work, but tried for two years to hire him.

During Ive's consulting activity with Apple, he worked for Robert Brunner, Apple's Chief of Industrial Design. Ive became a full-time employee of Apple in 1992 and designed the second generation of the Newton and the MessagePad 220.

In 1997, Ive became the Senior Vice President of Industrial Design after the return of Jobs to Apple and became head of the team responsible for most of Apple's hardware products. His first design assignment was the iMac, followed by designs, such as the iPod, iPhone, and iPad.

Jobs made design his main focus, which led to products that were functionally uncomplicated, aesthetically pleasing, and extremely popular. In *Time,* March 17, 2014, Ive described his working relation ship that had existed with Jobs:

> When we were looking at objects, what our eyes physically saw and what we came to perceive were exactly the same. And we would ask the same questions, have the same curiosity about things. Ive described Jobs as "so clever" with "bold" and "magnificent" ideas.

In 2011, Fortune.com cited some observations from Ive about the fragility of ideas:

> Steve used to say to me—and he used to say this a lot— "Hey, Jony, here's a dopey idea." And sometimes they were. Really dopey. Sometimes they were truly dreadful. But sometimes they took the air from the room and they left us both completely silent. Bold, crazy, magnificent ideas. Or quiet, simple ones, which in their subtlety, their detail, they were utterly profound . . . And just as Steve loved ideas, and he loved making stuff, he treated the process of creativity with a rare, wonderful reverence. You see, I think he knew better than anyone that while ideas ultimately can be so powerful, they begin as fragile, barely formed thoughts, so easily missed, so easily compromised, so easily squashed.

Ive runs his own laboratory at Apple. Only top executives and his core team, consisting of fifteen people from America, Australia, Britain, Japan, and New Zealand, who have worked together for twenty years, have access to his laboratory. On May 26, 2015, Ive was promoted to Chief Design Officer. He is the third C-level executive at Apple, along with CEO Tim Cook and CFO Luca Maestri.

In 2006, Ive was appointed Commander of the Order of the British Empire (CBE) for services to the design industry. In the 2012 New Years Honors, he was elevated to Knight Commander of the British Empire for "services to design and enterprise." He was knighted by Princess Anne at Buckingham Palace in a May 2012 ceremony. He said he was "both humbled and sincerely grateful." As of early 2014, Ives was a patent holder of over 730 U.S. design and utility patents, as well as many more patents around the world.

In 2014, Ive was quoted as saying:

> We are at the beginning of a remarkable time, when a remarkable number of products will be developed. When you think of technology and what it has enabled us to do and what it will enable us to do in the future, we're not even close to any kind of limit. It's still so new . . . At Apple, there's almost a joy at looking at your ignorance and realizing, "Wow," we're going to learn about this and, by the time we're done, we're going to really understand and do something great. Apple is imperfect, like every collection of people. But we have a rare quality. There is this almost pre-verbal, instinctive understanding about what we do, why we do it. We share the same values.

BIBLIOGRAPHY

INTRODUCTION

Catmull. Ed. *Creativity, Inc.,* New York: Random House, 2014.

De Bono, Edward. *Serious Creativity: Using the Power of Lateral Thinking to Create New Ideas.* New York: Harper Business, 1992.

Fritz, Robert. *Creating.* New York: Fawcett Columbine, 1991.

Goleman, Daniel, and Paul Kaufman and Michael Yay. *The Creative Spirit.* New York: Dutton, 1992.

Kelly, Tom, and David Kelley. *Creative Confidence: Unleashing the Creative Potential Within Us All.* New York: Crown Business, 2013.

Kent, Tami Lynn. *Wild Creative.* New York: Atria, 2014.

Lubart, Todd I. *Defying the Crowd: Cultivating Creativity in a Culture of Conformity.* New York: The Free Press, 1993.

Maisel, Eric, *The Creativity Book.* New York: Penguin Putnam, 2000.

Michalko, Michael. *Cracking Creativity: The Secrets of Creative Genius.* Berkeley, CA: Ten Speed Press, 1998.

Mihaly Csikszentmihalyi. *Creativity: Flow and the Psychology of Discovery and Invention.* New York: Harper Perennial, 1996.

Sternberg, Robert J., and Todd I. Lubart. *Defying the Crowd.* New York: The Free Press, 1995.

PAINTERS / SCULPTORS CHAPTER 1

LEONARDO DA VINCI

Kallen, Stuart A., and P. M. Boekhoff. *The Importance of Leonardo da Vinci.* San Diego: Lucent Books, 2000.

Lester, Toby. *Da Vinci's Ghost.* New York: Free Press, 2012

Marshall, Norman V. *Leonardo da Vinci: What Made Them Great.* Englewood Cliffs, NJ: Silver Burdett Press, 1990.

MICHELANGELO

Brandes, George. *Michelangelo: His Life, His Time, His Era.* New York: Frederick Ungar, 1963.

De Tolnay, Charles. *Michelangelo: Sculptor, Painter, Architect.* Princeton: Princeton University Press, 1975.

Jeffrey, David. "The Sistine Restoration: A Renaissance for Michelangelo." *National Geographic.* Dec. 1989: 688-713.

Seymour, Charles. *Michelangelo: The Sistine Chapel Ceiling*. New York: Norton, 1972.

Von Einem, Herbert. *Michelangelo*. London: Methuen, 1973.

VINCENT VAN GOGH

Bonafoux, Pascal. *Van Gogh: The Passionate Eye*. New York: Harry N. Abrams, n.d.

De Leeuw, Ronald, ed. *The Letters of Vincent Van Gogh* New York: Penguin, 1997.

Honour, Alan. *Tormented Genius: The Struggles of Vincent Van Gogh*. New York: William Morrow, 1967.

Hulsker, Jan. *Vincent and Theo Van Gogh: A Dual Biography*. Ann Arbor: Fuller, 1990.

Meier-Graefe, Julius. *Vincent Van Gogh*. New York: Harcourt, Brace, 1933.

Sweetman, David. *Van Gogh: His Life and His Art*. New York: Crown, 1990.

Wright, Frederick S. *Van Gogh*. New York: Beechurst, 1954.

PAUL GAUGUIN.

Cogniat, Raymond. *Gauguin*. New York: Harry N. Abrams, 1963.

Estienne, Charles. *Gauguin: Biographical and Critical Studies*. Cleveland: World, 1953.

Gauguin, Pola. *My Father Paul Gauguin*. New York: Alfred A. Knopf, 1937.

Hughes, Robert. "Seeing Gauguin Whole at Last," *Time Magazine,* 9 May 1988: 77.

Steinberg, Barbara Hope. *Gauguin*. New York: A & W Visual Library, 1976.

AMEDEO MODIGLIANI

Dale, Maud. *Modigliani*. New York: Alfred A. Knopf, 1929.

Modigliani, Jeanne. *Modigliani: Man and Myth*. New York: Orion, 1958.

Sichel, Pierre. *Modigliani: A Biography*. New York: E. P. Dutton, 1967.

SONGWRITERS / COMPOSERS CHAPTER 2

CHARLES IVES

Cowell, Henry and Sidney. *Charles Ives and His Music*. London: Oxford University Press, 1955.

Ewen, David. *The World of Twentieth-Century Music*. Englewood Cliffs: Prentice-Hall, 1968.

Machlis, Joseph. *American Composers of Our Time*. New York: Crowell, 1963.

Posell, Elsa Z. *American Composers*. Boston: Houghton Mifflin, 1963.

Sive, Helen R. *Music's Connecticut Yankee, An Introduction to the Life and Music of Charles Ives*. New York: Atheneum, 1977.

GEORGE GERSHWIN

Reef, Catherine. *George Gershwin: American Composer*. Greensboro, NC: Morgan Reynolds, 2000.

Rimler, Walter. *George Gershwin: An Intimate Portrait*. Urbana: University of Illinois Press, 2009.

COLE PORTER

Gill, Brendan. *Cole: A Biographical Essay*. New York: Holt, Rinehart & Winston, n.d.

McBrien, William. *Cole Porter, A Biography*. New York: Alfred A. Knopf, 1998.

ALEC WILDER

Balliet, Whitney. *Alec Wilder and His Friends*. Boston: Houghton Mifflin, 1974.

Stone, Desmond. *Alec Wilder in Spite of Himself: A Life of the Composer*. New York: Oxford University Press, 1996.

Zeltsman, Nancy, ed. *Alec Wilder (1907-1980)*. Newton Centre, MA, 1991.

BETTY COMDEN & ADOLPH GREEN

Comden, Betty. *Off Stage*. New York: Simon & Schuster, 1995.

Comden, Betty, and Adolph Green. *Singin' in the Rain: Story and Screenplay*. London: Lorrimer, 1986.

Robinson, Alice M. *Betty Comden and Adolph Green: A Bio-Bibliography*. Westport, Conn: Greenwood, 1994.

AUTHORS / POETS CHAPTER 3

JOHN MILTON

Bush, Douglas. *John Milton: A Sketch of His Life and Writings*. New York: Macmillan, 1965.

Ivimey, Joseph. *John Milton: His Life and Times*. New York: Appleton, 1833.

Reeves, James. *A Short History of English Poetry, 1340—1640*. New York: Dutton, 1962.

Untermeyer, Louis. *Lives of the Poets: The Story of One Thousand Years of English and American Poetry*. New York: Simon & Schuster, 1959.

Wilson, A. N. *The Life of John Milton*. New York: Oxford UP, 1983.

SIR WALTER SCOTT

Buchan, John. *Sir Walter Scott*. New York: Coward-McCann, 1932.

Daiches, David. *Sir Walter Scott and His World*. New York: Viking, 1971.

Johnson, Edgar. *Sir Walter Scott: The Great Unknown*. New York: Macmillan, 1970.

Keith, Christina. *The Author of Waverly: A Study in the Personality of Sir Walter Scott*. New York: Roy, 1964.

Lauber, John Francis. *Sir Walter Scott*. Boston: Twayne, 1966.

ELIZABETH BARRETT BROWNING

Forster, Margaret. *Elizabeth Barrett Browning: A Biography*. New York: Doubleday, 1988.

Markus, Julia. *Dared and Done: The Marriage of Elizabeth Barrett Browning and Robert Browning*. New York: Alfred A. Knopf, 1985.

Stack, V. E., ed. *How Do I Love Thee: The Love Letters of Robert Browning and Elizabeth Barrett*. G. P. Putnam's Sons, 1969.

EMILY DICKINSON

Dickenson, Donna. *Emily Dickinson*. Dover, NH: Berg, 1985.

Ferlazzo, Paul J. *Emily Dickinson*. Boston: Twayne, 1975.

Lingsworth, Polly. *Emily Dickinson: Her Letter to the World*. New York: Thomas Y. Crowell, 1965.

Olsen, Victoria. *Emily Dickinson*. New York: Chelsea House, 1990.

GEORGE BERNARD SHAW

Coolidge, Olivia. *George Bernard Shaw*. Boston: Houghton Mifflin, 1968.

Hill, Eldon C. *George Bernard Shaw*. Boston: Twayne, 1978.

Holroyd, Michael. *Bernard Shaw*. New York: Random House, 1988.

Matthews, John F. *George Bernard Shaw*. New York: Columbia UP, 1969.

Smith, J. Perry. *The Unrepentant Pilgrim: A Study of the Development of George Bernard Shaw*. Boston: Houghton Mifflin, 1965.

INVENTORS / RESEARCHERS CHAPTER 4

THOMAS EDISON
Cousins, Margaret. *The Story of Thomas Alva Edison*. New York:
Random House, 1965.
Egan, Louise. *Thomas Edison: The Great American Inventor*. New York:
Barron's Educational Series, 1987.

ORVILE WRIGHT & WILBUR WRIGHT
Crouch, Tom D. *The Bishop's Boys: A Life of Wilbur and Orville Wright*.
New York: Norton, 1989.
Howard, Fred. *Wilbur and Orville: A Biography of the Wright Brothers*.
Mineola, NY: Dover, 1998.
Jakab, Peter L. *Visions of a Flying Machine: The Wright Brothers and
the Process of Invention*. Washington: The Smithsonian Institution,
1990.
Kelly, Fred C. *The Wright Brothers*. New York: Harcourt Brace, 1943.

JOHN ATANASOFF
Burks, Alice R., and Arthur W. Burks. *The First Electronic Computer:
The Atanasoff Story*. Ann Arbor: University of Michigan Press, 1989.
Mollenkoff, Clark R. *Atanasoff: Forgotten Father of the Computer*.
Ames, Iowa: Iowa State University Press, 1988.
Smiley, Jane. *The Man Who Invented the Computer*. New York:
Doubleday, 2010.

ALAN TURING
Copeland, R. Jack. *Turing: Pioneer of the Information Age*.
London: Oxford University Press, 2012.
Hodges, Andrew. *Alan Turing: The Enigma*. Princeton:
Princeton University Press, 1983.

STEPHEN HAWKING
Ferguson, Kitty. *Stephen Hawking: Quest for a Theory of the Universe*.
New York: Franklin Watts, 1991.
Hawking, Stephen W. *Black Holes and Baby Universes and Other Essays*.
New York: Bantam, 1993.
White, Michael and John Gribben. *Stephen Hawking: A Life in Science*.
Minneapolis: Dutton, 1992.

ARCHITECTS / ENTREPRENEURS   CHAPTER 5

SIR CHRISTOPHER WREN

Gray, Ronald. *Christopher Wren and St. Paul's Cathedral*. Minneapolis:
  Lerner, 1979.
Lindsey, John. *Wren: His Work and Times*. New York:
  Philosophical Library, 1952.
Whinney, Margaret. *Christopher Wren*. New York: Praeger, 1971.
Whitaker-Wilson, C. *Sir Christopher Wren: His Life and Times*.
  New York: Robert M. McBride, 1932.

GEORGE EASTMAN

Ackerman, Carl W. *George Eastman*. Clifton, NJ: Augustus M. Kelley,
  1973.
Brayer, Elizabeth. *George Eastman: A Biography*. Baltimore:
  Johns Hopkins University Press, 1996.
Solbert, O. N. "George Eastman." *Images—The Journal of Photography
  of the George Eastman House, Inc. Vol. II, No. 8* Nov. 1953.

THOMAS J. WATSON

Belden, Thomas Graham, and Marva Robbins. *The Lengthening
  Shadow: The Life of Thomas J. Watson*. Boston: Little, Brown, 1962.
Rodgers, William. *THINK: A Biography of the Watsons and IBM*.
  New York: Stein and Day, 1969.

CHESTER CARLSON

Dessauer, John H. *My Years with Xerox: The Billions Nobody Wanted*.
  Garden City, NY: Doubleday, 1971.
Mort, J., *An Anatomy of Xerography: Its Invention and Evolution*.
  Jefferson, NC: McFarland & Company, 1989.

BILL GATES

Boyd, Aaron. *Smart Money: The Story of Bill Gates*. New York: Morgan
  Reynolds, 1995.
Ichbiah, Daniel, and Susan L. Knepper. *The Making of Microsoft*. Rocklin,
  CA: Prima, 1991.
Manes, Stephen, and Paul Andrews. *Gates*. New York: Doubleday, 1993.
Marshall, David. *Bill Gates and Microsoft*. New York: Exley, 1994.
Wallace, James, and Jim Erickson. *Hard Drive: Bill Gates and the Making
  of the Microsoft Empire*. New York: Harper, 1992.

ENGINEERS / SCIENTISTS CHAPTER 6

REGINALD MITCHELL
Collier, Basil. A *History of War*. New York: Macmillan, 1974.

Cooke, David C. *The Planes They Flew In World War Two*. New York: Dodd, Mead & Company, 1969.

Cooper, Bryan, and John Batchelor. *Fighter: A History of Fighter Aircraft*. New York: Scribner's, 1973.

Spitfire. Videocassette. Royal Sound Video Productions, 1942. 90 min.

Vader, John. *Spitfire*. New York: Ballantine, 1969.

ROBERT GODDARD
Coil, Suzanne M. *Robert Hutchings Goddard: Pioneer of Rocketry and Space Flight*. New York: Facts on File, 1992.

Dewey, Anne Perkins. *Robert Goddard: Space Pioneer*. Boston: Little, Brown, 1962.

Goddard, Robert H. *Rocket Development*. New York: Prentice-Hall, 1948.

Lehman, Milton. *This High Man: The Life of Robert H. Goddard*. New York: Farrar, Straus, 1963.

PALO ALTO RESEARCH CENTER
Butcher, Lee. *Accidental Millionaire: The Rise and Fall of Steve Jobs at Apple*. New York: Paragon House, 1988.

Smith, Douglas K., and Robert C. Alexander. *Fumbling the Future: How Xerox Invented, Then Ignored the First Personal Computer*. New York: William Morrow, 1988.

STEVE JOBS
Aaseng, Nathan. "Steve Jobs." *Business Builders in Computers* Minneapolis: Oliver, 2000.

Butcher, Lee. *Accidental Millionaire: The Rise and Fall of Steve Jobs at Apple*. New York: Paragon House, 1988.

Deutschman, Alan. *The Second Coming of Steve Jobs*. New York: Broadway Books, 2000.

Smith, Douglas K., and Robert C. Alexander. *Fumbling the Future*. New York: William Morrow, 1988.

SIR JONATHAN IVE
Arlidge, John. "Jonathan Ive Designs Tomorrow." *Time,* Time, Inc., 17 March 2014.

Elmer-Dewitt, Philip. "Jonathan Ive on Steve Jobs and the Fragility of Ideas." New York: Fortune.com. 24 October 2011.

Kahney, Leander. *Jony Ive: The Genius Behind Apple's Greatest Products*. New York: Portfolio / Penguin, 2013.

GENERAL

Allen, John, ed. *100 Great Lives*. NY: Journal of Living Publishing, 1944.

Bolton, Sarah K. *Famous Men of Science*. New York: Crowell, 1960.

Crowther, J. W. *Famous American Men of Science*. NY: Norton, 1937.

Hart, Michael A. *The 100: A Ranking of the Most Influential Persons in History*. New York: Hart, 1978.

Tripp, Rhoda Thomas, ed., *The International Thesaurus of Quotations*. New York: Harper & Row, 1970.

Untermeyer, Louis. *Makers of the Modern World*. New York: Simon & Schuster, 1955.